The World Needs Dialogue!
Two: Setting the Bearings

This edition first published in 2020

Dialogue Publications
The Firs, High Street
Chipping Campden
Glos GL55 6AL UK

All rights reserved

Book Copyright © Dialogue Publications, 2020
All individual authors featured in this publication retain copyright for their work

Without limiting individual author's rights reserved, no part of this publication may be reproduced, distributed or transmitted in any form or by any means, including photocopying, recording, or other electronic or mechanical methods, without the prior written permission of the publisher, except in the case of brief quotations embedded in critical reviews and certain other non-commercial uses permitted by copyright law. For permission requests, write to the publisher at the address above.

Typeset by Ellipsis, Glasgow, Scotland

Ordering Information:
Quantity sales – Special discounts are available on quantity purchases by libraries, associations and others. For details, contact the Special Sales Department at the address above.

The World Needs Dialogue! / Two – 1st ed.

Classifications:
UK: BIC – Society (JFC): Cultural Studies and JFF: Social Issues)
US: BISAC – SOC000000 Social Science

Hardback: 978-1-9161912-4-2
Ebook: 978-1-9161912-5-9

Printed in Great Britain and the USA

Contents

Chairman's Foreword   v
Editor's Introduction   vii

Section One
Dialogue in the Room

Dialogic Team Coaching in TAMK Proakatemia   3
Timo Nevalainen

Dialogue at School   17
Joop Boukes

Bohm Dialogue as a Way to Support Adult Development   33
Marie-Ève Marchand

Reflecting on Dialogue Facilitation   49
Kati Tikkamäki & Mirja Hämäläinen

Section Two
Dialogic Intervention

Dialogic Intervention in a Volatile Organisational Takeover   63
Jane Ball

Professional Dialogue as a Research Methodology   83
Peter Garrett

Putting Dialogue to Work in the Virginia Department of Corrections   105
Harold Clarke and Whitney Barton

Dialogue and a Healing Environment in the Virginia Department of Corrections   121
Harold Clarke and Susan Williams

Section Three
Systemic Dialogue

Trim-Tab Dialogues: Transformative Vision and Action in South Asia   141
William Isaacs

The Netherlands in Dialogue: A Structural Approach to Dialogue Across Society 165
Olga Plokhooij

Dialogue for Social Change: A Practical Case Study 191
Ove D Jakobsen and Vivi ML Storsletten

Participants 211

Chairman's Foreword

Nearly 50 of us – almost half the international membership of the Academy of Professional Dialogue – gathered for our second annual conference in October 2019, once again at the Roffey Park Institute in the quiet and wooded English countryside. Our Board of Trustees decided to carry the proclamatory theme of the first international conference forward into the second, with the title *The World Needs Dialogue!* Two: Setting the Bearings.

We held plenary sessions at the start and end of each day, at which all of us engaged in a single Dialogue, and at various times in the day we met in small Home Groups of five participants to digest the day's activities more personally. Everyone, whether leading a session or not, was present for the entire three days to interact with others over meals and coffee breaks.

As during the previous year's gathering, considerations of the various working papers authored by Member Dialogue Practitioners were at the heart of the conference. Each paper had two sessions attended by a third of the participants. The first was to understand the practitioners work. Talking about the work with others adds a different dimension from reading about it. The second session explored the implications of the work for the practices of all the participants. These are starting to evolve into a form of peer review for Professional Dialogue. Their publication in this volume is intended to inspire others to incorporate Dialogue into their way of working and to inform people of different ways to do so.

The conference was structured in a three-part sequence, as is this book. This design was an outgrowth of a year's work of the Academy's Professional Standards and Accreditation Board (PSAB), led by Peter Garrett (UK), Lars-Åke Almqvist (Sweden), Harold Clarke (USA) and Mark Seneschall (UK), to determine criteria for the accreditation of individual Professional Dialogue Practitioners. For this purpose the PSAB adopted Peter Garrett's design of a three-part framework: *Dialogue in the Room, Dialogic Intervention* and *Systemic Dialogue*. This structure proved very useful in bringing coherence to our gathering.

The foundational level of this framework is *Dialogue in the Room*. This involves understanding the face-to-face dynamics of awareness and participation amongst any grouping of people to enable a generative process and outcomes. Once a practitioner is competent with these facilitative skills, they can be utilised for the purpose of *Dialogic Intervention*. This second level includes the additional dialogic skills needed to address problems and issues within competing power structures and narratives, by turning them into creative opportunities to co-author change. The third level is *Systemic Dialogue,* where the understanding, theory and skills are developed to design and evolve an organisation into an adaptive Dialogic Organisation.

Part One of this book includes three Working Papers that focus on *Dialogue in the Room*. As it happens, they also all fall within the educational sector. Timo Nevaleinan, from

Finland, expands on the facilitative coaching model he has developed to support fledgling entrepreneurs as they set up businesses during their time with him at Tampere University. Joop Boukes, from the Netherlands, writes about a very different context: his paper concentrates on his work with adolescents who are mildly intellectually disabled and aggressive, and how dialogue helps them learn to manage their lives. Meanwhile, Marie-Ève Marchand, who lives and works in Canada, has remained faithful to the early conception of Dialogue in the Room by David Bohm, sustained over many years with her colleague Mario Cayer at Université Laval in Quebec. These are followed by a smaller conference event, conceived by Kati Tikkamaki and Mirja Hämäläinen, both of Finland, about reflecting on Dialogue. Their aim was not to offer a rigorous analysis of dialogic process, but rather to encourage reflection on the different ways people engage with Dialogue.

Part Two of this book features three working papers on *Dialogic Intervention* by Jane Ball, Peter Garrett, both of the UK, and Harold Clarke & Whitney Barton, both from the US. As it happens, they all work within the field of criminal justice. Jane Ball recounts what is involved in dialogically intervening in a prison in crisis, where their remarkable success is at least partially measured by the disasters that *didn't* take place. Peter Garrett makes an innovative and bold claim for Dialogue as a Research Methodology, using two detailed case studies to show how the processes of traditional and dialogic research contrast and sometimes converge. Harold Clarke and Whitney Barton from the Virginia Department of Corrections reveal how Dialogue has been incorporated into operational decision-making through a business practice they call the Working Dialogue. We also include Harold Clarke's and Susan Williams' paper from last year to provide organisational context for the Working Dialogue.

Part Three is comprised of three Working Papers: one by William Isaacs from the USA, one by Olga Plokhooij of the Netherlands and the third by Ove Jakobsen & Vivi Storsletten from Norway. They all consider Systemic Dialogue within social arenas. William Isaacs tackles the challenge of alignment of some of the most senior international decision-makers in South East Asia, to step beyond a fragmented political history to enable mutually generative outcomes. Olga Plokhooij has achieved something people often only dream of doing – establishing Dialogue at a national scale, and with the symbolic endorsement of Queen Beatrix – and writes with honesty and clarity about the process. Ove Jakobsen and Vivi Storsletten, who touched the heart of a provincial Norwegian town by engaging its population in a generative and utopian exploration, describe how they helped them imagine of what kind of future they might create together.

Peter Garrett
Chairman, International Board of Trustees,
Academy of Professional Dialogue

Editor's Introduction

It's a pleasure to write the introduction to this second volume of *The World Needs Dialogue!* collection—officially, we are a series! Where the first volume, subtitled *Gathering the Field*, was about discovering who we are as a far-flung community, this year's offering—*Setting the Bearings*—speaks to purpose and direction, and to determination for the journey ahead.

As before, the papers in this volume were distributed ahead of the conference to free up time for dialogue rather than spending hours "reading papers at each other," as often seems to be the case at such gatherings. Because the number of attendees was smaller by design than the previous year, there was time for conversations to move to depth. And if *Gathering the Field* is about finding out who might be interested in the journey, *Setting the Bearings* is about fixing a course for a shared, robust practice of professional Dialogue. Papers this year largely focus on dialogue sustained over time to fulfill long-term goals rather than one-time events.

Peter has outlined the structure of the conference, which this book mirrors, so I will speak a bit about the nature of the book itself. While the text is in English (UK, US and Canadian), several of the authors have translated terms and practices from their native tongue so that more of us can follow their narrative. Where possible we have kept the essence and cadence of the writers' style and, occasionally, the sentence structure to give a sense of their approach. Several of the papers were written from an academic perspective; we've worked with the authors to make these accessible to nonacademic professionals and practitioners.

As we did last year, we have included at the end of almost every paper a shortened transcript of the smaller-group consideration with the author(s) of each chapter. (The two exceptions are the session with Mirja Hämäläinen and Kati Tikkamäki—an experiment in present-moment reflection that resulted in the paper in this volume—and the reprinted article from Harold Clarke and Susan Williams, to provide context for this year's offering.)

Finally, my thanks to my co-editor and Academy chairman Peter Garrett, who spent many hours with each of the authors developing the ideas for their papers, and for his insightful and welcoming introductions to each of the sections.

– Cliff Penwell
Editor

Section One

Dialogue in the Room

The entry level for Professional Dialogue work is Dialogue in the Room. The primary focus of attention is within a circle in a single room. The skills it draws upon to help a grouping of people to talk and think together in one room are the foundation that make Dialogic Intervention and Systemic Dialogue possible. Dialogue in the Room is the unfolding process at the heart of the Professional Dialogue work. It is an art and a science – an intellectual, emotional, physical and perhaps spiritual undertaking. The challenge is always the same: to address the fragmentation of awareness, and the aim is to expand the common content of consciousness (the container) by understanding one another and oneself. There are many ways into Dialogue, but they all involve the same steps: gathering people into one room together; getting participants engaged with one another; managing the functionality of time and intention; creating an environment of high-quality interaction; and becoming conversant with the face-to-face dynamics of awareness and participation involved in enabling generative outcomes.

— P.G.

Dialogic Team Coaching in TAMK Proakatemia

Timo Nevalainen

This paper will explore the basic principles of dialogic team coaching in TAMK Proakatemia, a special unit of entrepreneurship education in Tampere University of Applied Sciences (TAMK) in Finland. Currently the learning community of Proakatemia consists of about 150 students studying in the Bachelor of Business Administration (BBA), Entrepreneurship and Team Leadership and physical therapist programmes; 11 coaches; about 20 students in the MBA in Entrepreneurship programme; and several hundred alumni who regularly take part in Proakatemia activities. In the Tampere region, TAMK Proakatemia is one of the most recognized university programmes and internationally it is quickly gaining more visibility. Proakatemia currently is developing an international BBA degree programme based on team learning and coaching, with the aim of developing the capability of students to work in the Finnish business environment, using both English and Finnish languages.

TAMK Proakatemia

Proakatemia was founded in 1999. It started as an initiative by two teachers in TAMK business, based on earlier work in the city of Jyväskylä, where they had posted a notice on a wall asking students, "Do you want to learn marketing and travel around the world?" They got 20 people to join the programme, and those people formed the first team enterprise in Proakatemia. They called it *Villivisio*, or 'Wild Vision'.

In the beginning, Proakatemia operated in small premises in the basement of the TAMK School of Arts & Media. Students had to take care of upkeep of both the exterior premises and its interior – some cleaning floors, some sewing window curtains. Studying in Proakatemia was also quite unstructured, with coaches and students creating new structural elements and ways to solve problems as questions arose. Over the years, Proakatemia grew, with two teams of about 20 students starting each year, and it moved to larger premises. The curriculum became more structured, and a spreadsheet-based personal study plan was devised for the students to follow the course of their own work and studies.

Several ideas have formed the core of Proakatemia from the beginning:

- **Student ownership of the community and team enterprises** (they are cooperative companies).
- **The students' leading role in all activities in Proakatemia.** This is a marked difference from almost all other university programs, where most of the activities are led by the faculty.
- **The role of the teaching staff as team coaches, employing shared principles that guide their work.** Any faculty member who would try to take the responsibility for learning and business away from students and transfer it to him- or herself by, for example, attempting to directly control the activities or business of the team he or she is coaching, would only cause confusion and demotivate students.
- **Support, openness and courage from TAMK leadership as the head coach of Proakatemia acts as a mediator between Proakatemia and TAMK leadership and management.** This has, in retrospect, proved especially critical, as other similar programmes in Finland and Europe have often withered away or been downright cancelled because their working practices can be difficult to understand for leaders and managers of the higher education institutions.

The students in the Proakatemia BBA programme in Entrepreneurship and Team Leadership begin their studies at the main campus by studying the basics of business through such topics as accounting and marketing for half a year. They also spend one day each week on the Proakatemia premises with a coach, with whom they have dialogic training sessions on various topics. Sometimes these are self-selected and include such areas as team learning and starting their own business as a team. This initial half year also prepares the new students for dialogic training sessions, led twice a week for several hours at a time by each team member in turn.

After this initial introduction the students, in teams of about 20, start and register their enterprise as a cooperative company. They begin contacting companies in the area to find out about customer needs and they negotiate with each other about the type of business they want to build, including its products or services, its initial brand image, vision and values and its leadership structures and practices. The type of the company is not set by Proakatemia but rather by the teams; so far all have settled on a Finnish-type cooperative company, as this designation affords its individual members some financial independence from the economy of the cooperative, as well as more relaxed legal responsibility for different roles than would be possible in a traditional limited liability corporation. The teams are free to decide on their leadership structures, but they commonly emulate previous teams' arrangements and choose a format that includes a Business Leader (a CEO without the legal responsibilities that would go with the title), an HR Leader, a Finances Leader and a Marketing Leader, each with their own small teams. The first people to take up these leadership roles are usually selected through voting after a short presentation by each applicant. Later on, however, when the team members know each other better, coaches encourage them to engage in dialogue about leadership and, after that, they decide on the leaders based on the goals of the team as a whole.

From a team-coach perspective it is important to take a somewhat passive role during the first months, especially when in training sessions with the whole team. This is to balance the coaches' often quite-strong tendency toward preconception about what the students should be doing. In training sessions, it is often important to help the students perceive their own role as the ones responsible for whatever takes place in the sessions; this applies to everyone taking part, not just the student whose turn it is to lead the session. This often is best achieved by the coach being silent and listening without intervening. Where the coach *can* take a more active role is in conversations with individual students and with the leadership team of the student-team enterprise. There the coach can draw the attention of the individual students back to their own role in the team and discuss their ideas about how to best contribute or give direct feedback on how they are performing in different roles. The coaches hold development discussions with each student twice a year in conversations can take anywhere between half an hour and two hours.

As a team coach I spend most of my working time on the Proakatemia premises in an open-door shared office next to the space where the teams work. Our policy is that if a coach is in the office, anyone can enter and start a conversation. This has made the office a somewhat busy place to work with constant interruptions, so we often go to work elsewhere (at home, in library, in a café) if we need to focus for a longer period of time. Each coach sees their own team at least twice a week for four-hour training sessions (led by the students, with 15 to 20 people in the room, usually seated in a circle with movable chairs and no tables). They also take part in team-leader meetings, conduct development discussions with each student every half a year, tutor thesis work, and engage in countless informal conversations with students from their own team as well as those of others. (These informal conversations are such an important part of the learning process that Proakatemia has a dedicated cafeteria space in the middle for them.)

The team coaches' role mostly is not to deliver information or instruction – at least in the traditional sense – but rather to help the team build and manage an effective business organization as the students manage their own learning processes. All of the coaches are experts in pedagogy and learning processes, but we come from a wide variety of academic and professional backgrounds, including maths and language teaching to economics and marketing, as well as positive psychology and entrepreneurship.

Team-Entrepreneur Students in Proakatemia

The Proakatemia student body is relatively diverse. Some have just graduated from high school, while others have over 10 years of professional experience before coming to the programme. The age of students ranges from 18 or 19 to over 40, while most of them could be categorized as millennials, members of generation Y, between 21 and 28 years of age. Most of the students still have an ethnic Finnish background, but there also those whose parents have immigrated to Finland, or who themselves moved to Finland when they were younger. Currently a high level of Finnish language skill is required of all degree students in Proakatemia, which limits the possibility of taking international applicants, but this will change with the starting of an international programme next year (2020). The students who come to Proakatemia have a wide range of different personal goals and interests, which necessitates continuous dialogue and negotiation about what kind of business the team wants to run together. Many of the students are interested in entrepreneurship because it allows them to set up a company to provide a living for themselves and others while working in a sustainable and ethical way (as with a group of male students, for example, who started an ethical cosmetics business). Others are more interested in the opportunity to become economically successful entrepreneurs, while still others want to set up a small business where they can work with something in which they are intensely interested, in a way that suits their personalities. Some of the students want to continue their family business or, in case of those associated with larger companies, become its leaders. (At the moment, for example, the CEO of a major food-producing family business in Tampere is a Proakatemia graduate.)

Generally, the students drawn to Proakatemia are more interested in trying out things in practice than in reading and learning theories in a classroom. However, it is fascinating to see how quickly they become interested in reading for their own development when they themselves can select their books, helped by an extensive list of resources and reading suggestions from the community. With regard to academic skills, the students who come to the programme are a diverse group. Some have done very well in high school, while others have struggled with reading or writing, with language or with maths. The entrance exam to Proakatemia does not qualify students based on their prior success at school – at the moment, in fact, the previous grades are not even taken into account (although this may change with the upcoming revisions to the general university admission process in Finland). Many of the problems the students have previously experienced are alleviated by the emphasis on teamwork and building on people's different strengths instead of focusing on grading their weaknesses. For example, the Proakatemia curriculum carries the requirement for more reading and writing than most professional university studies, and all essays written by the students are published on the open Internet (esseepankki.proakatemia.fi) but students who have struggled with reading and writing before often find out that in a different environment, with the support of the team, the community and the coaches, their weakness becomes less of an issue.

Values and Roles in Proakatemia

Proakatemia operates on a principle of giving students centre stage. The coaches are strictly here to help students develop in ways they themselves see as important for their entrepreneurial careers. Proakatemia curriculum provides a generic framework for an entrepreneurial development process, including the development of competencies that are generally deemed necessary for succeeding as an entrepreneur. Proakatemia's path of five values ('Path to Entrepreneurship') provides the core of the curriculum:

1. **Trust** is critical for the development of a team enterprise or successful coaching relationship. Trust at its core means being vulnerable – making something that I value vulnerable to the choices and actions of others, because I trust them to respect my trust in them. In Proakatemia, we witness over and over that fundamental trust in students in important matters gives rise to their trustworthiness. For example, team entrepreneurs in Proakatemia often manage tasks and decisions that in other schools require decisions from the faculty members or even school management. This fundamental trust does not require a basis in previous actions but, instead, becomes a basis for future actions.
2. **Courage** is needed when team entrepreneurs need to challenge their own fears and feelings of inadequacy and find new customers to expand the team's business network. Courage has trust as its fundamental precondition.
3. **Doing** is necessary for reflection and learning in action. It is also very much needed as a basis for any meaningful feedback. Talk and theoretical reflection is not enough for building a capable enterprise together with others. When people trust each other and act with courage, their energy is directed to constructive action together with others rather than safeguarding their own individual positions.
4. **Learning** may follow from all of the above, but it is also necessary to keep this value in focus as an opportunity even when (or especially when) the team fails to achieve what they have set out to achieve. Failure can be a great – if not *the* greatest – source of entrepreneurial learning when a team has the trust and courage to look things in the eye together.
5. **Success** is not an individual value but one that transcends the personal self and its concern for its own advancement. In practice it means that an individual in Proakatemia should consider their choices and actions from the perspective of the long-term success of the team and others in it. Over the years, many visitors to Proakatemia have asked whether success should really feature in Proakatemia's value path, as it is usually thought of as something that an individual has relatively little control over. In Proakatemia, however, we emphasize how our choices and actions affect the success of the whole team rather than how our individual accomplishments advance us personally.

The role of a team coach in TAMK Proakatemia consists of five major coaching roles and their related activities: *1) modelling* the shared path; *2) building* safe shared space; *3) challenging* and acting as a sparring partner; *4) supporting* growth and offering encouragement; and *5) seeing* and making visible. These coaching roles may sometimes be held in tension with each other. For example, coaches may sometimes be perceived by the students as their friends, but they must still maintain enough distance to be able to bring up, when necessary, difficult and conflict-risking themes that the team members are neither capable of nor willing to take up with their colleagues. They must be willing to challenge the team and individual students, perhaps causing the kind of 'friction' which is sometimes necessary for learning and growth.

Team coaching is a holistic form of guidance and counselling that connects the growth processes of the team with the students in it. The team is a platform of mutual and personal growth for its members: the coach supports the development of the team through coaching individual persons and by promoting positive dynamics in the interaction of the team. The members of the team together create the conditions of growth for each other and the team enterprise.

The work of the coach *appears* to change surprisingly little during the course of studies. This may be due to the coach spending a lot of time growing with the team. At first, the focus is more on building trust, which requires a high degree of student agency, ensuring that the students know that the coach is on their side, and that there will not be a 'catch', or risk of failing to satisfy the goals set by the coach. Gradually, once the safe space has been firmly established, challenging students to move outside their comfort zones becomes more important. While many programmes gradually allow students more say over their activities and the learning process, in Proakatemia the students are fully empowered from the very beginning. This is also reflected in the leadership structure of the programme, as well as the strategic planning processes (Nevalainen & Maijala, 2012).

While it naturally becomes easier for the coach to treat students as younger colleagues – often as more competent experts in many topics – when they have known the students for a longer time, this should be the aim from day one. For example, when working with team entrepreneurs from different teams, the coaches usually never distinguish between first-, second-, third- or fourth-year students. The Proakatemia curriculum reflects a developmental process for both teams and individual students, but it has very little to do with how students are treated. Right from the beginning they are treated as capable team entrepreneurs with full participation and decision-making rights, including decisions over the direction of their company and the whole community. With these rights, they are also trusted to be responsible in their actions. For example, every student in Proakatemia has 24-hour access to all the premises (although there is a rule against spending whole nights on the property) and there are few locked spaces. Most of the international activities and almost all of the marketing activities in Proakatemia are expertly carried out by the student teams, and each May students organise Proakatemia's annual 'Academic Adventures' international week.

It is relatively easy for a coach to spot, even early on, where individual student strengths lie, but coaching different personalities to develop these strengths can be challenging. Engaging in dialogue with a student who has rather similar personality and preferences to the coach is often quite straightforward and easy, but working with those whose communications style is very different from that of the coach can be more challenging. For many coaches, extending the capacity to work with students with a wide range of different personalities becomes a major professional development goal. For example, I have always found it relatively easy to work with students who share my preference for lively conversation, easily flowing from one topic to another, as well as those with a strong focus on the meaning of the topic at hand. However,

I have sometimes struggled with the more introverted and careful students, or those who focus on *power* or *emotion* rather than *meaning* in their communication.

My Personal Path as a Dialogic Coach

The first time I came in contact with the idea of dialogue must have been during my qualification training to become a subject teacher in the English language. Our didactics tutor was very philosophically oriented, and introduced us to the thinking of humanistic psychologists, including that of Carl Rogers, who had studied dialogue extensively in educational contexts, and the work of Paulo Freire in critical pedagogy and Mikhail Bakhtin in literature. It was at that time I begun to rethink my own ideas of pedagogy and teaching, becoming enamoured with the idea of education as emancipatory dialogic work. During the teaching observation phase of my studies I also started paying more attention to the presence of the teacher and the various ways they engaged in dialogue with the elementary school pupils and high school students. If I had to select one person who had most influence on my dialogic coaching practice in the beginning, I would point to my didactics tutor.

One formative experience was a week of teacher training and observations that I did in southern Sweden, following third- and fourth-grade teachers in a midsized elementary school. There the pupils had no school bell, as we did at that time in virtually all Finnish schools. When the lessons were timed to start, the pupils came to the classroom, picked up their workbooks and started to work in small groups at their own pace. The teacher and the school assistant came in a few minutes later. (I later learned that there was one pupil who had a learning problem in the class and the school assistant was there for him, although he mostly appeared to work with anyone who needed help.) The pupils could also move freely between the classroom, the corridor where there was space for those who wanted to work by themselves in a quieter environment, and another classroom where there were classes in other subjects, like biology or geography. The teacher and the school assistant worked with whoever needed help in the class and engaged in dialogue with individual pupils and groups. At the time in 2003-04, the degree of self-direction of the pupils was very different from what I had experienced at schools in Finland.

I completed my MA thesis on the topic of authentic dialogue in communicative EFL (English as a Foreign Language) classes in a university in 2006, and it was based mainly on the work of Paulo Freire, Carl Rogers and David Bohm. It made me reflect more deeply on how I wanted to teach, and it gave me a solid basis on which to build more dialogic practices. This work helped me in training sessions I held with colleagues in a technical communication company, where I had also worked before my teacher training. It also helped a great deal when I later began my teaching career in 2007 at TAMK as a lecturer in English language for engineering and IT students, project management and website design. Many of my classes at the time were evening classes for adults who were already in their working life; in many of these classes I was the youngest person in the room and very often one of the least experienced on the topic I was supposed to teach. In my previous work as a trainer I had learned to respect the experience of the participants as a source of learning content. Having become somewhat adept at drawing out and exploring in dialogue that experience together must have been what enabled me to work as a teacher with participants who were senior to me in so many ways.

These experiences, and my continuous experimenting in all of my classes, made me realise that I could often draw on younger students with little or no 'professional' expertise or experience – and that experience, when shared, is the main 'tool' and material with which I must work as an educator.

Beginning My Team-Coaching Career

My career as a team coach began officially in 2008 when I started coaching first-year Information and Communication Technology (ICT) students in TAMK Business Information Systems programme, working in small teams on various cases and projects. I quickly noticed that self-direction by the students and a dialogic approach to coaching motivated many of the students and allowed them to develop their ICT skills more rapidly. Often, however, this conflicted with the structures and practices of the school, where most of teaching was still based on lectures, workshops and exams.

In 2010 I started working in TAMK Proakatemia as a team coach for a tea enterprise called *Versio Osk*. In Proakatemia, I learned to rely on the core values of the unit as well as constant dialogue with the team-entrepreneur students and my coach colleagues. However, it was not always easy: I often realised that I had given advice (often bad advice!) instead of engaging in dialogue. Learning to give up the role of an expert advisor was, at times, difficult, when nearly my whole university training had emphasised the value of my knowledge ('know-what') and expertise ('know-how'), instead of facilitating a process in which experience is shared and explored and understanding of its meaning developed in dialogue.

What helped me greatly in reflecting on how I was doing as a dialogic team coach was the set of shared core values in Proakatemia, formulated into a 'Values Path', as described earlier. The path allowed me to review my actions to see if I had acted and facilitated the values with the team, or if I had strayed and done something that did not promote – or was even detrimental – to them. For example, I might have inadvertently promoted my own expertise by giving direct advice (as truth) based solely on my own past experience or from a theory learned from studies or through reading, when the team actually needed was for me to help them explore their own past experience or figure out (as a team, not based on my expert opinions) how to find relevant information needed for the task. I realized that in the beginning, when I promoted my own experience or handed out expert advice like teachers are often expected to do, I often was acting directly against the core values of *trust* (in the ability of the team and in the value of their own experience), *courage* (to get in contact with the relevant experts in their own networks), *doing* (trying out things in practice, rather than me as an expert predicting how things might go) and *learning* (by finding information and applying it in practice). Quite quickly I learned that handing out expert advice neither increased the students' sense of agency nor contributed to their success, and that a dialogic approach often brought better results; it offered a learning process that was much more effective for everyone, myself included. Indeed, suspending the attitude of a teacher as an expert was crucial to success. After a while, the students started joking about me knowing a lot more about the topics we discussed than I would allow myself to reveal. This was only partially true, as I suspect that many of the gains that the students interpreted as signs of my superior knowledge actually emerged because of the dialogic sharing of experience and knowledge construction rather than because of my prior experience. In a way, I think the team I was coaching allowed me to access a much wider knowledge base than I would have been able to without them.

Besides the continuous conversations with my colleagues and students, participating in professional networks like the Academy of Professional Dialogue and taking part in courses and trainings in facilitation and coaching, knowledge management, education and logotherapy, my current ways of developing the art of dialogic coaching also include practices that are seemingly unrelated to dialogic coaching. These include Chinese martial arts (*Yiquan* and *Tai chi*) to train for sensitivity and situational awareness, and to explore and train my reactions to what is taking place, and the Alexander Technique to learn about my own reactions and how to better deal with potentially stressful and high-stakes situations in coaching. The latter practices often enable me to suspend my judgements so that I can pay attention to what is actually taking place in situations where stress or anxiety would likely work against it, or against dialogue.

Knowledge as Reflective Dialogue in Action

When discussing the pedagogical practices in Proakatemia with people who have not visited the unit, one question often comes up (besides the usual ones related to grading and assessment): How do coaches ensure that students get the right type and amount of knowledge during their studies? This question may be motivated by a non-dialogic conception of knowledge, or *knowledge as facts* within higher education. According to this view, knowledge is a valued 'thing' that can be 'possessed' by an expert, who then can derive various social advantages because of this possession. According to Chris Argyris and Donald Schön in *Theory in Practice: Increasing Professional Effectiveness*, knowledge as a possessed thing can consist of facts gained through scholarship, research or experience, as well as knowledge of rules and procedures. If one works within this conception of knowledge, teaching becomes information delivery (often through lecturing) or facilitation of information acquisition (reading assignments), alongside examining and monitoring this acquired information, rules and procedures.

A second view of knowledge suggested by Argyris and Schön is *knowledge as thinking like an expert*. This includes utilizing cognitive procedures similar to those of the experts when solving real-life problems – for example, thinking like a doctor when diagnosing patients or like an engineer when designing engine parts to fit together as a whole and work with maximum fuel efficiency. In this view of knowledge, the teacher takes on the role of a tutor or a mentor who works alongside the student, looking at how he or she diagnoses and solves problems, praising the student after success, pointing out flaws in thinking and, perhaps, handing out appropriate qualifications after the student has successfully completed certain tasks.

A third view of knowledge they suggest is *knowledge as reflection in action*. This view states that knowledge is constructed within action through reflection on that action. This kind of knowledge cannot be separated from action, taught or examined outside it. Knowledge as reflection in action is always woven into a situation and cannot be separated from it. One example of this would be the way that an object being designed informs the designer as it is being made, and how she, through continuous reflection on that feedback and by organizing her own actions, can guide both the process and the way the object comes into being. A similar process can take place in a sales meeting: A salesperson gives a short presentation about the product while at the same time focusing and reflecting on the reactions of the potential buyers, continuously revising the speech as it emerges. The presenter skilfully aligns actions to the reactions of the buyers with the aim of bringing about a certain kind of action-oriented relationship. Similar processes take place when skilled leaders engage with their employees or stakeholders.

Thinking of these models as they relate to Proakatemia, even though all conceptions of knowledge are crucial for higher education, I would suggest that it is the third, often ignored view of *knowledge as reflection in action* that must be brought to the forefront in dialogic team coaching. In Proakatemia it must be extended to something like shared dialogic reflection in action, or *reflective dialogue in action*.

How can a coach then facilitate this reflective dialogue? The first thing would be to exemplify it in one's own actions. When working with students a coach has to be present, attentive to the experience of the students, listening actively, always respecting what they bring out and open up in their own talk. After setting an example, the coach has to help team members train their attention to each other's experience and how they contribute to (or harm) the overall dialogic space. If, for example, a student appears to take up too much floor time, the coach may have a private conversation with the student (who often might not have noticed that he or she is making it more difficult for others to take part), or encourage others to bring forth their experiences more courageously. Here the coach has to exemplify both trust and courage and encourage others to do so as well.

References

Argyris, C., & Schön, D. A. (1992). *Theory in Practice: Increasing Profes-sional Effectiveness* (first edition). San Francisco: Jossey-Bass.

Nevalainen, T., & Maijala, M. (2012). "Creative management in TAMK Pro-academy". *Development and Learning in Organizations: An Inter-national Journal, 26*(6), 17–19.

Conference Session Extracts

From a conversation with participants considering the paper with the author

Speaker 1: What interests me about what you're doing, Timo, is that you have a business, and it'll fail or make money, and work or not work, so we have to find out how to do it. So I'm interested in the element of it succeeding. It is a real business where people put up their own money and have to make work. That allows everything else to start to fall in behind it.

Speaker 2: That was one of my thoughts too. How to create more project-based teaching in addition to teaching in a more traditional way? Because in my view, it's just as important to listen to people that have a lot of knowledge and wisdom. I have learned a lot by just sitting there listening. This combination of approaches – learning by doing, and this traditional listening to deep knowledge, is very important, I think.

Speaker 3: I had an interesting experience with a not-for-profit organisation that I've been working with in South Africa. A friend of mine and I are working on it together. They have 40 staff, mostly young people, and really diverse in terms of different cultures. We've been running a series of dialogues for them. But the Managing Director specifically requested, based on some experimental dialogues we did for six months, that we should not have any education up front. No theory. Because she really believes dialogue lives within us, and it is part of who we are. She went back to some of the ancient, different tribes, and sitting around the fire, and she really wanted to experiment with this. And as we got going, I noticed, I could see questions coming up – and complexity, like what are we doing? And why are we doing it? So in between each session I wrote to the staff. I noticed in myself that I did a lot of what I'd call invisible work, like container work, holding them in my awareness in a specific way. I thought there was going to be complexity, and there was. There were lots of questions, like, What are we doing? Why are we doing this? What is this process? So eventually, after three or four sessions, the Managing Director said, "Yeah, I think I was wrong. I think maybe we could do a day or two days of training". So do you just keep the thing implicit and create a real container?

Speaker 1: Functional familiarity means an appropriate level of development. I sometimes wonder whether we're teaching people too much dialogue, and not enough enabling them to do what they're trying to do.

Speaker 4: Well, it's turning some of the thinking on its head. In a lot of the most recent work we didn't teach anybody anything ever. No instruction. Never. It was never about that. It was always that there's a certain result sought. You have to interact together, you have to create a pattern where the interaction unfolds in a certain way. I think the focus is what's needed – what are you trying to do?

Speaker 1: But in a way, that's a distraction from the idea of how we learn, isn't it? The fundamental here is do we learn by being given answers and ways and means? Or do we learn by doing something and asking for, or reading or finding out from other sources, what's needed to get there? And they can be worked together, but they are different methods, aren't they? The one is: We'll go on a course and learn how to do it. The other is: We'll try to find out what's needed as we get going.

Speaker 5: What you're saying brings to my mind the difference between the team that doesn't have a project yet, and a team that's working together on a project. Because they are . . . .

Speaker 1: Different animals.

Speaker 5: It's a different animal because when a team doesn't have a project yet, the feedback that they give to each other is, "Oh, you were so nice to me in the morning". It's like so introspective that they would go crazy if they continued like that. Because there's no outlet for their energy besides the team dynamics. When they actually have a project, it could be called a shared object of attention or intention. When they have a shared object, they start working intensely on something. They see their friends being interested in that same thing, and they become more interested in it themselves. Then you get another person joining in, and it's like there's a lot of teamwork. That's where the teamwork starts. They're going to be doing something. It can be staged. You don't have to learn how to do everything simultaneously.

Speaker 1: I experienced this in a maximum-security prison. We had offenders who were antisocial and wouldn't participate in anything, but I managed to get a couple of them to come to the dialogue group. They enjoyed the fact they could talk about anything and they did. For a long time, they talked about things, and they would still not go an any therapeutic courses or any educational stuff, but their interest in the dialogue was strong. Eventually, the conversation got onto how's your life working out? And what's going on and why are you in the situation you're in? Gradually, the conversation shifted to, Where am I going in my life? It became quite self-reflective, and they challenged each other really personally.

Speaker 4: Yeah, something must have happened so that they were talking about themselves. How did that transition occur?

Speaker 1: The way I facilitated it, our dialogue was a conversational dialogue. So we'd start off talking about football scores or whatever, gradually getting everyone involved. We'd get everyone talking and, gradually, it comes onto my family and my brother, or whatever. Slowly people get more and more involved in thinking about their lives and what they're doing – and there are very few places to talk about that kind of stuff safely, because normally in a prison you get taken advantage of. So you build a container that has a bit of safety.

Speaker 5: We try to create that, or help build that as coaches. In development-stage discussions, people talk about their life goals. They have signed up for Proakatemia for three years. And sometimes their life goals are sort of going in a very different direction from where the team is going. So as a coach, I try to remind them to think about whether or not this is going to help their team to succeed.

Postscript

The author's reflections, written some months after the conference

Writing a paper for and taking part in the 2019 The World Needs Dialogue! conference certainly became a real learning journey for me. The initial idea for my paper was based on my work and experiences as a team coach and almost 10 years of experience in dialogue as part of the approach we call 'entrepreneurial team learning'. The idea and the paper developed much further in online conversations with Peter Garrett and Jane Ball, through which the paper more or less 'wrote itself'.

During the dialogue in the conference, we talked about our doubts about the basic role of dialogue alone in learning or constructing new knowledge. This perception mirrors a very common attitude that specialists hold towards knowledge, as information content that can be acquired and possessed by a specialist and which they can then disseminate to others. An alternative to the idea of knowledge as something to be acquired and then possessed could be taking the process aspect of knowledge more seriously – the training of people, through the disciplined practice of dialogue, to reflect together on what they are trying to achieve while they are trying to achieve it.

Other themes that came up in the dialogue were the significance and context of experience, and the goals that are shared by or at least relevant to the lives of those engaging in dialogue. We also talked about shifting attention from the individual experience to shared consciousness of the group or the team, and how a university degree program can provide an architecture for dialogic learning with a high level of student agency, dialogic spaces, entrepreneurial practices, traditions and relationships between the participants (the team entrepreneurs and their team coaches, and whether similar architectures could be implemented in different contexts like, for example, in correctional institutions.

Going back to the dialogue, I can now see that the process that began with the paper is still ongoing and the theme is resonant with much of the work I have undertaken after the conference. In January 2020 we started a research group 'Learning & Growth in Teams' (LeGiT) in TAMK, where I have continued to study topics such as the role of collective reflection within the team and dialogue in team learning, and the changes needed in the practice architectures of conventional educational institutions. All of these are important if organisations want to create spaces for entrepreneurial team learning – including the core practices of dialogue and dialogic team coaching.

Dialogue at School

Joop Boukes

> *To reform the world – means to reform upbringing*
> – Janusz Korczak

I am enthusiastic about explaining how I came to want to give Dialogue a broad place in schools, about the added value Dialogue offers in that setting and how it benefits students and our society.

My first practical experiences with Dialogue took place at work. I had been working in Driehuis, the Netherlands, as a senior youthcare worker with an organization called *Lijn5*, delivering treatment to disadvantaged youth (primarily boys between 13 and 18 years) with mild intellectual disabilities, behavioural disorders, attachment disorders and psychopathologies. Many of them had experienced neglect and abuse within an unhealthy and inadequate home environment, and often they used aggression as a coping mechanism. *Lijn5* has many years of experience in the diagnosis and treatment of behavioural and social-emotional problems in children and adolescents (6-23 years), and it offers treatment, family-crisis intervention, after-school day treatment, stay-in care at one of the treatment groups or independence training for young adults.

The treatment I delivered was within group-home settings that offered varying degrees of freedom and restrictions. By mid-2000 I became aware that, through our guidance and control – including physical control – we were moulding the youths to display socially desirable behaviour with us but, when they left the facility, their oppositionality returned. In fact their resistance and hostility to adults in general grew, and we were often frustrated in our attempts to help the youths heal and adopt healthy strategies and behaviours.

I decided to quit my job because I could not keep on doing what was not working. Luckily my supervising psychologist, Gerard Kocken, was interested to know why I wanted to leave the organization.

Gerard Kocken and I discussed my observations and I explained what I thought should be done to achieve a healthier treatment environment. At this time, along with my work, I was studying Transpersonal Counselling and took inspiration from the teachings and experiences of Don Bosco, the 19th-century priest, educator and writer from Turin who encouraged street youth to talk about choosing better and healthier ways of living. He developed teaching methods based on Dialogue and love rather than on punishment. I wanted all youth workers to connect and communicate with young people in way that was different from what we were doing.

In all the years I worked with these disadvantaged youth they had never been aggressive towards me personally. (I broke my ribs and nose a few times, but that was because I had to interfere in fights between others.) I was always open to talking about anything with them, even after being hurt by them, and that made a mutual relationship more possible. They told me that because I was open and not resentful they trusted me and were more eager to talk with me than with others.

Developing New Training Pilots

Gerard was interested enough that he offered to supervise a pilot project utilizing methods which encouraged the youths to Dialogue, and to develop long-term healthy ways to manage themselves in the world. Our organization was supportive. The project wanted to eliminate the 'screw you' stance of the youths and to show that desirable treatment results were possible.

Two treatment groups totalling 16 youths and 20 educators (youthcare workers) were involved. I trained the educators in the protocols, including Dialogue, and collected data. After three months we found that resistance and aggression had markedly diminished, and the youth were increasingly willing and able to develop an internal locus of control and to engage in their treatment, learning goals and personal perspectives. (Details of this pilot are elaborated further on in this paper.) The results were so successful that Gerard embarked on another study and research project, building upon the findings of the pilot project. This research is finished and the thesis embodying the research is expected to be completed by the end of 2019.

The research, named 'Screw You', investigated whether social, cognitive and contextual factors influence communication between young people with mild intellectual disability and behavioural problems and their youthcare workers in an orthopedagogical treatment centre, based in a holistic approach that does not see children as fundamentally 'damaged'. Because youthcare workers play an important role in teaching correct behaviour, training was developed to help them use effective communication (which we refer to as *De Dialoog*, or 'the Dialogue'). The findings of the research underline the importance of the use of Dialogue. It is a flag to the treatment centre and its staff that solutions for dealing with miscommunications and stressors need to be found and that these solutions need to facilitate replacement of 'screw you' attitudes with ones that focus on 'looking out for you and caring for you'.

During the research of Gerard Kocken, it became clear that when people were approached through Dialogue, their social information process became easier and better; they felt safer. They used their higher brain functions (executive functions) more effectively, thinking about what they wanted to say or do instead of just being reactive. Because of this, they experienced that their voice mattered – they were taken seriously. This had a positive effect on their self-esteem and also on their experience of Self-efficacy. They began to have confidence in their ability to perform specific behaviours in different circumstances. Because of this confidence and self-esteem, they were more willing to engage and cooperate in their treatment. By repeating the use of Dialogue, this series of consequences only became stronger and the youths became clearer in their thinking and more cooperative.

Executive Functions and Dialogue

Executive functions belong to the mind. They are higher thinking processes needed to plan and manage activities. You can see them as 'conductors', because they help with all types of tasks. They ensure efficient, social- and goal-oriented behaviour. The executive functions are also called executive attention.

You can roughly divide this attention into four types: impulse control, concentration, flexibility, and prioritizing. Researchers Peg Dawson and Richard Guare even distinguish eleven types in three broad categories: *response inhibition* (thinking before doing something, working memory, emotion regulation, persistent attention, task initiation, planning / prioritization, organization); *time management* (time estimation and division, goal-oriented behaviour, flexibility in dealing with changes and setbacks); and *metacognition* (taking a step back to oversee and evaluate yourself and the situation). These are all characteristics that are so important to have a healthy Dialogue. Helping to develop these executive functions can also be achieved by learning early on how to conduct a Dialogue with another.

Training, Part One: Dialogue and the Factors that Influence It
For the three-month pilot project, we developed a four-day training for the research groups. This was an intensive training that would mean a major change in the interaction and treatment of these youths. The training had the following structure:

In Training, Part One we explained how the information that comes to the young person is processed. We looked at the patterns that have developed in thinking and behaviour. By exploring the functioning of social information processing, we showed which thinking steps precede different behaviours. Subsequently we considered the thoughts and patterns that give us the ability to participate in a Dialogue, as the executive functions regulate such aspects of behaviour as flexibility and frustration tolerance. Finally, we considered the concept of self-esteem. We explained why positive self-esteem is so important for healthy development, and we discussed the link between Dialogue and self-esteem development. We explained what Dialogue entails, what core aspects it has and what Dialogue skills someone needs to be able to enter into Dialogue. These skills include adopting a 'learning' attitude, showing radical respect, being open, speaking from the heart, listening, delaying, suspending assumptions and assessments, structural reasoning, having a questioning attitude and observing yourself as an observer.

We think of Dialogue as a form of interchange aimed at fostering mutual insight and common purpose. The process involves listening with empathy, searching for common ground, exploring new ideas and perspectives, and bringing unexamined assumptions into the open. In this, we discussed the stages that Dialogue goes through. We provided instructions for a good Dialogue, and included its pitfalls: interrupting each other, completing or filling in someone else's thoughts, holding unexamined assumptions, moving too fast, talking too much, staying too abstract and judging. We explained in this context the right form of Dialogue-oriented presence.

Many colleagues were curious about our approach to Dialogue. Deep down, most of them felt resistance to using physical intervention to manage aggression. People were looking for other ways to prevent incidents. In Training, Part One we also used aspects of transactional analysis – looking at the person's interactions and relationships – to show how people end up in a negative spiral.

Training, Part Two: Dialogue-Oriented Communication During Daily Interaction
In this part of the training, we introduced Dialogue in a professional learning and treatment environment, as we were dealing with educators. The professionalization was a key condition for Dialogue to be carried out in this setting. With this in mind, we focused on the development patterns that influenced the pursuit of the profession by the educators.

In this context it was important that the professional educators had studied the development processes upon which we based *De Dialoog*. We looked at the motivations of our actions. We did not promote Dialogue as just a conversation technique, but rather we hoped that, during daily activities, the educators would see moments in which they could apply Dialogue. During this part we also discussed the tension between the educator as a profession and as a person. Everyone has their own values and norms, their own frame of reference, and we discussed the tension between what we have to do (our profession) and what we personally think of it (each of us as a person). We saw that many colleagues have strong ideas about aggression, resistance and punishment, which made Dialogue difficult.

Training, Part Three: Dialogue-Oriented Communication and Personal Growth Plans
In Training, Part Three, we explored Dialogue in the context of the creation of a personal growth plan for the children. In developing plans with the youth, youthcare workers learned how to ask the children to express his or her learning goals. This was communicated with the help of Dialogue. We discussed the appropriate Dialogue technique (listening, suspending one's thoughts for others to understand, not interrupting, supplementing or filling in, talking quietly and checking to see if you are well understood). This was partly in light of the young person's initial resistance and limitations. Furthermore, we offered guidelines for

facilitating the Dialogues and for conducting personal interviews. We also gave instructions on how to record a Personal Growth Plan interview. These planning sessions were important, as for many young people it was the first time, after years in institutions, that they were really asked how they thought about themselves and about their future perspective. They felt taken seriously for the first time and felt that their opinion really mattered.

In this part of the training we promoted the learning process by using role plays that were recorded on video and later watched and reviewed. As mentioned, we also focused on conducting group Dialogues. As our young people are mostly in groups, it was important to focus on creating the skills needed to conduct a group Dialogue through the use of 'round-table discussions'. We looked at what a round-table discussion entails and its ultimate goals. This kind of conversation is a group intervention and therefore has a specific dynamic. Youthcare workers were trained to cope with interruptions, emotions, not participating and negative interactions.

Following this, the youth can be encouraged to actively participate in the group Dialogue. The size of the group was about eight people – a challenge in itself because the various psychopathologies made it difficult to maintain concentration. Some young people really wanted to talk a lot and others were very quiet and expectant. The interaction between the different young people often needed a lot of guidance.

Training, Part Four: Dialogue in Challenging Circumstances

In this section, we gave attention to conducting Dialogue sessions when stressful moments arise. A range of feelings, including anger, powerlessness and aggression, can be channelled differently with the help of Dialogue. The researchers and educators learned how to help youth deal with these tense moments by becoming aware and applying the necessary steps to deal with them effectively by means of becoming aware and applying professional steps (*stop, think, do*). This was the most exciting training goal because many colleagues experienced powerlessness when the youth showed aggression – other people's emotions do something with our emotions. It was very important during the training to learn how to stay calm. Very often aggression was translated as aimed at the person, while often it actually was about fear, misunderstanding or despair. It was also important to start the conversation as soon as possible when peace returned and to investigate together the cause and the process that followed the disturbance. Understanding each other's responses was just as important as looking for solutions. In this way, a different relationship with the youngsters emerged.

We regularly used video recordings during the training sessions with the purpose of allowing participants to see themselves and receive feedback on their behaviour.

We wrote a special section for the trainers at *De Dialoog*. Trainers were expected to be unambiguous and well-founded in both theory and practice, and we provided instruction on how to encourage these conditions. The trainers were expected to delve deeper into the theories applied during this course, and to base their professional Dialogue accordingly.

A number of behavioural scientists, together with Gerard Kocken, have written 'the

Marked Dialogue', a document designed to provide tools for daily interaction with young people with a mild mental disability who also have had a psychological / psychiatric referral for help (including Attention Deficit/Hyperactivity Disorder, Pervasive Developmental Disorder, Oppositional Defiant Disorder and Attachment Disorder.)

The Next Steps: Closing One Chapter and Beginning Another

After we completed the required basic data for the study, I was finally allowed to train all the other treatment groups at the institute. The groups and teams are spread throughout the Netherlands at different treatment facilities. In total it involved more than 400 youthcare workers.

The then-director of the institute wanted to keep informed of the progress and results of the training, so we had monthly meetings to share our progress. At a certain point we recognized that everyone within the organization needed to know of the added value of Dialogue, which resulted in a request to give everyone within the organization training in Dialogue. Altogether over 900 people, including not only management but also support services, were familiarized with Dialogue. We established an implementation group to help further Dialogue within the organization. This brought several major and generative changes: management became more communicative, and the youths gradually began to understand that a conversation was more desirable than threatening or anger. Colleagues met and talked with each other differently and more effectively. *De Dialoog* had found a place within the organization. A dialogical environment arose among the youths, which was noticeable by the sharp increase in productive conversations which took the place of angry outbursts and aggression behaviours.

During this time our national government made the decision that the task of youthcare would be decentralized and transferred to municipalities. This was a result of the desire to invest in youthcare at the management level closest to youth, their educators and parents. Decentralization was also fiscally driven by the premise that, by divesting responsibility to municipalities, money could be diverted to prevention, support and outpatient services. This would result in less-expensive care by reducing the need for 24-hour residential care and other specialized and more expensive services.

Our organization, providing 24-hour care within a residential setting with specialized services, had to shrink from more than 900 employees to just over 400. Many groups and locations had to close and there was – and still is – great financial pressure to survive as an organization. Reorganization and redundancies led to the loss of the use of Dialogue.

Of course, I was disappointed and frustrated that a major investment in time and energy suddenly disappeared. We also noticed that the old parenting patterns took over again quickly. Fortunately, because of the experience I had at *Lijn5,* in combination with my work as a teacher at the academy for integral human sciences where I lectured in adolescence and adolescence-problems, I saw opportunities for Dialogue in education in general.

I started my own business in training and guiding Dialogue with *Mens in Dialoog* (Mankind in Dialogue), and had some inspiring experiences with Dialogue at school. I will mention the most impressive one.

I was asked to help guide a Dialogue for over 200 people following the suicides of two students who were bullied. The Dialogue would be between police, sports clubs, youth workers, religious institutions, municipality and school staff. The groups wanted to talk together and see what could be done to prevent bullying. When they asked if I could arrange 20 facilitators for the guidance of a large World Café Dialogue, I suggested that 20 students could become familiar with this role. The students received training and were very enthusiastic and driven to do well. After all, it was about their school and their friends. It was their own idea to all wear the same T-shirt, with 'I see you' on the front and 'Do you see me?' on the back. Even better was that they had created a kind of arrival ceremony for all participants, giving loud applause when someone came in. They were very serious during the Dialogue and perfectly capable of providing even the mayor with tips for a Dialogue.

Why Starting with Dialogue at School Is Important

It is impossible to conceive of successful school reform without the active support of the community. Knowing how to bring stakeholders into the tent, rather than leaving them outside, is also best practice for democracy.

– Daniel Yankelovich

Dialogue is becoming more well known and is used increasingly to come jointly to solutions. Unfortunately, this often only happens when there are problems or challenges to address. Since most people do not grow up with the awareness or skills of Dialogue, people must first become familiar with or trained in Dialogue. This is often difficult because most adults have already developed their own patterns in communicating that do not match those of Dialogue. Children learn at school to present themselves and their ideas, to discuss and to debate, but they do not learn how to enter into Dialogue. But Dialogue not only helps with the development of certain brain functions, it also increases precisely those thinking capacities that help people slow down, respond more proactively, focus better and listen more attentively. Because of this they are better able to deal with other perspectives, work together, find solutions and become more creative.

For better understanding of the importance of Dialogue in school we have to address the meaning of the word *Dialogue*. I think I have more than 50 definitions and translations of the word.

So what is Dialogue? I like to use the definition made by William Isaacs in *Dialogue and the Art of Thinking Together*:

Dialogue . . . is a conversation with a center, not sides. It is a way of taking the energy of our differences and channelling it toward something that has never been created before. It lifts us out of polarization and into a greater common sense, and is thereby a means for accessing the intelligence and coordinated power of groups of people. Dialogue is a conversation in which people think together in relationship. Thinking together implies that you no longer take your own position as final. You relax your grip on certainty and listen to possibilities that result simply from being in relationship with others and possibilities that might not otherwise have occurred. To listen respectfully to others, to cultivate and speak your own voice, to suspend your opinions about others—these bring out the intelligence that lives at the very center of ourselves—the intelligence that exists when we are alert to possibilities around us and thinking freshly.

What would it be like if Dialogue became a regular part of education? What would it be like if all schools were to familiarize their pupils with Dialogue as a way to discuss topics that matter to them? Would we become a society in which people would be more easily able to engage in difficult conversations with each other? Would students be better able to embrace diversity, and would action be more based on inclusion? Would they be more able to jointly tackle problems? Would people listen to each other sooner and better, because they know that everyone's voice is of value and can be seriously explored together? I believe so, but it will require a major effort.

The school is of course the most important place to introduce children and young people to the power of Dialogue – and not just an interfaith Dialogue, an intercultural Dialogue or a Dialogue that is initiated because other forms of consultation have been unsuccessful. No, I'm thinking of Dialogue as a basic skill of living, where we learn to listen to others and ask questions freely.

For students, teachers, staff and parents/family I might explain Dialogue more easily:

A Dialogue is about the free exchange of insights, ideas, opinions, or feelings between two or more people. The aim is to promote the idea that everyone's contribution adds to the goal of the group and strengthens mutual cooperation. The core of this is that a group sees the value of 'making room for everyone's input', and that they know real space is created. Everyone has a piece of the puzzle. Together we will find the best approach. New insights can arise in Dialogue so that something new can emerge. Dialogue is not a discussion, where it's all about winning. A different spirit reigns in Dialogue: *win-win*. Everyone wins, and only together can we move forward.

And the younger the better. Even at primary school you can start Dialogue with children.

De Dialoog circles are an effective way of Dialogue. These circles are gatherings in which all participants sit in a circle facing each other to facilitate open, direct communication. Dialogue circles provide a safe, supportive space where all school community members can talk about sensitive topics, work through differences, and build consensus. Being able to think critically comes in handy with every professional and in every aspect of life.

Dialogue is also a social activity. Children learn to listen, respect each other and see through the eyes of another. Moreover, it can be formative: children discover how they think about the world, learn to articulate their thoughts better – and they dare to speak them. Dialogue can also give a wonderful feeling of freedom. There are no wrong answers.

Dialogue is also interesting for teachers. With it, they get to know children in a very different way. They learn not only what children think, but also *how* they think. A child's reasoning is often moving, original, creative and also amazingly clever. Moreover, dialogue is good for their social, emotional, moral and language development as they learn to think critically and creatively.

In contrast to most other European countries, schools in the Netherlands pay little explicit attention to Dialogue about social issues or to discussing relevant experiences in class together. Many teachers find it difficult to conduct a Dialogue with pupils (Veugelers, 2009), although Dialogue and reflection on events inside and outside the school can make an important contribution to the formation of critical-democratic citizens. Conducting Dialogue requires communication skills such as argumentation, reasoning, perspective, nuance and listening. Skills such as taking a stand, respecting other opinions, making moral discernment, being able to empathize with the opinions of others, critically dealing with sources and information and coming to an agreement with others are all important in the context of citizenship development. Many now assume that Dialogue not only promotes a deeper understanding of the topic of the conversation, but also contributes to social cohesion in the group or class (Castelijns, Koster & Vermeulen, 2009; Verhoeven, 2012).

Dialogue creates a bond. Social cohesion, or the awareness of interdependence between the members of a group, is seen as a form of social capital, as Ruben Gowricharn, Dirk Willem Postma and Sandra Trienekens have pointed out. Robert Putnam uses the term 'bonding capital' in this context. By this he means the mutual bond that you create through socialization and interaction with your own group.

Dialogue and Lessons in Current Events

Obviously, the use of Dialogue works well within the lessons on social studies or citizenship education. However, there will always be current topics that require a Dialogue. Pupils may have different opinions as a result of a news item, causing tensions. In the dynamics of the class there may be a natural role for Dialogue, or a subject that asks for Dialogue might emerge from the lesson content. In the Netherlands, classes have a mentor, a teacher who discusses the school atmosphere with students, including how people are feeling and what they might have problems with. And, of course, topics such as bullying, drug use, use of social media, sexual behaviour and violence can be discussed through Dialogue. Even charged topics such as radicalization and polarization can be addressed with Dialogue. A teacher can have a Dialogue with a student about motivation, learning difficulties, absence or behaviour in the classroom.

Class Management with Dialogue

Dialogue can also be used by the teacher to achieve healthy class management. I myself have been giving classes in class management for 12 years based on Dialogue. The training teaches teachers how to reach a consensus with the students on positive rules of conduct that give the teacher the opportunity to transfer knowledge and teach students at rest. Class management based on Dialogue is done together with the students. Rules are drawn up together and instead of punishment there are consequences if the rules are not followed. Students better accept the consequences because they were allowed to think about the rules and co-create them.

Dialogue Between Teachers

Teachers can use Dialogue between themselves to achieve more clarity about teaching in the interest of the students. They can employ clarity in control and rules, to be sure. But they can also learn to conduct student discussions based on Dialogue in which they work together in solving learning problems, exploring motivation, talking about disability and engaging with other topics. Dialogue between fellow professionals about the quality and intended results of their work, based on the exchange of personal experiences to arrive at a joint vision on educational developments, could be a useful goal. This way everyone can take responsibility for school development from their own position. In all of this, Dialogue can promote the contact culture in a respectful way, thereby improving the working environment.

Dialogue Teachers with Parents and Family

Having conversations with parents through Dialogue yields much more than what is possible in the standard 10-minute conversation. Parents who work with teachers and the school on the learning process of their children are invaluable. Teachers can better coordinate what is needed for a specific student in consultation with parents. Many families are not adequately informed about what their children need to learn in order to succeed in a complex global society, so the sharing of information and a dedicated space for making meaning is essential. And while all families want their children to do well, many need guidance in how to amplify their voices on behalf of their own children and those in the community as a whole.

Making time for the concrete questions parents have about care of their children is a good starting point. Another important element in the dialogue between parents, teacher and school is the recognition of the important role parents play in the child's welfare. Every parent has unique knowledge about his or her child at home, and that insight about the character, sensitivities, interests and talents of a child is a great addition to the teacher's professional knowledge. Teachers know the child in the classroom: how they behave and feel in the group, as well as how they deal with assignments and agreements. When the school can incorporate all of this knowledge in an equivalent way, acknowledging the contribution each person makes to the child's wellbeing, parents and teachers become full partners in the upbringing of the child.

Dialogue Between Teachers and Management

Teachers can enter into Dialogue with school management about shaping education within their school. Teachers often feel excluded from discussions about school redesign. They experience it as something that is happening to them, not as something in which they have a direct stake. But when teachers have a chance to be at the table, to be a genuine part of the decision-making process, they are often receptive to changes and offer their own ideas for how to best implement them.

What Is Needed Next?

In order to give Dialogue a full place in schools, it is important to start sharing Dialogue now, with beginning teachers. Next year I will start giving a Dialogue training at a Pedagogic Academy Primary Education facility (in Dutch, a *PABO*) and dialogue classes at the Hogeschool Inholland in The Hague in the course called 'Learning and Innovation' for teachers working towards a Master of Education degree. These teachers contribute to educational development in their organization in primary, secondary and higher education because they act as so-called 'change agents' within their team. They initiate and guide educational innovations, thereby contributing to the professionalization of colleagues. Hopefully other teacher training programs will follow. Dialogue as a citizenship instrument is developed by the *Hogeschool Rotterdam,* and the *Hogeschool van Amsterdam* (higher professional education) uses Dialogue as a methodology for the second-degree curriculum of teacher training courses. I will promote the use of Dialogue in other education for teachers.

    I am writing a small book about Dialogue (*The Little Dialogue Book*) that contains steps to make Dialogue more possible. This booklet provides a few dos and don'ts for conducting Dialogue in a simple way, and I hope it will be given to all pupils, teachers (and parents) in schools as a reminder and reference. In addition, I hope to write a manual for teachers on how to use Dialogue at school and in lessons. I am building a website with a lot of information about Dialogue and its use. There will also be a network of people available who can give lessons or training in Dialogue to students, teachers and staff. The purpose of the website is to encourage educators to make Dialogue part of the curriculum as well as part of daily use. Starting next year I plan to offer training courses for teachers, mentors and school management.

Unfortunately, education in the Netherlands is currently very unsettled. There is a huge shortage of teachers and a new curriculum is being worked on for all schools. Since the spring of 2018, about 150 teachers and school leaders in development teams within nine learning areas have been working on proposals for revising national attainment targets and targets for primary and secondary education. It is the first time that these targets have been revised in a coherent way, and that teachers from primary, secondary and special education are the ones to take the initiative. There is a great deal of disagreement among teaching staff about the usefulness and potential of this initiative. Nevertheless, I will continue to connect with people who want to contribute ideas and work with me on giving a place to Dialogue within education.

While it takes a village to raise a child, it takes a school to teach them Dialogue. There has to be a 'dialogical environment' for children to learn these skills, and it is not enough to engage in Dialogue infrequently. You learn Dialogue by doing it repeatedly. Dialogue can be widely used within education. In every lesson can there be a question or moment in which Dialogue can be used. Teachers need knowledge of and experience with Dialogue skills. All people involved with education have to have at least some knowledge of Dialogue.

The Invitation

I would like to invite you, as a reader, as a member of the Academy of Professional Dialogue, to think along with me about dialogue at school. Share with me what you know about dialogue at school (articles, books, websites), start dialogue within your own community at school, connect with me on LinkedIn or put me in contact with others. You can contact me personally at joop@mensindialoog.nl.

References

Dawson, P. & Guare, R. (2008). *Executieve functies bij kinderen en adolescenten* [Dutch edition of *Executive Skills in Children and Adolescents*]. Amsterdam: Hogrefe Uitgevers BV.

Gowricharn, R., Postma, D.W., & Trienekens, S. (ed.) (2012). *Geleefd burgerschap* [*Living Citizenship*]. Amsterdam: SWP Uitgeverij B.V.

Isaacs, W. (1999). *Dialogue and the Art of Thinking Together: A Pioneering Approach to Communicating in Business and in Life*. New York: Currency/Doubleday.

Castelijns J. & Verhoeven S. (2013). *Dialoog in de klas*, [*Classroom Dialogue*]. 's-Hertogenbosch: KPC Groep.

Veugelers, Pedagogiek en Onderwijskunde Radboud Universiteit (2009). *Docenten en waardenvormende dialogen*. [Teachers and value-forming dialogues]. Amsterdam: Instituut voor de Lerarenopleiding / Universiteit van Amsterdam.

Conference Session Extracts

From a conversation with participants considering the paper with the author

Speaker 1: At UCLA, they train their teachers to be social justice minded. They use Paulo Friere's work and they talk about positionality. The research we did with these teachers was to see if you could you get to a deeper self-reflective space if you brought dialogue in. A place where the teachers are really thinking about their experience and their own identity before they engage, and actually doing ethnographic studies of the communities they're going to work in before they start to work there. The teachers are also trained in culturally responsive pedagogy. Yet even with all of that, the teachers will talk about how, if they make room for things to come up in the classroom, they're so uncomfortable with navigating that afterwards. The feelings, these are important feelings, and right now social emotional learning is being promoted at the kindergarten level in California. But there are teachers who are just not comfortable. They say that if a child talks about how they're feeling that day, and they want to talk about "my father's in prison", then those teachers just aren't comfortable. They've made space, because they told to me these things that show that, but they still don't know how to navigate it.

Speaker 3: You can't lead anyone else further than you actually have gone yourself. I really, really understand the teacher who is afraid of letting those feelings come out and dealing with those kinds of feelings from the kids if they haven't been doing this themselves in a safe environment before. I think that's pretty scary. Which means we need to make sure that all the teachers can have a safe environment to train, and to hold this space in that situation.

Speaker 4: Can I just ask, why is it scary? Is it because you are worried about these children afterwards? They have been in the classroom and then they're left alone? Or it is scary for the teachers?

Speaker 5: For the teachers, I think.

Speaker 4: Okay, I thought it was more scary for the children.

Speaker 6: Well, I would think that it be scary for humans to hold those kind of feelings, and things happening in the room, if you are actually scared of your own feelings. So if you haven't tried out that in a safe environment . . .

Speaker 3: I guess I'll defer to your judgment, but if I'm a teacher in the U S and I kind of get into difficult territory, I'm starting to worry about – am I facing the risk of litigation? Am I going to create a situation there that I'm going to find myself getting quite deeply embedded into the legal structure? I just think that there's a layer beyond what's happening in the room in terms of the surrounding environment, social climate, legal structure . . .

Speaker 1: We do our dialogues around the intersectionality of identities. So we consider, what are all of their different identities that may be coming up to play because of their position? Whether it's their socio-economic status, so they can't take a risk to have any parents or administrators upset with them – or if they don't have that concern. The majority of teachers in the U.S. are still white, and with all that privilege, in the study we did find there were many who said that they felt they could take a risk. But then there are many teachers who talked about how they couldn't. There's political, there's social . . .there's a lot different things at play, a parent's response, admin response, student's response . . .it's about all of that for them.

Speaker 7: One of the problems we have in the UK is that as social services and youth services have been cut back and cut back, so schools are basically having to deal with a lot of social problems – the kind of problems like knife crime. In the UK, one of the patterns I've seen is that badly behaved children get excluded from school. Nobody will have them. Then they're on the street. Then they're vulnerable. Then they're carrying knives, and then they're involved in antisocial, very high-risk situations for them. At our school we try very hard. They call it 'off-rolling' when you get rid of the kid. We try very hard not to 'off-roll' any children. We keep them all on our pupil roll. We don't exclude unless something really, really terrible has happened. Even then we keep them on our roll, but we send them to a different place to do something else.

Speaker 8: Earlier you talked about the idea that other entities should own the problem. Well, what we find often is that all of those other entities do not want to come through, and do not want to be a part of the solution. So how do you get the other entities to the table, so that can help those kids in a very dialogical fashion? That's challenging.

Speaker 5: We did one thing with our son. We told him when we started at that school . . . we told him that we are going to help you and we are going to talk to the school and tell them what you need. You can tell us on the way everything that you have to tell us. We did this and he saw that things changed, so suddenly he understood that if I tell what I need or what's my problem to the adults or to my parents or to the school, they actually take me seriously and it gets better. Now he's 13 years old and he's growing up amazingly good. He has Asperger, so that's why we have had a lot of contact also, but it's that one thing. The school really saw the kid and took him seriously and they took us seriously as parents. That's something we haven't talked that much about in here, but the communication between school and parents is so important because who knows the child best? That's the parents.

Speaker 6: You and the school gave your son a very important thing. It's called locus of control. The way you have control of the situation in your own life and that's exactly what the children I work with never had. They were never taken seriously. We think about the treatment goals you get. We think about what you have to learn. From dialogue we started, "What do you think? Explain why. What's your dream? What do you want to be?"

Postscript
The author's reflections, written some months after the conference

I started writing my paper dialogue with passion at school. Because of my experience in working with dialogue within youth-care in the Netherlands, I became convinced that dialogue could make an important contribution if it was taught at school.

The writing of the paper also came at a good time. I had just joined the Academy of Professional Dialogue, and I was keen to share my ideas and vision with people who also have an affinity for dialogue. The writing itself was difficult because I'm not used to writing so much in English. My thanks go out to Peter Garrett, Jane Ball, Cliff Penwell, Monique Cartesan and my wife, Sandra, who helped me a lot with this.

In my paper I describe how I developed my enthusiasm for dialogue within school. During the conference, where I was allowed to share my paper with interested parties, I had the opportunity to explain in different ways how and why a dialogue with young people works so well. I mainly work with young people with mild intellectual disabilities and behavioral disorders, but I got the same results with all young people with whom I have used the dialogue. They feel taken seriously, they are really listened to and their voice really counts.

Especially in this time of transformation, in which many things are going differently than we are used to, you see that young people adapt very quickly. In addition, they have also become very articulate and want to be heard. Just think of the protests for climate change, black lives matter and more.

During the conference I had the opportunity to talk to people not only while discussing my paper, but especially afterwards, during lunch, dinner and during a walk. I learned that there was a great affinity with the paper that I was allowed to share and the way I have used this way of conducting a dialogue to set up a training.

As I write this Postscript I realize that writing, presenting and sharing my paper only makes me more motivated to give dialogue a place in the lives of young people. Not just in and at school, but in the broadest sense of the word. Children and young people of today live in a world and grow towards a world that needs a lot of dialogue to remain a liveable world.

Bohm Dialogue as a Way to Support Adult Development

Marie-Ève Marchand

Among dialogue practitioners few, if any, have continued to use group dialogue in the original format proposed in 1991 by David Bohm and his colleagues Peter Garrett and Donald Factor.[*] In the United States, despite major efforts by William Isaacs and his colleagues at his firm Dialogos to introduce this mode of "thinking together"[†] in organizations, the method in its "pure form" did not take root. In Quebec, Canada, efforts were made to use Bohm dialogue with managers and professionals of the public health system.[‡] That early experience continued for a while but did not last. The difficulties encountered gave rise in North America and Europe to many adaptations of the original format in an effort to embody its basic principles in different ways. One might wonder, Is there still a place for the practice of Bohm dialogue in its original format?

In this paper I suggest that there is such a place in the context of educational programs aimed at facilitating, in individuals, the passage from conventional orders of consciousness to post-conventional orders—in other words, from an "either/or" mindset to a "both-and" way of thinking. (I will explore these ideas in more depth below.) The paper will describe how dialogue became part of a course for leaders and managers at Laval University in Quebec, how the impact of the course was measured and how these orders of consciousness relate to Bohm dialogue. Other ongoing initiatives will be presented in support of the observations that Bohm dialogue can be a very useful educational method, particularly when it is part of a curriculum that uses other means of sensitizing adult students to the role of presuppositions, or mental models, in perception and thinking, the interconnectedness of people and systems and the power of inquiry that is both thorough and caring.

---

[*] Bohm, D., Factor, D., & Garrett, P. (1991). Dialogue—a Proposal. England: Mickleton, Glos.

[†] Isaacs, W. (1993). "Taking flight: Dialogue, collective thinking, and organizational learning". *Organizational Dynamics*, 22(2), 24-39.; Isaacs, W. (1999). Dialogue and the *Art of Thinking Together*. New York: Currency.

[‡] Pauchant, Thierry, et al. (2002). *Guérir la Santé*. Canada: Éditions Fides.

How We Experimented and What We Discovered

At the turn of 2000 in Quebec, Canada, my colleague Mario Cayer and I were two researchers who had completed, separately, our doctoral dissertations on Bohm dialogue. Mario had studied at Saybrook University in California[*], and I did my PhD at the University of Montreal.[†] We shared David Bohm's hope that group dialogue, conducted in the manner that he had proposed, would prevent fragmentation and bring coherence to decision-making processes in the scientific, political and organizational fields. A better world would be the happy consequence of Bohm's method of group dialogue if it were widely taught and practiced.

At that time—at least in North America—we saw the rise of interest in what eventually became "the mindfulness movement". Meditation and yoga were gaining rapidly in popularity at the fringes of the population. It took another decade before an interest in "mindfulness" could find any legitimacy in the field of management. In fact, until a few years ago, meditation was regarded with suspicion in nearly all North American faculties of management. Nevertheless, my colleague and I were convinced that cultivating presence (mindfulness) was essential for managers. We wanted to contribute to the field of management by creating a program that encouraged self-observation as well more conscious ways of relating, exploring ideas and making decisions.

The program we designed targeted working managers (mostly senior managers) who wished to further their education. We entitled it "Complexity, Consciousness and Management". We gave the program in the Department of Management of Laval University over three semesters, for a total of 135 hours of classroom time spread over 17 full days of attendance. The course could be taken as continuing education or as part of an MBA. In the latter case, there were requirements to produce papers and undergo formal evaluation. The program was offered in more or less its original form from 2001 to 2017, but the content was adapted over the years to include new research and to respond to participants' feedback.

The main objectives of the program included:

- A better understanding of how mental models (presuppositions) affect perceptions and decisions;
- An increased capacity to be present to one's inner experience and to the environment;
- A more developed intuition and emotional intelligence;
- An increased ability to deal with paradoxes, ambiguity and complexity;
- A more authentic way of relating and communicating.

---

[*] Cayer, M. (1996). "An Inquiry into the Experience of Bohm's Dialogue." Doctoral dissertation, Saybrook Institute, San Francisco.

[†] Marchand, M.E. (2000). "L'exploration réflexive dans la pratique du dialogue de Bohm: une expérience avec des gestionnaires, conseillers et formateurs en gestion." Thèse de doctorat, Université de Montréal, Québec, Canada.

The curriculum included different elements such as a study of the stages in human development, theories of complexity and change, emotional intelligence, compassion and gratitude and the link between creativity, flow and performance. It also included the requirement for a daily practice of meditation as taught by Jon Kabat-Zinn* and a two-day introduction to Bohm dialogue. For a number of years, after the two-day introduction, we offered opportunities to practice Bohm dialogue at different points in the one-year program. For a while, under the initiative of enthusiastic students, additional dialogue practices were made available outside the course structure.

We were hopeful that this curriculum, with its particular mix of theories and practices, would support the embodiment of capacities associated with post-conventional orders of development. We were convinced by Robert Kegan (1994)† that, in order to live at ease in the complexity of the modern world, one needed more than new skills. Another way of thinking that embraces rather than fears ambiguity, paradoxes and uncertainty was—and is—called for. It is particularly imperative for leaders and managers to learn new ways of operating in order to fulfill their role without too much anxiety. We were hoping that those among our students in the conventional orders of consciousness—where one's view of the world relies primarily on social rules and/or scientific results—would initiate a move towards *post-conventional* orders of consciousness, where there is greater capacity to question the existing social order and dogmas, and accept complexity. We anticipated that our few students who already rated at post-conventional orders would feel supported in their worldview by the contents of the course and by the community created during those 10 months, where the sharing of ideas and experience was actively encouraged.‡

Human Development and Orders of Consciousness

To understand the potential of dialogue to support a passage from conventional to post-conventional orders or "action logic", I include here a graphic representation of the stages by Susan Cook-Greuter who is a major contributor to the theory and measurement of human development within the framework of "orders of consciousness". It is worth noting here that there is a considerable body of new literature on stages of adult development. Theoreticians and researchers are remarkably consistent in their description of stages, even though different terms are used to designate them, such as "orders of consciousness", "ego

---

* Jon Kabat-Zinn founded the Stress Reduction Clinic in Massachusetts and became a prominent figure in the teaching of meditation in a secular manner. My colleague and I were trained by him.

† Kegan, R. (1994). In Over Our Heads: The Mental Demands of Modern Life. Cambridge: Harvard Business Press.

‡ We used a sentence completion test originally developed by Loevinger and later adapted by Susan Cook-Greuter, to measure the stage of development before the course and after the end of the course.

states" and "action-logic". I have opted here for "order of consciousness", the term used by Robert Kegan.*

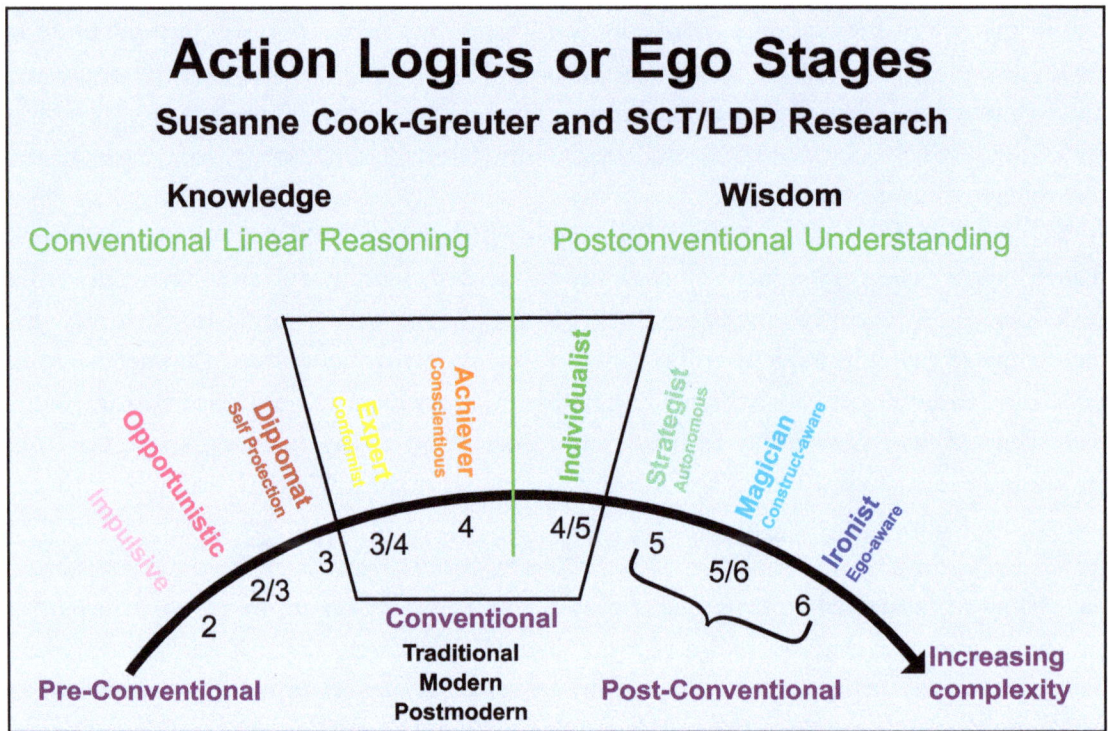

Characteristics of Post-Conventional Orders

As the name suggests, a person operating from a post-conventional order of consciousness is able to maintain some distance in regard to social rules and conventions. He/she will try to identify the assumptions underlying these rules and conventions in order to free himself/herself from them. For these persons, beliefs and values are viewed as an interpretation of reality emanating from a given culture and a historic context. The person understands that the meaning given to events represents a construct based upon personal experiences. Thus, many interpretations of the same event may be relevant. People with a post-conventional mindset naturally listen to many perspectives. This ability is particularly useful in resolving conflicts in a creative way.

At the Post-Conventional order of consciousness, a person has developed a greater capability to grasp interrelations between people, events or elements of a system. He/she will be

---

* In the following graphic, the terms to designate each stage are attributable to W. Torbert and D. Rooke. In 2005, they changed some of the names of their post-conventional stages but not the description. Ken Wilber, Frederic Laloux, and Beck & Cowan use colours rather than words.

freed from the tendency to find a unique cause to an event and will adopt a systemic way of thinking. For instance, this expanded awareness of interrelations will cause managers to be more concerned with the long-term impact their decisions will have on different parts of the organization, the community to which it belongs and the world at large. Juggling so many variables requires complex thinking capable of handling, among other things, paradoxes and contradictions.

Another characteristic typical of the person who has moved beyond conventional stages is an interest in the process, not just in the results. This attention to process calls for the use of forms of intelligence other than just the conceptual intelligence that focuses on analysis of measurable facts. Thus people with a post-conventional mindset value their inner experience as part of understanding what lies underneath the apparent reality. Sensitivity to context, energy and emotions is included in what matters. External goals are held within a larger perspective and expected to change, since life is viewed as a continuous process of transformation. Meaning must be created and re-created in a constantly shifting context. In this, we move from sole reliance on knowledge and facts to reliance on wisdom acquired through many ways of seeing and listening. Intuition is greatly valued; multiple forms of intelligence are solicited to understand what is really going on.

Research on orders of development in the general population is scarce. Kegan (1994), Beck & Cowan (1996), Cook-Greuter (2004-2015) as well as W. Torbert (1991-2005) have administered tests in different contexts and in different countries. These tests show that a majority of people, including leaders, have not reached the needed post-conventional orders that would allow them to live at ease and make enlightened decisions in today's world. Despite this troubling data, little attention has been paid to ways of supporting adult development in order that a majority of people—and, most importantly, decision-makers—live well and think clearly with a sense of the emerging reality.

As a result of adults being unequipped for the complexity of life today, we notice a widespread longing for the good old days when life was simpler. This is exemplified by the recent American elections and the Brexit vote in England, both driven by confused, fearful citizens in search for something solid and familiar.

To my knowledge, the field of adult education has paid little attention to educational programs that would specifically support the passage from one order to the other, even though Mezirow (2000)* laid the foundation with his work on the attitudes linked with maturity in adults.

In the field of management, Rooke (1997)† gave some advice stemming from his work with executives. He observed that the following elements could contribute to changes toward a post-conventional awareness:

---

* Mezirow, J, et. al. (2000). *Learning as Transformation: Critical Perspectives on a Theory in Progress*. San Francisco: Jossey Bass.

† Rooke, D. (1997). "Organizational transformation requires the presence of leaders who are strategists or magicians." Organizations and People, 4(3), 16-23.

- a mentor or model who has reached the post-conventional stage;
- involvement in a reflective process such as writing a personal journal;
- reading biographies of people having reached the post-conventional stage;
- therapy, and participation in an action-inquiry group.

To this list, it seems legitimate to add participation in a dialogue group in the form proposed by Bohm because it cultivates self-awareness, disidentification with one's opinions, and the ability to question culturally acquired suppositions. We can see it as a powerful way "to make talk developmental", in the words of Nancy Dixon (1998).[*]

A parallel can easily be drawn between the characteristics of post-conventional orders and what Bohm dialogue seeks to accomplish. This is explicit in various writings on dialogue. Also, two empirical studies, one conducted by Cayer[†] (1996) and one by myself[‡] (2000) highlight these similarities.

Challenging Assumptions

The capacity to expose tacit social rules and conventions and question their underlying assumptions is at the very core of the practice of dialogue. In fact Bohm, Factor and Garrett (1991) present dialogue in the following way: "We are proposing a type of collective exploration of not only the content of our words, thoughts and feelings, but also of underlying motivations, assumptions and beliefs" (p. 1). During the practice of dialogue, participants are invited to question everything from individual and collective assumptions to emotions, thought function and the experience of the present moment. This is what Isaacs (1993) noted in his definition of dialogue: "Dialogue can be initially defined as a sustained collective inquiry into the process, assumptions, and certainties that compose everyday experience".[§]

Cayer, in interviewing practitioners of dialogue, discovered that one of the effects of the practice of dialogue was a greater awareness of hidden assumptions that are both personal and prevailing in the practitioner's culture. The study I conducted showed that managers involved in weekly dialogue sessions over a period of five months saw an increase in readiness to expose their own assumptions in a dialogue group—assumptions that they would not have dared reveal (even to themselves, as one participant put it) before they started to practice Bohm dialogue. The same research demonstrated that, through practice, the participants had developed the capacity to

---

[*] Dixon, N. (1998). *Dialogue at Work*. England: Lemos & Crane.

[†] Op. cit.

[‡] Op. cit.

[§] Isaacs, W. (1993). "Taking flight: Dialogue, collective thinking and organizational learning." *Organizational Dynamics*, 22(2), 24-39.

challenge other people's assumptions without lapsing into confrontation. They could pay attention to both: the idea and the relationship. They questioned with a sense of caring.

Suspending Assumptions to Listen Better

Suspension is a central concept in the practice of Bohm dialogue. In a text where they invite people to practice dialogue, Bohm, Factor and Garrett (1991) state:

"Suspension of thoughts, impulsions, judgements, etc., that is the very essence of dialogue. It is one of its most important new aspects . . . Not holding on to them, repressing them or postponing them. It simply means giving them special attention in order to take note of their structures at the moment they appear" (p. 9).*

Suspension of immediate reactions and judgements allows a person to listen attentively to other people's opinions and ideas and, consequently, enables him/her to consider different points of view without prematurely dismissing any of them. In Cayer's study, many participants noted this relationship between suspension of judgements and becoming better listeners. Following the same line of thought, the managers who participated in my research mentioned being surprised by how welcomed and listened to they felt in a form of dialogue that advocates "impersonal fellowship". They felt at least as appreciated as one would be in groups that make a great deal of each person's uniqueness and emotional state. They attributed this experience of empathy to the *quality of attention* prevailing in the group while they were speaking. They felt truly listened to. This corresponds to a capacity shown by people at the post-conventional stages: listening with curiosity to multiple perspectives without becoming defensive.

Dealing with Paradoxes, Ambiguities and Uncertainty

One of the capacities that is most looked for in managers and leaders nowadays is being able to face the complexity of the organizational world. It implies dealing with paradoxes and ambiguities and sustaining one's commitment when things are uncertain while, paradoxically, remaining flexible. According to supporters of the developmental approach, individuals who have reached the post-conventional orders would display this capacity much more than individuals operating from a conventional mindset.

According to Isaacs (1993), many paradoxes stem from the very practice of dialogue: "While [dialogue] seeks to allow greater coherence to emerge among a group of people (not necessarily agreement), it does not impose coherence. Beginning a dialogue exposes another paradox: while the process encourages people to have a shared intention for inquiry, it does

---

* Op. cit.

not have an agenda, a leader, or a task" (p. 32).* Inherent in its form, independently of the contents, Bohm dialogue is a practice in the tolerance of uncertainty, paradox and ambiguity.

People practicing dialogue also have stated that they sometimes find themselves confronted with situations where they have difficulty choosing between two behaviours or two attitudes that apparently could not be manifested at the same time. For example, how does one reconcile the individual and the collective, the personal and the impersonal, the content and the process? Participation in a dialogue group enables participants to face all these paradoxical situations. In the study I conducted, the moment participants (all managers) appreciated the experience of dialogue was when individual and group perspectives were broadened because of the capacity to stay with contradictions, paradoxes and grey areas until something new unfolded. They experienced spaciousness when realizing that *a view and its contrary* could be true at the same time.

Interest in Process and Connectedness

As mentioned earlier, people who have reached the post-conventional order take an interest in processes and connectedness, as opposed to people in the conventional stages who tend to keep an eye on expected results to the detriment of the process. Being attuned to the many dimensions of what is happening here and now is highly informative. It contains the seeds of what will emerge in the future. This advantage of being able to sense the invisible beginnings of what will become visible to all later is well described by Otto Scharmer in his book *Theory U*.

Bohm dialogue invites participants to observe and explore their full experience of the present moment. They are asked to pay attention to various aspects: to their own thought process, the collective thought process, the emotional tone and the energy of the group, as well as their own energy, emotional state and sensations. This is seen as important because fragmentation can be found in the interface of any of these facets of reality. According to Bohm, Factor and Garrett, dialogue can help explore the roots of the crises our society faces precisely because of its broad view of what needs to be taken into consideration when people are communicating. First and foremost, it recognizes the interconnectedness of people and events.

Bohm Dialogue in the Passage to a Post-Conventional Order

As mentioned in the introduction, many consultants who have attempted to introduce Bohm dialogue in organizational settings have been disappointed. They have found very little

---

* Op. cit.

patience there for such an open-ended method of exploration. When they have attempted the experience, the initial enthusiasm soon dwindled. The world of organization is still deeply anchored in a conventional mindset, with the exception of some avant-garde organizations such as those listed by Frederic Laloux (2014) in his book *Reinventing Organizations*.

At Laval University we had more freedom to experiment than in most organizations in the private or public sectors. We were allowed to try a very new approach to the development of managers.* We wanted to know if our "Complexity, Consciousness and Management" program had an impact on the order of consciousness of our participants. So we decided to test it, using a control group to compare. One group was composed of participants registered in the course. The control group was composed of managers on the waiting list for registration at a subsequent course. Both groups had to undergo the Sentence Completion Test developed by Cook-Greuter at the beginning of the one-year program and, again, a year later. There was no significant change in the results of the control group but we found a significant move from conventional to post-conventional orders in the group that took the course (Baron, 2019).†

In earlier research, interviews conducted by Cayer showed that long-term dialogue practitioners attributed significant elements of their personal evolution to their sustained practice of dialogue. As one person mentioned, "First, the self-knowledge is tremendous, and is different. Also it's very empowering, self-empowering . . . ." Another stated, "I think I have more of a steady, less-mobile kind of personality. Less mobility, less scattered and more integrated kind of. I think I've become a more integrated kind of person". In the study I conducted executives commented that experiencing Bohm dialogue had contributed to something more than the acquisition of specific skills related to challenging assumptions, listening, or building collective meaning. They had come to see themselves and others differently as they engaged in a process of searching together. Their personal positions became less important than the expansion of their minds and hearts to include more aspects and more people.

The following list gives an overall, brief overview of Cayer's findings from inquiring about the effects of the practice of dialogue on the long-term practitioners :

Positive Effects
- Greater aptitude for communicating and entering into relationship with others
- Greater aptitude for dealing with conflicts and controversies
- Greater ability to listen and to express oneself

---

* Nevertheless, we were very careful with the vocabulary we were using and also in the way we justified each element of the program.

† It is anticipated that the results of this study will be published in 2020 in a peer-review management journal. A second study, conducted a few years later, with participants in the same program, gave less convincing results on the impact of the curriculum on their development. It is to be considered that the workplace in Quebec, in both the public and the private sectors, is increasingly placed under stress by an accumulation of performance measures and a diminution of resources. In our view, this stress could even drive one who is already in a post-conventional order to regress to a conventional order.

- More respect and consideration of others
- Changes in self-perception
- A stronger self
- More inner spaciousness
- An experience of the transpersonal
- A more subtle intelligence
- Greater clarity and understanding
- More consciousness of one's own suppositions
- More creativity
- More openness
- Less fear

Unintended effects
- Confusion and identity crisis
- Suffering linked with greater awareness
- Use of the group by some to enhance one's self image

In sum, in two studies using a self-reporting methodology (Cayer 1996 and Marchand 2000), regular participants in Bohm dialogue attested to the acquisition of abilities that can be associated with post-conventional orders of consciousness. In one conventional research using a control group in 2006, the passage from a conventional to a post-conventional order was evident for a number of participants.

Current Experience in Bohm Dialogue

Since 2017 I have offered four introductory courses in Bohm dialogue as a prerequisite to participating in an ongoing practice group that meets once a month in Montreal for a two-hour practice. About 70 participants have taken this course. Of these, 15 have been regular participants in the monthly meetings. The two main sources of recruitment have been graduates from a well-regarded American Integral Coaching School called New Venture West (operating in French, in Quebec, under the name of *Convivium*) and from La Maison des leaders, a Quebec-based leadership training organization with a mission that corresponds to a post-conventional worldview. These people have in common a true interest in their own development, a desire to be of service and a belief that rigid organizational structures hinder rather than help people to live a fulfilling life and contribute to a healthy society.

In 2018-19, after a year of participation in the monthly practice, some participants expressed the desire to go further in order to increase their self-awareness, their presence and their inquiring skills, as well as their understanding of orders of development. They were interested in the link between these elements and the capacity to sustain dialogue in the various circumstances of their lives. So, in addition to the practice group, I offered four, one-day sessions under the title "Dialogue and the Development of Consciousness".

In June 2019, the same students who took the four-session course asked to go even further in their development, so I designed another series of four sessions called "Autobiographical Awareness and Dialogue". In this course, they will share written autobiographical texts on four major areas of life where key presuppositions have greatly changed in the past decades—at least in the Western world. The role of autobiographical work in the development of consciousness has been documented by William Torbert,[*] based on an experiment with his MBA students. Numerous writings in psychotherapy and adult education assert the importance of autobiographical work in the process of becoming self-aware, and in the development of a capacity to make a distance between oneself and one's story. The selection of themes was influenced by Robert Kegan's observations of areas where life is very different for adults now than it was for their parents and grandparents.

Conclusion

Twenty years of experience and research on Bohm dialogue in the form that it was originally proposed have led me to believe that it is a powerful method to support the passage from conventional orders of consciousness to post-conventional ones, but as one element of a fuller curriculum such as my colleague Mario Cayer and I intuited many years ago. When the participants in my current dialogue group requested complementary teachings it confirmed my observation that the practice of Bohm dialogue takes its full meaning when it is part of a program with other components that highlight the importance of self-awareness, presence and inquiry as well as an understanding of the impact of world views (orders of consciousness) on of human and social development.

The new program that I will offer from December 2019 to June 2020 is called "Autobiographical Awareness and Dialogue"; it will be offered at a more advanced level. These experiments are not done in a university context. Therefore, there is no plan to measure their impact. However, practitioners who have remained part of the dialogue group I started in 2017 have recently been asked to answer a questionnaire where some of the questions are similar to those asked by Mario Cayer in his original research. I am currently looking for self-reports on the effect of long-term practice of Bohm dialogue.

---

[*] Torbert, W. & Fisher D. (1992) "Autobiographical awareness as a catalyst for managerial and organizational development." *Journal of Management and Education Development*, 23(3), 184-198.

References

Bohm, D., Factor, D., & Garrett, P. (1991). *Dialogue – A Proposal*. England: Mickleton, Glos.

Baron, C. & Cayer, M. (2011). "Fostering post-conventional thinking in leaders: Why and how?" *Journal of Management Development, 30*(4), 344-365.

Baron, C. (2019). "Fostering mindfulness and post-conventional consciousness in organizational leaders: An executive program." Unpublished paper, submitted for publication in 2020.

Cayer, M. (1996). "An Inquiry into the Experience of Bohm's Dialogue." Doctoral dissertation, San Francisco: Saybrook Institute.

Cayer, M., Marchand, M.E. & Roy L. (2002). Développement d'un leadership transformationnel par la pratique du dialogue. In *Actes du 12è congrès de psychologie du travail et des organisations*. Belgique: Louvain la Neuve:

Cook-Greuter, S.R. (1990). "Maps for living: Ego-development stages from symbiosis to conscious universal embeddedness". In Commons, M.L., Grotzer, T. & Sinnott, J. (Eds.), *Adult Development: Models and Methods in the Study of Adolescent and Adult Thought*, Praeger, 79-103.

Cook-Greuter, S.R. (2001). *The Leadership Development Framework: Training for Consultants and Coaches*. Wayland, MA : Harthill USA.

Cook-Greuter, S.R. (2013). *Nine Levels of Increasing Embrace in Ego Development*. https://www.semanticscholar.org.

Dixon, N. (1998). *Dialogue at Work*. London, England: Lemos & Crane.

Fisher, D., & Torbert, W. (1991). "Transforming managerial practice: Beyond the achiever stage." *Research in Organizational Change and Development, 5*, 143-173.

Fisher, D., Rooke, D., & Torbert, B. (2000). *Personal and Organisational Transformations Through Action Inquiry*. Boston: Edgework Press.

Isaacs, W. (1993). "Taking flight: Dialogue, collective thinking, and organizational learning". *Organizational Dynamics, 22*(2), 24-39.

Isaacs, W. (1999). *Dialogue and the Art of Thinking Together: A Pioneering Approach to Communicating in Business and Life*. New York: Currency.

Kegan, R. (1994). *In Over Our Heads: The Mental Demands of Modern Life*. Cambridge: Harvard Business Press.

Kegan, R. (2000). "What 'form' transforms? A constructive-developmental approach to transformational learning". In Mezirow, J. (Ed.), *Learning as Transformation*, San Francisco: Jossey-Bass, 35-70.

Kegan, R. & Lahey, L. (2017). *An Everyone Culture: Becoming a Deliberately Developmental Organization*. Boston: HBR.

Laloux, F. (2014). Reinventing Organizations: A Guide to Creating Organizations Inspired by the Next Stage of Human Consciousness. Millis, MA: Nelson Parker:

Loevinger, J. (1976). *Ego Development: Conception and Theories*. San Francisco: Jossey-Bass.

Marchand, M.E. (2000). *L'exploration réflexive dans la pratique du dialogue de Bohm: Une expérience avec des gestionnaires, conseillers et formateurs en gestion*. Thèse de doctorat, Université de Montréal, Québec, Canada.

Mezirow, J. (1991). "How Critical Reflection Triggers Transformative Learning." In Mezirow, J. (Ed.), *Fostering Critical Education in Adulthood: A Guide to Transformative and Emancipatory Learning*, San Francisco: Jossey-Bass, 1-20.

Mezirow, J. (2000). "Learning to think like an adult: Core concepts of transformation theory". In Mezirow, J. (Ed.), *Learning as Transformation*, San Francisco: Jossey-Bass, 3-34.

Mezirow, J. (2000). *Learning as Transformation*. San Francisco: Jossey-Bass.

Pauchant, T. et al. (2002). *Guérir la Santé*. Montréal : Éditions Fides.

Rooke, D. (1997). "Organisational transformation requires the presence of leaders who are strategists and magicians." *Organisations and People*, 4(3), 64-79.

Rooke, D. & Torbert, W.R. (1998). "Organizational transformation as a function of CEOs' developmental stage." *Organization Development Journal*, 6(1), 11-28.

Rooke, D. & Torbert W. (2005). "Seven transformations of leadership." *HBR*, April 2005.

Scharmer, O. (2007). *Theory U: Leading from the Future as It Emerges*. Cambridge, MA: The Society for Organizational Learning.

Torbert, W.R. (1987). *Managing the Corporate Dream: Restructuring for Long-Term Success*. Homewood, IL: Dow Jones Irwin.

Torbert, W. (1991). *The Power of Balance—Transforming Self, Society, and Scientific Inquiry*. San Francisco: Sage.

Tobert, W. and Fisher D. (1992). "Autobiographical awareness as a catalyst for managerial and organizational development." *Journal of Management and Education Development*, 23(3), 184-198.

Wilber, K. (2000). *Integral Psychology: Consciousness, Spirit, Psychology, Therapy*. Boston: Shambhala Publications, Inc.

Conference Session Extracts

From a conversation with participants considering the paper with the author

Speaker 1: So I'm kind of coming back to where we started. You made this connection between levels of consciousness, and the activity of dialogue. So I'm wondering if that the goal of dialogue, to help individuals raise their levels of consciousness?

Speaker 2: No, it's not the goal of dialogue. It's my goal as an adult educator, and dialogue helps, but it's not the goal of dialogue.

Speaker 1: So then what is the goal of dialogue? A lot of the reading about dialogue says nothing about levels of consciousness. I mean it's not even part of the discussion. So what is the goal of dialogue? When we say the world needs dialogue, what are we saying. What are we trying to solve?

Speaker 3: Reduction of fragmentation.

Speaker 1: Yeah. I like that answer, I like the answer that it is the reduction and fragmentation. Are there other things you think that dialogue is about? Again, the role of dialogue is . . . ?

Speaker 2: Meeting. It's a meeting, because otherwise it's too lonely. We are linked in our consciousness, and it's about meeting. But let's say that we take people who are at a certain level of consciousness. Say we put all people that are achievers together. This is their way – they believe in progress. They believe that we always have to be better. This is their logic, and if you put them together, they're going to have a very good dialogue. But the challenge of our time is to take people who have a different logic and to sort of weave something with them, meet them and create new things. This is why I find the spiral dynamics and all its stages interesting. What we long for most is to be met at the soul.

Speaker 1: Connection. Yes, it's connection, isn't it?

Speaker 4: Let me tell a short story that's true, and it has some relation to Peter. He convened a dialogue circle, I don't know, about 10 or 15 years ago, I've forgotten, with about 35 people. It was for Skip Griffin, a fellow who had been working with Civil Rights in the US. He was an African-American man who was prominent in the Civil Rights movement, and that was the focus of the dialogue. The circle was formed like this, perhaps a bit bigger, and we were checking in. We had started some place and went around.

Peter was checking in, he was telling his story and experiences. Then all of a sudden, a woman on the other side of the circle started to whimper, and then sob, and then heave in great, uncontrollable wailing. She was out of control. I think we were in the first morning of a four-day dialogue. And I'm thinking, what the hell is this about? Am I going to make it through four days of this? And I suppose a lot of people were thinking some variation of that. Peter went silent. We all went silent. What do you say? So we sort of sat respectfully for this woman to recompose herself. Skip was the facilitator of the group. He remained silent. And finally, she gathered herself together in order to say, "All you ever do it talk." And she resumed crying. And of course, she was right. We're a dialogue circle, and all we ever did when we got together was talk. Finally, she calmed down. The woman next to her put her arm around her shoulder, comforted her.

And after about five minutes, Skip leaned into the circle, because no one knew what to say. He leaned into the circle. He looked at her straight in the eyes, and said, "Thank you on behalf of all of us here for witnessing the pain we all feel at not being able to deal in action with the issues that we are able to discuss". And then he leaned back, and after another couple minutes, he went back to Peter, asked him to complete his check in. We went on around the circle. When we got to her, she did her check in, and all was well.

Speaker 1: So is that the answer then, connection?

Speaker 5: I struggle with this idea of the goal of dialogue being connection. I'm not saying it isn't, but if you asked Bill Isaacs, or read on his book, he would say it's actually about a new way of thinking. It's about a collective form of thought, and a way of connecting our experiences, our deeper experiences in the world, to create a new vision of what's possible. He would say it in those terms. He's got a phrase about how, given the crises we face in the world, we need a new way of thinking. That's how he frames dialogue.

But for me, my experience of dialogue, I would say has been about shifting my own awareness, my own consciousness and the way I think. So for me personally, I would say, dialogue is a form of personal development, and a unique one. You can't do it in any other way, I think. You can only do it sitting in this group. And Bohm would say yes, of course there is this impersonal friendship, which is a kind of connection, but that's almost a byproduct. It's what goes on in understanding the kind of mechanics of our thoughts. That what he seems to be saying to me.

Speaker 6: And I think for me, connection is no longer the goal, although I became aware through dialogue, and the journey it took me on, that we are all connected, and as a human being I can experience that I am connected within this dialogue, or within a dialogue. It's rediscovering that we are connected, and what it feels like to be in that state.

Speaker 3: To bring an end to the fragmentation, you need to learn to see our wholeness, our collective wholeness. I really think that what he was trying to do with his proposal of dialogue, ultimately, was to help us humble humans figure out a way to stop bumping into each other and causing great harm out in the universe with our actions based on our separate knowing rather than our collective knowing.

Postscript

The author's reflections, written some months after the conference

In addition to sharing the contents of the paper, I also presented the results of a questionnaire on the effects of a sustained practice of Bohm dialogue. The respondents were the participants in my current dialogue groups in Montreal. The results drew interest among those who attended my workshop. They brought up that even if they do not use the original model of Bohm Dialogue, their dialogical activities, based on the same principles, lead to similar results: a notable a reduction in the rigidity of participants' thinking and a greater sensitivity to what moves them to talk. Many use David Kantor's model and they shared that, in their dialogical activities, participants became more aware of what prompts them to initiate a topic, observe, oppose or support. Colleagues reported that they saw a change in their participants regarding pleasure taken in uncovering individual and group assumptions, rather than fear. Hearing about their experience opened my mind to the fact that many ways of engaging in dialogue can support the development of consciousness in adults.

What pleased me most is the interest in my account of an experiment I was conducting with long-term dialogue practitioners. I refer here to the program 'Autobiographical Awareness and Dialogue'. This four-day program focuses on an autobiographical exploration of specific themes, where mental models are likely to evolve greatly over the years (working, being a citizen, sexuality and spirituality). This experiment inspired two colleagues who were intrigued by the potential of the autobiographical route to uncover deep-seated assumptions. They have now included an autobiographical element in some of their dialogue activities in Germany and Holland. I feel privileged that my work enriched their collection of resources and initiated a rich dialogue between the three of us.

Reflecting on Dialogue Facilitation

Kati Tikkamäki & Mirja Hämäläinen

In this paper, we will describe a process of reflecting on facilitation that started in our workshop at the second The World Needs Dialogue! international conference organised by the Academy of Professional Dialogue in 2019. For this event, the papers are usually distributed to participants beforehand and, at the conference, dialogues are held on the topics of the papers. Our workshop proceeded in a reverse order. We invited participants to reflect on dialogue facilitation in the workshop without us providing any other reading than our invitation. After the conference, the reflection continued online in three Zoom meetings. This paper is a report of the whole process, including feedback from the participants on the reflection that we provide in this paper.

In addition to describing the process, we aim to describe the main contents of the participants' reflections. However, including all the voices in full, and in any 'objective' manner, is not possible. We do not hesitate to acknowledge the fact that our personal interpretations of the reflections are inevitable. In addition, we will provide our own reflections on the process and the topics that came up in the dialogues. As we have different backgrounds (see 'About the Authors' at the end of the text) we hope, in a dialogic way, to make use of our approaches and perspectives rather than trying to come up with a common understanding of the process and the topics. We both are enthusiastic about promoting dialogue in working life and dialogue skills for future professionals and professionals in their working life.

Kati: *Mirja, why did you want to inquire about dialogue facilitation at the conference? What kind of expectations did you have?*

Mirja: *I am a practicing teacher at a university, and I teach English for academic and working-life purposes. I teach a dialogue course and I value the opportunity to find out about other practitioners' experiences and reflections on dialogue facilitation. What about you, Kati?*

Kati: *I wanted to create together with you a space for people interested in dialogue to reflect on their experiences, to offer an opportunity to suspend understanding, interpretations and assumptions – to think and learn together. As facilitators and teachers we have these kinds of possibilities too rarely, I think.*

About the Process and Method

The second *The World Needs Dialogue* conference was held in Roffey Park from 22-24 October, 2019. The invitation to our workshop, with the title *Inquiring into Dialogue Facilitation: Methods and Reflection*, was sent to the conference participants in advance through email:

> Won't you come to this dialogue session and bring your experiences and contribution to reflecting about ways of facilitating dialogue?
>
> - How do you create a generative dialogue that draws people's passion and creates insights?
> - What works well in your facilitation?
> - What else could you do that may work better?
> - What are your strengths as a facilitator?
> - Where do you hit a dead end?
> - What are you learning to do differently?
> - What do you wish you could provide as a dialogue facilitator?
>
> *Reflecting experiences.* We ask each participant to share one eye-opening facilitation experience. The experience may have been awakening in good or bad, but it is in some way meaningful. First we share, then we reflect and afterwards we reflect again! And all through thinking together in dialogue.
>
> *Developing methods for facilitating reflection.* The dialogue will be audio-recorded and we all can consider the potential of using video-recording for reflection as an experiment to develop facilitation methods. We also suggest that reflection on action could take place after the conference in Zoom. Kati and Mirja will write a paper for the conference publication based on this dialogue session. The recording supports writing the paper, and the recorded dialogue will be available for all in the AofPD online resources for reflection and learning.

The workshop session was planned to be held just before dinner on the second day of the conference, with a small number of participants (maximum 15). Eight conference participants came to the hour-long workshop in the early evening. Kati facilitated the session and Mirja took the role of participant-observer, making notes of the discussion; the session was also recorded on audio. Steve Marshall organised our check-out as a video-recording for those who agreed to be recorded. Jonathan Drury and Kati took this opportunity, and the rest of the workshop participants followed the recording with interest.

Our aim as session facilitators was to give as much space as possible to the participants to speak. We sat in the circle with the participants. First, Kati introduced the idea of the session and paper to be written afterwards. After that she did not participate in the conversation by talking or commenting. Mirja made notes and did not take part in the discussion. We didn't want to lead the conversation into any directions and wanted to offer participants the possibility to share their experiences after introducing the topic. This conversation provided preparation and context for what would follow after the conference sessions.

After the conference, we continued our reflection on facilitation in three Zoom meetings at the beginning of 2020. We will describe the content of these meetings below. The participants (in the conference session and the Zoom dialogues) had the opportunity to read this paper before publishing. It is interesting to think about whether the participants reflected on their work differently, or more, in the interim period between the Zoom meetings, and whether this inquiry changed their way of facilitating dialogue.

To summarize our inquiry process:

1. APPLYING ACTION RESEARCH: We didn't carry out action research in detail, but applied the cycle of action research: planning, acting, observing and reflecting. The first-hand data was generated in four dialogue spaces: the conference session and the three Zoom meetings that followed. These were recorded by the facilitators (Kati & Mirja). This data and facilitators' experiences were used as data for reflection on what happened (see below). At the end of the process, we asked participants to respond to our version of reflection. Our assumption is that participants reflected on the way they facilitated (reflection-in-action); they reflected between sessions; they facilitated other dialogues; and they returned to reflect together in the Zoom meetings on what they had done (reflection-on-action). We as facilitators *planned* this process, were *acting* together with the participants, together *observed* and *reflected* on what happened and finally put the different individual learnings into this collective paper.
2. REFLECTIVE FOCUS GROUPS: We invited participants to join our Zoom sessions. The number of participants varied in each session. Only a couple of people took part in two sessions – most came and went over the course of the three Zoom dialogues. We did not reach a longer joint process with the participants, but instead got a variety of views. We asked the participants to reflect on their most meaningful facilitation experiences. We summarized the earlier dialogues before each meeting. We gathered the range of responses to the question (checking the recordings where needed) and organised/summarized them in a way that will hopefully help other practitioners to learn more about their own approach to facilitation and reflection.
3. EXAMINING A FRAMEWORK: We had an open plan for this inquiry process. We were curious to explore what kind of experiences people have with facilitating dialogue. We explored our proposed framework for facilitation and for reflection in organised sessions. We noted what was reinforced, what changed during the process and what areas emerged for further consideration.
4. WRITERS' REFLECTIVE CO-ENQUIRY: Given our previous experience, and given everything we heard in the sessions, we did an in-depth enquiry of each other. We helped each other to reflect on our own facilitation styles. We shared each of our approaches to facilitation, and what we learnt reflecting on them. We also learned from the participants' feedback.
5. UTILIZING THEORETICAL CONCEPTS: We reviewed the literature and utilized what others have been thinking about dialogue and facilitation. We used the theoretical frameworks and cited

examples to make sense of the sessions we ran. We tried to choose the type of models and concepts that may be of help to us and other practitioners. We limited our review on the content of the dialogue sessions.

6. EVALUATION OF THE PROCESS: We asked for feedback from the participants, by inquiring of them what experience they have in facilitation, and for any feedback about our paper. We evaluated and reflected on this process together and have thought about what we have learned for our future facilitation.

Findings – Reflection about Facilitation in the Room and by Zoom

Mirja: *Kati, what do you mean by* facilitation? *And how do you facilitate?*

Kati: *My background is in education, so I see the terms* reflecting *and* facilitating *as very crucial. I see myself as a dialogue facilitator acting in different roles: as a developer, a teacher, a work supervisor and a trainer. Facilitating is like playing in a jazz band – improvisation, but still playing the same piece of music with others. I want to promote thinking together by reflective work practice. As a facilitator I do this by asking a lot of questions, making sure that I and other participants understand things in the way participants mean to be understood. I promote appreciative culture and free expression, giving space for participants' experiences and voices. What about you, Mirja?*

Mirja: *I have sometimes introduced myself as a facilitator in the dialogue course that I teach. But when I compare my role to a facilitator's role in a dialogue outside of the educational context, I would think there is a difference. Your description of your facilitator role as playing in a jazz band is beautiful! But I think I play my part in a different way as I step aside after I have given the first notes by introducing a dialogue concept at the beginning of each session and some exercises to highlight the concept. When you and I talked about this the other day, we came up with the idea that everybody facilitates. That is what I hope the participants in the dialogue course get; everybody is a member of the band!*

Kati: *So this outlines something of our earlier experiences and idea about facilitating, which formed the background for planning and carrying out this conference session and Zooms.*

Our aim was to create a space for inquiring into our experiences of dialogue facilitation. We saw it as valuable to raise awareness together, think about the facilitation experiences together and reflect on our use of theories. We could give and receive peer support, learn new ways of seeing, listening and doing. Facilitating learning and dialogue can happen in the role of a teacher, a trainer or a consultant. The participants of the conference session were acting in these different roles. Next, we will summarise our session and the Zoom participants' reflections about facilitating dialogue.

REFLECTION TASK FOR THE READER: *What kind of facilitation experiences have you had? Think about a couple of your own most meaningful facilitation experiences – when you have been facilitating or facilitated by someone else. What does it mean to facilitate something?*

Dialogue in the Room – Experiences and Thoughts about Facilitation

Based on the Kati´s introduction at the beginning of the conference session, the participants started the dialogue by evaluating the different ways of defining the concept of dialogue. Do we as facilitators define *dialogue* together with the participants or do we give our own definition of *dialogue* as a starting point for the collective definition?

The facilitator can start the dialogue session in many ways. One might first tell her/his own understanding of dialogue or start from the participants' understanding. Either way, it is important to listen to the participants' understandings and experiences about dialogue carefully. We can't take a shared understanding as self-evident. All participants should have the possibility to clarify their own understanding and become conscious about it.

We also discussed the invitation to dialogue. Who is invited to dialogue? Who is the inviter? Is the participation in dialogue voluntary or not? All of these questions have an influence on dialogue, and it is good to reflect on them before the start of the session. Facilitators do not work alone.

For our in-person dialogue at the conference, an hour of reflection with check-in and check-out certainly was a short time. We couldn't help admiring how committed the participants were, coming to this dialogue circle to reflect after a full day of dialogues behind them. The general feeling was that reflecting on facilitation was interesting and useful, and there is a need for this type of collective reflection.

Dialogue by Zoom – Reflections on Our Dialogues

We had three Zoom meetings after the conference. There were five participants in the first Zoom meeting in early January 2020. There were some technical problems with the second Zoom meeting and, in the end, only two participants met. A third meeting was held in March, with four participants.

The First Zoom

Our first Zoom meeting, after check-in, started with the question of how to define what we mean by *facilitation*. We discussed this definition: 'the act of making something easier'. The participants agreed that the facilitator's role is not static; that is, it changes during the process from active to observant. We also considered the complexity of the relationship between the facilitator and participants. Facilitator and participant roles can and may often be intertwined. Social identities influence participation; questions of power related to gender, age, being housed or not-housed were brought up in the group reflection. We saw that facilitators need to be aware of how they use power in their work. At best, facilitation can be seen as being open and sensitive to a whole range of aspects and contexts. Facilitators would need to be aware of their Self and their role as facilitators. They would need to be aware of, for example, how they engage with the world and what principles guide their actions. We considered responsibility as a primary value. We finished with the consensus that the Zoom dialogue had been valuable and should continue. The following topics were mentioned as possible areas for our next Zoom meeting(s): the role of culture in dialogue, facilitation and participation, intention, trust and responsibility.

The Second Zoom
The second Zoom started with the sharing of ideas about power in the room. Different ways of using power can be recognised in social interaction. One can be loud or quiet when using power. Finding and constructing the truth about a topic might be one of the goals in dialogue. But whose truth is finally the truth? Being quiet was seen as an interesting and challenging part of dialogue. Should there be some empty space in the room so that the participants would have time to think together and suspend their own and others' thoughts? Does suspending call for quiet moments? We also talked about the role of dialogue in consulting.

When considering the process of dialogue, the term *generative dialogue* came up. We saw it as a possibility to become aware of something that wasn't recognised earlier, a possibility of creating something new.

The jewel of the dialogue was one participant's comment: *I try not to be the authority myself as a facilitator but help the participants to find the authority in themselves.*

The Third Zoom
The first topic that came up in this Zoom dialogue was how to engage people in dialogues. The reasons why people do not participate may be many, and it was agreed that time limitations often can be the main reason. People often simply have to prioritise their tasks at work and how they use their time in general. It can perhaps be questionable to order people in organisations to take part in dialogue circles at work. On the other hand, people may not have had experience in dialogue and therefore they can be encouraged to come. Whether people have an understanding of what dialogue is can be a decisive factor.

Understanding the meaning and purpose of dialogue is important, as is helping people see that they have the capacity to participate in dialogue. The facilitator needs to be able to motivate and empower the participants. The facilitator's sharing of his or her own personal experiences, and being interested in the participants' personal experiences, can motivate people to participate. It is important to be open and ready to show one's vulnerability. A facilitator on occasion can and maybe should also practice participation without being a facilitator.

Who is in the room is also important. People will not feel safe if they have a feeling that they will be judged. A supervisor's presence, for example, can make a difference in the perceived safety level of the dialogue. We wondered whose responsibility it is to decide who the participants are. It was suggested that deciding who comes is beyond facilitation. When in the room, participation in the dialogue is not only the facilitator's responsibility but the participants are also responsible for their participation. The facilitator can encourage the participants in different ways, including through asking questions and summarising the topics every once in a while. The facilitator is a participant in the dialogue through listening and paying attention. Even without speaking, is it even possible *not* to participate?

Dialogue groups can be challenging, and not all groups are able to have skilful conversation. Sometimes a participant may dominate, or strong emotions and reactions may derail the dialogue. The facilitator can appreciate people's reactions and make them aware of what is happening. Facilitators can indeed encounter challenging groups. (In this regard, teaching dialogue skills in a university language education context is different; although the goal may be to overcome barriers in communication, no real conflicts usually emerge in class during a short two-credit course.)

We finished the session by considering the role of agenda in dialogue. Originally, in Bohmian dialogue, the agenda was to understand human consciousness, how people think. In the dialogues that the participants in our Zoom session most often facilitate, there is a given agenda.

After the third Zoom we reflected on the question, What if *all* the participants in the room or Zoom could be defined as facilitators? There may be one person that carries the legitimised status to facilitate, but ideally all the participants would engage in facilitating; they would take the responsibility to carry out the dialogue.

Kati: *I have learned that there are many functional but different ways of facilitating dialogue. Facilitators can be active 'on the stage' or stay more in the background, and/or regulate their level of activeness during the process. Referring back to the jazz metaphor, even if every instrument has its solo, the band is still playing together, improvising collectively. It is important to be conscious about one's own facilitation. We should reflect on our thinking and behaviour alone and together with other facilitators. Listening to other facilitators' experiences opens up an opportunity to reflect our own assumptions and routines. When speaking about our own experiences and understanding, maybe we are seeking justifications for our ways of facilitation. At its best, these reflections help us learn new ways to facilitate dialogue from others.*

Mirja: *My role is so different in the dialogue course that I teach. Referring back to our Zoom dialogue, I suppose I do participate in the dialogue and facilitate it too by creating the container and then listening to students' dialogue. I seldom interfere when the students are working on their group task through dialogue.*

Kati: *This sounds so interesting! I want to do that more in my teaching, too.*

REFLECTION TASK FOR THE READER: *What themes might you have brought up in these Zoom dialogues if you had participated in them? What do you see as important when inquiring into your dialogue facilitation and that of your colleagues?*

Promoting Dialogue: Strengthening Enablers and Reducing Barriers

Based on this inquiry, we see that we can promote dialogue in many ways as facilitators. The nature of the session defines our actions as facilitators – are we facilitating a structured or unstructured situation, and what are the goals of that session? Is dialogue more like a tool to reach, for example, comprehension of some theme or is the dialogue the content itself in that situation?

Though dialogue is more than a method (Isaacs 1999), we can also use different kinds of 'tools' or methods in facilitation for encouraging dialogue, or to develop as a dialogical interaction partner. Methods promoting dialogue might be, for instance, asking open (and appreciative) questions, sitting in a circle or utilizing different kinds of symbols (e.g., dialogue cards). Structuring the session in phases of checking-in and checking-out might promote the dialogue. Sometimes a talking stick might be useful to draw forth each participant's voice. Playing a dialogue board game could be an interesting way to have a dialogue and to practice dialogue skills.

The four cornerstones of dialogue skills are voicing, listening, appreciating and suspending. We can't force dialogue to happen, but we can enable it in many ways. What is important is our willingness and courage to hear, see, feel and learn. Our conscious presence and willingness to understand are crucial, too. Facilitators need to be aware of their own skills of reflection (self-reflection and collective reflection) and critical reflection (Mezirow 1991). They also need to recognise and demolish prejudices, become conscious about values and their own assumptions.

As facilitators we are weaving a synthesis, promoting inquiring, suspending, wondering and asking open questions, encouraging different viewpoints and reflecting. In practice, we often summarise what has been said so far and ask about what we are still missing.

Egocentrism, low self-confidence, blind spots and ignorance, a feeling of fear, an atmosphere of distrust and harassment are barriers to dialogue. In her book *The Spirit of Dialogue in the Digital Age*, Marie-Ève Marchand (2019) reports that the practitioners that she interviewed listed four aspects that are detrimental to dialogue: dominance exercised by one group member, lack of attention, escape into abstract thinking and refusal to question certain assumptions.

Dialogue is a developing process. When a group of people first meet, they generally carry out a dialogue of politeness. People behave based on inferred norms about how to interact – formal protocols. (Scharmer, as cited by Isaacs 1999, 279-280.) We also often unconsciously defend our opinions and ways of doing (Bohm 1996, 13). We might feel that if someone attacks our idea, they are attacking us (Isaacs 1999, 135). At this first stage, conversation consists of shared monologues and still lacks reflection (Scharmer, as cited by Isaacs 1999). The facilitator's role is to give room for each participant's voice and create an atmosphere of trust. In the second stage, participants are carrying out controlled discussion. The nature of this discussion can be called skilful conversation, in which people say aloud what they think. There might be power battles: whose meaning will have more power? Facilitators need to accept and deal with a range of emotions. It is important to keep the focus on themes and opinions, not people themselves. People are not their point of views.

Proceeding from level two forward requires reflection. At the level of reflective dialogue, people are examining and exploring the nature of the structures that guide their behaviour and action (Scharmer, as cited by Isaacs 1999). The facilitator can promote this level of dialogue by feeding the spirit of curiosity. Generative dialogue, the fourth stage of interaction in which genuinely new possibilities come into being, is only possible when people become aware of being part of a whole that is more important than their egos. Many new possibilities and options can be seen that were hidden before. In this stage, people often feel the collective flow. (Scharmer, as cited by Isaacs 1999) Isaacs points out that this stage is rare. The three other fields of conversation in the container that he describes are more common. As a facilitator, it is important to give space for new possibilities to come into existence by regulating one's own participation and encouraging participants to think aloud.

REFLECTION TASK FOR THE READER: What do you think are the enablers and barriers of dialogue in your facilitation?

Reflections on Reflection

In the *Cambridge English Dictionary, facilitation* is defined as 'the process of making something possible or easier', as noted earlier. A related word is *cooperation*. Facilitation can also be defined as 'an act of engaging participants in creating, discovering, and applying learning insights'.

What are we trying to reach by dialogue facilitation, then? According to Bohm (1996, 10), dialogue affects the whole thought process and aims to change the way the thought process occurs collectively. To follow this, we must first create a space for developing thinking and being. After this, we might see changes in people's behaviour and level of interaction. Maybe the most important aim in facilitation is to create a space and give tools for participants' reflection, and to empower them to think together. As facilitators, we are developing the meta-competencies and skills of dialogue: voicing, listening, suspending and respecting, and creating meaningfulness. We enable people to become aware of their own potential.

Reflection is an inseparable part of dialogue. Reflection can be seen as a core of (adult) learning and professional growth, transformation and empowerment. Numerous definitions for reflection exist, but often they are related to becoming conscious of, analysing, evaluating, questioning and criticizing experiences, assumptions, beliefs or emotions (Hilden & Tikkamäki 2016). Reflecting can be done, for example, by speaking, writing or drawing. Working with symbols (e.g. cards, photos) might also promote reflective thinking.

Suspension is at the core of dialogue. As we slow down and suspend our thoughts and reactions, dialogue becomes possible. Suspending involves changing direction, stopping, stepping back, seeing things with new eyes. It is the art of loosening our grip and gaining perspective (Isaacs 1999, 135). This sounds very close to what educators mean by a concept of reflection.

Reflection can be done individually, as self-reflection. Through self-reflection individuals have the opportunity to become conscious of their interpretations, assumptions and values that guide their thinking and behaving. Concepts, experiences and assumptions can also be reflected upon collectively. Collective reflection takes place in the processes of social interaction, sharing of opinions, asking for feedback, challenging groupthink and experimentation. Reflection always takes place in certain structures and processes, contexts. The type of culture, leadership, organisational structures and work processes create an architecture for reflection. (Hilden & Tikkamäki 2016) Reflection taking place while doing is called reflection-in-action and reflection done afterwards is reflection-on-action (Argyris & Schön 1978).

This process opened many interesting windows for our own inquiry into dialogue facilitation. Limited time in the conference session and a variable set of participants in each Zoom session affected the nature of our dialogues. We started many important routes but we have not yet reached the destination. However, in the session and in the Zoom dialogues we were thinking together and inquiring about dialogue facilitation from different angles. The participants were internally motivated and appreciated each other's professionalism. But you can't force dialogue to happen. Sometimes this might be frustrating. As a facilitator it is important to create a container to encourage dialogue to happen.

Kati: *You and I facilitate in different ways in different contexts, but despite that I see many common features and aims in our professional activities. We both want to promote dialogue, but do that in our personal ways. We both want to find justifications for our actions, yes, and to be sensitive to our strengths and weaknesses as dialogue facilitators/promoters. We believe in dialogue and its power in making the world and working life better places.*

Mirja: *Yes, I am an idealist and I believe in the possibility of making the world and working life better places through dialogue. As I work in language education, I want to believe that more awareness of dialogue in the educational context will make a difference.*

Kati: *One of our participants gave us feedback and said that these Zoom dialogues went straight into the topic and they were focused dialogues. So, maybe we managed quite well in our facilitation – or what do you think?*

Mirja: *I appreciate the feedback and I do think that all went well. This was likely due to us all being dialogue practitioners; everybody facilitated!*

REFLECTION TASK FOR THE READER: *What have you been reflecting on recently, related to your work or profession? What did you learn?*

To Conclude – How to Continue?

Many important themes were raised in the conference session and in the Zoom dialogues. Conversations generated rich data with different points of views, angles, and experiences. The challenge is to go deeper in certain themes. There was focus in these conversations but the time limitation did not allow us to consider the themes in more depth. Yet this was an important beginning. We feel that we should carry on this type of dialogue with the aim of developing a reflective facilitation approach. Here are some themes that could be discussed more in the future:

- How does one develop oneself as a dialogue facilitator?
- How can we best facilitate multilingual/multicultural groups?
- What ethical aspects are there to consider in dialogue in the room and in dialogue in the Zoom?

We finalised this paper in the time of the Coronavirus pandemic outbreak. The world is now shaken. The question is: Are we experiencing the same world? Thinking of all the different ways we are reacting to this dystopia and how differently it affects people's lives financially, we seem to live on the same planet but in different worlds. With all these crises around us, dialogue may be the only way to save the planet and make this one world. Facilitating dialogue involves a lot of potential and responsibility in raising this awareness. *The World Needs Dialogue!*

About the authors

Kati Tikkamäki, D.Ed., is a Senior Researcher and a professional in development at the Work Research Center of Tampere University, Finland. At the moment she is working in the European Social Fund Development Project (2019–2021): Renewing Dialogues in Social and Health Care – Leadership, Well-being and Productivity. https://projects.tuni.fi/sotedialogit/english/

She is also a part-time entrepreneur who works as a work supervisor, lecturer and trainer. Her dissertation (2006) dealt with learning at work and in organizational changes. A research and development program of Dialogic Leadership during 2011-2013 was a starting point for her dialogical journey. Especially William Isaacs' (1999) book *Dialogue and the Art of Thinking Together* raised the need and motivation for promoting dialogue. Since then, her research and development projects, teaching and training has strongly related to promoting dialogue and dialogical skills in working life.

Mirja Hämäläinen, Phil. Lic., is a lecturer in English at the Language Centre of Tampere University, Finland. University students in Finland have twelve years of English studies in school behind them. Many of them have acquired English outside classrooms through media, gaming, travelling and so forth. In other words, they are quite proficient in English (approximately at least B2 on the Common European Framework of Reference proficiency levels). All Finnish university degrees include language studies that aim to develop students' language and communication skills needed during studies and in working life. Tampere University Language Centre curriculum offers a variety of English language courses. Since 2013, one of the optional courses has been the two-credit course, *Dialogue: Constructive Talk at Work* (https://blogs.tuni.fi/elfdialogue/), created and taught by Mirja. The course is based on the dialogue approach proposed by Bohm, Factor and Garrett in "Dialogue: A Proposal" (1991). In this course, participants sit in a dialogue circle, practice dialogue skills and attitude, and philosophise on dialogue concepts in the spirit of equal communication. The teacher, Mirja, acts as a facilitator.

References

Argyris, C., & Schön, D. (1978) *Organizational Learning: A theory of Action Perspective*, Reading, Mass: Addison Wesley.

Bohm, D. Nichol, L. (1996). *On Dialogue.* London: Routledge, 1996.

Bohm, D., Factor, D., & Garrett, P. (1991). Dialogue: A proposal. Retrieved 17 February 2020 from http://www.dialogue-associates.com/files/files/Dialogue%20A%20Proposal.pdf

Hilden, S. & Tikkamäki, K. (2016). "Reflective practice as a fuel for organizational learning". *Administrative Sciences,* 2013, 3, 1, open access: www.mdpi.com/journal/admsci

Isaacs, W. (1999). *Dialogue and the Art of Thinking Together.* (First ed.) New York: Currency.

Marchand, M-È (2019). *The Spirit of Dialogue in a Digital Age*. Chipping Campden: Dialogue Publications.

Mezirow, J. (1991). *Transformative dimensions of Adult Learning*. San Francisco: Jossey-Bass.

[Note: *Because this paper was set up as an experiment in reflection, there was no separate conference consideration from which to draw extracts. The reflection participants did at the conference, and continuing with Mirja and Kati afterward,* was *the group consideration.*]

Section Two

Dialogic Intervention

Once a practitioner is competent with the Dialogue in the Room facilitative skills, they can be utilised for the purpose of Dialogic Intervention. This second level requires all the capability of Dialogue in the Room, and yet more. The Dialogic Intervention practitioner draws a larger circle that encompasses a particular problem, challenge, issue or opportunity. There are many ways to intervene to create generative co-created outcomes, but all of them must accomplish important objectives, some of them simultaneously. They need to shift collective thought patterns held by sub-cultural groupings and manage competing power structures; change the collective narrative and address accountability as well as authority through a sequence of Dialogues. The artistry is to transform an apparently unwelcome problem into a welcome opportunity.

– P.G.

Dialogic Intervention in a Volatile Organisational Takeover

Jane Ball

This is the story of a six-month intervention that enabled the successful handover of a government-run prison in the UK to a private company in 2011. I will be describing the mobilisation phase of privatisation; it is one chapter in a longer story of the transformation of the prison in private hands, and – although I won't be covering it in detail here – nine years later the collapse of safety and security at the same prison to the point it was returned to government management. This is itself part of the 25-year story of Professional Dialogue work in UK prisons and US corrections. The story is significant in part because the situation was unprecedented – Her Majesty's Prison Birmingham was the first prison in the UK to be transferred from the public to the private sector. The situation was also high stakes, with a cast of politicians, militant unions, a multinational corporation, prisoners, and the media, and the widespread anticipation of a drama that would become a crisis. Instead, using Professional Dialogue with the benefit of professional partners in this work, the handover was a non-event to the outside world.

A Container-Based Professional Dialogue Intervention

At a high level, the success of this intervention was based on the development of a *Container* that allowed a complex situation – deeply fragmented, volatile and riddled with conflict – to work out constructively. Those outcomes were at the personal level, supporting individuals in making decisions about their futures, and the level of organisational planning of changes that affected many people. The Container (described more fully under *Our Principles*, below) provides the conditions for the potential in any situation to unfold, and therefore affects the outcome as much as the activities in the foreground. Using a range of design, engagement and facilitation skills, and a genuine, open disposition, I intentionally built, sustained and enriched the container at HMP Birmingham. The Dialogic Practices are key to the development of the container; these figured highly in my work. The intervention also required a range of *Modes for Talking and Thinking* together, the extensive use of *Conversation, Skilful Conversation* and *Dialogue*, replacing the traditional use of *Monologue* and *Debate* in the prison culture. We needed to design a sequence of meetings, considering different sub-cultural mixes, agendas and facilitation processes, to achieve the desired outcome.

This paper should be of interest to anyone working on organisational intervention and volatile situations, not solely within a prison or corrections context.

HMP Birmingham: A Thorn in the Side of Her Majesty's Prison Service

HMP Birmingham was opened in 1849 as Winson Green Prison, a Victorian facility built to the radial design, intended to separate prisoners, and allow for easy observation. It was a menacing institution built in the city as a visual deterrent to would-be criminals, in the thinking of the time. When I first started working at another prison in the same area in 1999, it was still known as The Green, and staff and prisoners alike had stories to tell about the attitude of the staff, the state of the building or the overcrowded conditions.

Beyond the reputation, a report of the Chief Inspector of Prisons in 2001 described HMP Birmingham as having "some of the worst conditions for prisoners we have seen anywhere", with a "deep and longstanding negative culture". Despite valiant attempts and some improvements at times, (particularly with a multimillion-pound investment programme that added a building and new facilities to the site, and along with it the challenge of managing 1400 prisoners), not enough changed over the following 10 years. Staff behaviour was still cited as the most frequent cause of prisoners feeling unsafe; basic building, hygiene and food conditions were poor (the rubbish, rats, pigeons within the site were horrendous); purposeful activity, resettlement and other rehabilitation interventions were well below what was expected; and rates of prisoner self-harm were unacceptable.

In addition, Birmingham had a strong local branch of the Prison Officers Association (POA), the union representing uniformed grade staff, viewed as militant by managers and politicians and blamed by many for holding back progress and improvement at the prison.

Dividing Lines Drawn
In 2009 Labour Justice Secretary Jack Straw began a market testing process allowing private companies to bid for the contract to run HMP Birmingham. For him, the goal was to achieve cost efficiencies and modern practices that were otherwise blocked by unions.

For the unions and prison campaigners on the other side of the argument, privatisation was seen as simply a way to achieve prisons on the cheap. Unions feared for their members' jobs and talked about the 'betrayal' of public sector workers. Many believed this was 'a punishment' for unions over failure to accept workforce modernisation proposals put forward by the prison service. In the words of one Birmingham Prison Officer, "The other prisons are looking at us and shitting themselves because if they can privatise Birmingham, they can privatise any other prison on the basis of cost. Plus, in terms of the POA they'll have taken on the biggest bully to make the other bullies crumble and give up fighting."* The POA campaigned vigorously with the slogan *Prisons are not for Profit*.

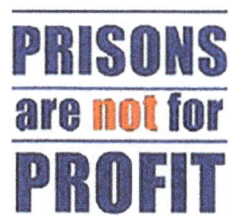

A Solid Partnership with G4S

Whilst the conflict was escalating in Birmingham, in the background the UK already had 13 private prisons with a successful track record. G4S ran four of those. The world's largest security company by revenue and one of the world's largest employers, operating in 90 countries, the Custodial & Detention Services (C&DS) division was a small business in their portfolio.

My colleague (and fellow Director in Dialogue Associates) Peter Garrett and I had partnered with the Managing Director of C&DS for eight years, first when he was working in the public sector. (I will call him the MD from here.) Over that time, I had worked as a consultant, coach, and interventionist within his region of the government-run prison service, then his business, using Professional Dialogue individually, facilitating challenging meetings and at an organisational level. The first work in 2003 paralleled the situation at Birmingham: a poorly performing prison with an adversarial union. With our Professional Dialogue intervention, HMP Dorchester – one of the prisons within his region at the time – rose from its status as one of the worst-performing prisons in the country to one of the best within a couple of years. More recently in 2010, I facilitated an intervention between the MD's leadership team and the GMB (General, Municipal, Boilermakers) union at their Joint Negotiation & Consultation Committee, where the exceptional way they had been able to talk and think together had astounded all the participants.

This shared experience meant we were trusted by the MD and his organisation to intervene where there were strongly divided subgroups, to enable constructive relationships to develop, take necessary decisions and actions and, ultimately, to change culture. We were recognised as professional partners with an expertise in Dialogue that could be relied upon in any situation, however high the stakes.

Peter and I were pleased to add our expertise to the G4S bid for HMP Birmingham. The proposal extended over a two-year period and included three phases: **Mobilisation**: a six-month period from contract announcement to the day G4S assumed control of the prison (and the subject of this paper); **Transition**: the period of handover and completion of employee transfers; and **Transformation**: introducing innovations in prison management, technology, business practices and cultural change.

---

* From *Privatising Prisons Labour Law and the Procurement Process* by Amy Ludlow. Reports of how shocking things were at the prison, the animosity between the POA, Prison Service management and government and the political context are easily accessible online and in Amy Ludlow's book.

Houses of Parliament, London 31st March 2011
On 31st March Ken Clarke, the Conservative Justice Secretary, announced the contract to run HMP Birmingham had been awarded to G4S. He claimed there would be cumulative savings of £216m from Birmingham and two other prisons involved in the market testing process over the 14-year contract. He also said contingency plans were in place to prevent violence and disorder inside prisons. The Government anticipated widespread walkouts by prison staff in wildcat action. Up to 3000 military personnel had been trained to work in prison and were on standby to take the staff's place. All bids had also been required to provide contingencies for rehousing prisoners in other prisons, should staff walk out on strike or prisoners take advantage of the situation and start a riot, so all G4S prisons were on standby.

One third of the 752 Birmingham staff walked out, and there were dramatic scenes outside the prison as they gathered there. The Birmingham POA branch chairman stated, "Our union has a policy of industrial action, up to and including strike action, should a public sector prison be handed to a private sector operator. The policy of the union will be followed by this branch". The POA also immediately launched a judicial review into the process.

The Action Begins

Our Principles
We began our consultation with some principles that would be the foundation for our approach. Container development is fundamental to the Professional Dialogue practice that Peter and I have been establishing. The ***Container*** provides the conditions for the potential in any situation to be realised. There is always a container; the skill is understanding how to affect the *quality* of the container to support the developing situation. Qualities of a container include strength, to manage challenges and crises; safety and security, to allow openness and vulnerability; energy, to bring about change; and the presence and awareness of potential. Intervention requires the development of a container fit for the change. The more conflict and challenge in a situation, the more robust the container needs to be, and the more skill and attention is required.

The concept of a container is understood in sports, without the language. We expect sporting competitions to have a home leg and an away leg. The container favours the home team, so when a team repeatedly loses at home fans really wonder what is wrong with the container. (Yesterday, for example, ninth-ranked Japan, playing on their home turf, beat Ireland, ranked second, in the rugby World Cup.) The womb provides a container – it must be safe, strong and steady to protect the foetus as it grows. It is flexible and changes size and shape through a pregnancy. Within the womb is the energy and potential for the foetus to grow to maturity for a successful birth and survival. If our children are in a school performance, we take care with their preparations and give them attention while they're on stage to help them do well. We all work tacitly with containers all the time.

Given the volatile context for the start of the work, we knew we needed the right quality of container. Built on many years working together, Peter and I have a steady and generative partnership to carry the most challenging work. Our partnership with G4S was also built on a solid understanding with the MD. In our preparations, we had carefully included the team working around him on this contract, sharing our motivations, hopes and fears for the work to come.

The **Dialogic Practices** need to be active to develop the container. The four Practices are **Voice, Listening, Respect** and **Suspension**. They are not technical skills; they can be developed through practice and have a profound impact as they deepen. *Voice* first means speaking up, then saying publicly what you say privately, then adding your unique perspective as a contribution to the situation. *Listening* requires hearing others, understanding their meaning. and receiving their unique contribution. *Respect* requires taking other people and their views seriously, even when they think very differently or in opposition, and finding out how to include their difference. *Suspension* is the practice of noticing how you are forming your views, explaining, and checking your thinking.

We also knew that our stance was important. The stance we take is to be a peer to all, whether they are the Head of the Prison Service, a prison officer, the Chief Executive of G4S, a prisoner, the union representative, a news reporter, or anyone else. As their equal we can talk on-the-level, without any limitation in our use of the full range and depth of the Dialogic Practices. This stance would prove crucial.

Addressing the Biggest Risk and Power

As we sat down with G4S to agree our first steps, POA industrial action posed the most immediate risk, both within HMP Birmingham and in the prison service nationally. National POA leaders in the newspapers were predicting the prison service could go into 'meltdown'. The union had the power to stop progress, or worse, and we knew this power had to be met directly and immediately. We had to address this risk first and, despite nervousness from many people in G4S, we agreed to set up and facilitate a meeting of relevant POA leaders with the senior G4S team.

Convening the meeting was unique in my experience. The MD was in touch with the National Chair of the POA. They were both experienced men who had known each other for many years, albeit on different sides of the fence, and they respected each other. The POA *Chair* agreed that a meeting might ease the situation and he was happy to talk with me about the possibility. Everything was arranged by phone. I called him, and after hearing his story and views in depth, he gave me a number to call the POA *National General Secretary*. I called him and we also spoke at length and in depth, and he gave me a number to call the *Regional* representative on the National Executive Committee. After an equally frank and cordial conversation he gave me details to call the *Branch Chair* at the Prison. I spoke with both him and his *Branch Secretary*. Once they agreed to the meeting, everyone else agreed to attend.

In each call I introduced myself and explained my role, asked one or two questions about the situation and invited them to the meeting. I listened and extended respect to each person and we began to establish a rapport that would be crucial when we met.

It was obvious that the sequence of calls respected the power dynamic within the union and was necessary to get everyone to the table. The local Branch has the power – they vote in the national officers, and the officers act on their behalf. National and Regional representatives could not tell the Branch what to do, but they could facilitate introductions. National and Regional representatives could not agree to attend the meeting until the Branch agreed – otherwise they would appear to be betraying their members. Each call felt like a test, and presumably I passed.

Around the Kitchen Table
The day of the meeting was preceded by dinner at a local hotel. A meeting room was booked there but, based on what I had heard on my calls, we agreed to move location to the Dialogue Associates office. Our office has a unique quality – the meeting room has the design of a bright kitchen-dining room with flip charts along one wall; we sit around a large oak kitchen table, and the tea- and coffee-making facilities are on hand. Symbolically the room signifies the integration of home and work, personal and professional values. It was just right for this occasion.

A crisis occurred at the start of the day. Everyone had arranged to drive down from the hotel in convoy, but a misunderstanding meant the Chair and Secretary of the Birmingham POA Branch were stranded without directions. By the time they arrived they were angry. "We never leave one of ours behind", said the Chair. The situation symbolised everything they were feeling about betrayal, and the meeting seemed to be on the brink of collapse. We could not ignore what had happened – like everything, this had to be discussable. Peter pointed out that it was inevitable we would feel let down by each other down at times, the question was how we managed the situation when it happened. After a range of authentic reassurances from others we agreed to proceed.

Given the significance of all the stories I had heard on my preparatory calls, I suggested we take time for a longer round of introductions to hear what each person was thinking and feeling about the privatisation of HMP Birmingham. In my opinion, one of the most significant introductions was by the Birmingham Branch Chair, who emotionally described his commitment to his members, his pride in HMP Birmingham, and his hopes and disappointments during prison modernisation and then privatisation. "I would treat my dog better than they (the prison service) have treated us", he commented. He appeared like a wounded lion, and as he talked his hostility begin to be replaced by the voice of a loyal colleague and proud public servant. A second significant statement was the Head of G4S Care and Justice, the most senior person in the room, who defended the private sector after comments from the POA about the lack of values in commercial organisations. He explained the value G4S contributed to many pension funds, including those of public sector workers. These were the two extremes in the room, and while they were developing a cautious respect for each other, there was no doubt that in the wrong conditions they would defend their own position and attack each other.

The atmosphere, the container, was transformed after the check-in and the day proceeded with an open respectful Dialogue addressing a range of issues that were of interest to each side. This ranged from ethical business to union recognition rights, the profit taken from a prison contract to the calibre of Birmingham staff, and from explanations about the due diligence process to arranging regular tours of the prison together. Everyone heard what others had to say about all these subjects and they were able to build a common view of the whole situation.

Outside the room the POA were maintaining a public stance that was critical of the government's decision, and during our breaks they were approving press releases denouncing the privatisation. However, over the next few days a more positive message to members emerged from both National and Branch officials. A letter sent the following week by one of the POA participants said the opportunity had "allowed the POA and G4S to expel some myths about each other and the meeting was both positive and professional". More than that, there was no industrial action, and the adversarial narrative had started to shift. Within weeks the Branch Chair and Mobilisation Project Manager were working together looking at staffing profiles. They did not always agree but they listened to each other, respected each other, and they could work together.

Mobilisation

During the six-month Mobilisation phase the G4S team had a long list of technical work to accomplish, including:

- conducting due diligence (which entailed an extensive survey of buildings and equipment)
- initiating a TUPE process, or Transfer of Undertakings (Protection of Employment) – UK law to protect employee rights when a business is transferred
- establishing a risk register
- purchasing and distributing new uniforms for every member of staff
- setting up the system to pay salaries to over 700 staff in October, and more.

Our role was to prepare staff for the transition to G4S on 1st October and initiate a change of culture. This preparation would include the opportunity for staff to talk through how they were feeling and thinking about working for a private company and the changes they knew or suspected would happen. Preparation would also mean enabling people to make informed personal and professional decisions, with an understanding about the implications of those decisions for them and others.

Off-site, Peter and I had designed a framework for the six-month Mobilisation process, including Engagement, Discovery and Preparation (described below). Each of these phases had a different goal, and were convened, designed and facilitated differently as a result. I talked offline with Peter regularly to reflect on what had happened and what was needed next, and the intervention adapted to the needs and opportunities that arose.

First Get People Engaged

The Engagement phase was designed to allow Birmingham managers and staff to meet the G4S Executives and Mobilisation Team, establish a common understanding and mutual respect and lay a foundation for working together. The first session brought together the incumbent Governor,

Deputy Governor and senior members of the leadership team to meet with the MD and senior peers in G4S. Only the day before, I had entered the prison for the first time with the Mobilisation Team Leader and Project Manager, but the meeting was off-site – on neutral ground.

We used facilitation patterns that we have used successfully in other settings. A *pattern* has a series of steps that make a difference to the quality of engagement and effectiveness with which people talk and think together, without participants needing new skills. One of the patterns we used required people to line up according to how long they had been working in prisons and, in turn, starting with the longest serving, tell the date they started and list the prisons they had worked in. On both sides they could respect the experience of the others – the G4S staff had a long public sector background as well as commercial experience. Then, we asked them to line up according to the length of time they had worked in HMP Birmingham. Once again, the line extended from the person who had served longest at Birmingham to those in the recent G4S Mobilisation team, and we heard the date they started and a story from their first day. In this round G4S were the inexperienced group, with less to say, and the Birmingham staff could speak with humour and pride about the prison. "We are passionate about Birmingham. It runs through us", one said. Mutual respect and understanding began to emerge.

Next in small groups, each with a mix of G4S and HMP Birmingham managers we introduced our Five-Question Pattern. In turn, each person on the group answered the question: *Why you did you join HMP Birmingham or G4S?* This was followed by: *What has been your most fulfilling experience?* Then: *What has been your most devastating experience?* And: *Why do you stay?* And finally: *What would make you proud that you stayed and saw this through, in two years?* Of course, the *most fulfilling* experience for most of the G4S staff was the announcement that G4S had won the contract to run HMP Birmingham, and the *most devastating* experience for many of the Birmingham staff was the announcement that G4S had won the contract to run HMP Birmingham. From these different feelings about the same event, they found they had very similar answers to the final questions – they all wanted to see Birmingham be a successful, high-performing prison. Having begun in different stories about what had happened, they finished with a common story about the future.

The Engagement phase progressed with these sessions for every level to first-level leaders (senior officers). Respecting the hierarchy and power structure, we cascaded through the ranks. Some of the responses to the experience were remarkable. People were hungry to be heard, and eager to meet and talk with anyone in G4S. The bidding process had taken two years, in which period staff felt that they were on a knife edge. One common story was this: *"The announcement was made in the gym on the other side of the prison. After, we were told we had to walk past four residential wings the prisoners were shouting 'you're gonna lose your job'"*. Many people talked about shedding tears when the announcement was made. The sessions enabled the collective organisational trauma to be processed. There were also many unhappy individual stories. One older officer explained through tears of anger how he had already lost one pension in his early career in industry, and now he feared the pension he had built in the prison service would be lost too as they moved to a private employer.

Who Are You? Signs of Pervasive Fragmentation

Once in the prison and talking to people, I found that the fragmentation was more extreme than I had anticipated. For example, in addition to the POA, several other unions represented staff. They never spoke to each other beyond formal meetings, and the POA drove the agenda. In an Engagement session they finally talked openly and began to find common ground with each other, as well as with G4S. In the same way I found an entire rank of uniformed staff! The Principal Officer (PO) rank had been replaced nationally by a non-uniformed senior management position, but those who refused to sign up to the new role were not penalised. POs were permitted to remain POs. Birmingham's organisational chart and briefing had not shown that they retained seven Principal Officers. They each had decades of experience, hundreds of years between them, but were pushed out and under-utilised. Engaging them led to their useful participation in Mobilisation, supporting areas such as staff care and communication, which benefitted from their reputation and strong connection with the prison and the staff. Finally, as we reached middle- and lower-management levels, staff who had worked in the prison for some years met each other for the first time!

As a result of the engagement sessions relationships were forming, people were gaining a better understanding of each other, the history and culture of the prison was clearer, and G4S were showing Birmingham staff how they did business. "It's great to be spoken to like a grown up", commented one manager. Our intervention design and my facilitation were focussed on evoking the Dialogic Practices, building the container, and preparing the ground for the complex work to be done. Engagement was also a phase of research, or what we called Discovery – with the goal of understanding more about the culture of the prison from the point of view of staff and prisoners. I spoke widely with people about what I was noticing and including the Mobilisation Team, to help them in their work.

Engagement with prisoners included one-to-one conversations, Dialogues for a range of groups with distinct characteristics such as foreign nationals, elderly prisoners, ethnic minority prisoners, and those at a different stage of their journey through the prison, such as on reception into the prison or on remand versus being long-term prisoners. Interestingly, these were straightforward sessions, where the prisoners were unsurprisingly critical of prison conditions and staff attitude and interested to understand what changes were planned. The signalling to Birmingham staff that G4S wanted to engage and hear from prisoners was more significant than the content.

Everything Changes and Nothing Changes: Preparation

Three months after the bid announcement, and with three months to go until the prison was transferred to G4S, staff were still understandably tired, anxious, sensitive and feeling disempowered. The aim of the Preparation Phase was, therefore, to help the staff, managers and prisoners establish a sound and shared understanding of what would happen during the Transition period and think together about what they could do to prepare effectively. Thus, they would realise that they could themselves manage and influence the situation rather than simply be subject to what was happening.

[Figure: Transition Road Map — hand-drawn chart spanning July to January 2012, covering MEUS/Unions/The Prison swim-lanes with items including TUPE, 121 interviews, Critical Training, People Leaving, G4S Employee, Sue Saunders Director, New Uniform, Redundancy Consultation, Selection Criteria, New Teams Forming, Implementing the "New Way", Road Map for Prisoners, Other Key Stakeholders, Contracted Colleagues]

Working in partnership with the head of each department, we appointed up to 20 people from mixed ranks and roles who worked in that area to attend meetings in the Preparation Phase. The structure was simple. I had created a six-month Transition Road Map (see figure) and started each session using this to explain what would be happening. I used the same roadmap, covering four flip charts taped together, in every session, adding anything that people had heard about that was not already written up, and dispelling myths when I heard them. Together we talked about the key issues that might arise for that team, what they could do to prepare, risks and how they could be mitigated. We recorded decisions publicly on a flip chart and shared with all the participants afterwards to circulate to their colleagues and staff.

The feeling of pain was still widespread. The break with public sector was emotional as well as practical for staff, and some degree of preparation for this was required. Many people were proud to work for her Majesty's prison service as a public servant and felt diminished by the prospect of working for a private company. This was symbolised by the change of uniform from Prison Service 'Black and Whites' to the G4S uniform that was likened to that of a coach driver. Staff had joined Birmingham for a steady job, or because their parents or grandparents had worked there. The upheaval and drama of the last few years had undermined their sense of security.

As staff talked about how they felt, and why, they began to take in the situation and think constructively about the future. The opportunity changed a negative and reactive disposition into a positive and proactive one. As well as making practical plans, Birmingham staff started to recognise they were going to be leading the transition and transformation of the prison – there was no big G4S team going to turn up to do it. Cross-hierarchical groups thinking things through together was a different way of working, and one that G4S intended to introduce to the culture at Birmingham. There was greater awareness of what was happening across the prison, greater participation, and people were able to act in a coherent and constructive way.

Preparation sessions were held with prisoner groups on every residential unit. Most had heard little that was concrete but had high expectations of what was to come (for example, in-cell showers and telephones) because they had been in G4S prisons, or other private prisons, before, or had heard stories about better conditions in private prisons. My aim was to manage their expectations, as the changes would be small initially (such as wearing their own clothes), and some of their expectations would never be met as this was an old building with significant limitations. What I could prepare them for, and the one or two staff members who participated in each session, was the quality of communication and relationship between staff and prisoners that G4S expected.

Much Can Be Achieved with the Right Mode for Talking and Thinking Together
While the formal sessions were taking place, I was talking informally daily with staff and prisoners, individually and in small groupings. In our work we distinguish seven Modes for Talking and Thinking Together, and an intervention requires a range of these Modes to achieve different outcomes. Monologue, one person holding the floor, is the most basic Mode and is commonly used in prisons. People were used to briefing others and telling them what to do. The message is "I know, and I am in charge", and at times that is needed. Debate was another familiar Mode – making your point to beat the other side and, if necessary, playing dirty to win. Our intervention required Conversation, enriching relationships, enabling mutual respect to develop, and providing a foundation to work together. Skilful conversation brought out reasoning and the chance to think through consequences and hence enable better decision-making. For more complex issues Dialogue included a range of stakeholders to talk and think together to reach a common understanding. There was no requirement for consensus, just a desire for a good overall picture to emerge from which each person or group could make decisions.

To engage basic-grade uniformed officers and non-security staff, it was not possible to convene large groups – after all, they were doing the work! Instead I walked and talked my way around the prison. I did not have a set of keys to get around as I wanted to be clear that I was a guest in their prison. Consequently, I had to be escorted everywhere and this gave me good opportunity to talk with my escort and ask them to introduce me to others. In *Conversation* I built great rapport and relationships with people – they realised that I was working with them, not doing anything to them or for them. The starting point for good Conversation is an interest in the other person. As you listen to what they say, and what they don't say, it is remarkable what you can pick up on – follow that thread and a deeper connection is formed. Most people were thirsty for that connection, especially as they associated me with their future employers, and they had been expecting a distant and impenetrable face from a commercial organisation. Good Conversation also requires a willingness to reveal yourself to others, and thus you easily find common ground. Remarkably a conversation that began with me asking one of the influential old-guard officers why he wasn't joining me for a cup of tea, to break the ice, led to the discovery that his wife had been treated by my brother, who is a consultant Nephrologist. The officer held my brother in high regard – "somewhere above God", he said. Did that help? Absolutely.

This may not sound that clever. We all get to know people and make friends, at the school gate or local bar, but the implicit rules of organisations define what you can and cannot talk about and with whom, dictating personal and professional boundaries, and constraining conversation. Attitudes towards the value conversation adds to organisational life tend to be dismissive or soft. I believe the tougher the situation, the more important the conversation.

The MD would regularly come to the prison and be guided by me about where he should go and to whom he should talk to go to the tough nuts, address risks or opportunities and build the container for change. This applied to prisoners as well as staff. I found an almost self-sufficient community of some 80 Vietnamese prisoners living in one housing unit. If understood and managed, this sort of community can be positive, but unmanaged there is a risk that they control the staff and their area of the prison. I took the MD to Buddhist Chapel to meet and talk with these men. Respectfully, he removed his shoes and sat cross-legged on the floor, deep in conversation.

Once relationships were established, I was able to drop into Skilful Conversation with individuals and smaller groups. Skilful Conversation takes some time and focus, as people consider what they are thinking and feeling and why, take on new information and think through the implications. Staff frequently raised issues with me, usually about G4S and what the prison would be like to work in. Many were considering whether to stay at the prison and work for G4S or try to transfer out to another prison within the public sector. A Skilful Conversation about G4S, Birmingham, future privatisation, other prisons, and their own aspirations helped them to think through their decision. Skilful Conversations would also be about aspects of their work, and how to manage situations given the changes that were happening. I was able to support and challenge the way they were thinking or introduce them to the right person to talk to.

As well as the Dialogue in the Engagement and Preparation process, at times complex issues were raised that required the Mode of Dialogue. These involved a range of perspectives, sometimes including external stakeholders such as education or treatment providers. Some had longer-term decision-making consequences, and always implications for a range of staff. Where staff raised such an issue with me, I would convene the right group from G4S and elsewhere to talk about it. The wide-ranging relationships I had developed through the intervention gave me the power to convene. One such situation arose with a complex contractual issue for the Drug Treatment provision, which affected the uniformed prison officers who were doing the work. The Dialogue brought out the range of perspectives, short- and long-term possibilities, risks and opportunities – everything was included and those who had immediate decisions to make were better informed.

Decision-Making

The process to help individual and collective decision-making was critical. Many decisions were having to be made amid the emotion and uncertainty of the situation. G4S could not recommend what anyone should do and the transitional Governor of the prison did not know what would be happening in the long term, so he was not able to advise his staff. The union were more subdued. People had to decide for themselves, and many were not used to doing that. The Dialogic Intervention created a container in which those decisions could be thought through and made constructively.

Sort Yourselves Out Too – Mobilisation Team Alignment
The G4S leaders and staff involved in Mobilisation were committed to doing a good job, proud of what they had achieved by winning the bid and of being the first to manage a prison privatisation. They were also warm-hearted colleagues. Yet they also had very different interests to manage during the Mobilisation process. The MD was in regular communication with the G4S Executive, who knew nothing about running prisons so could not understand the steps that were being taken and was anxious about the financial and reputational risks to the business. He also was the point of contact for the National agencies – the Prison Service, unions, and the media. The Head of the Mobilisation team, who was in line to take over as Governor of Birmingham, was trying to understand the operation, build relationships and prepare for the changes and innovations she knew she would be required to deliver after Transition. The Project Manager was ensuring delivery of the due diligence process. The Head of Human Resources was very concerned about ensuring a legal and professional process to take on the public sector employees. There was also the Facilities Director and Head of Finance, who had other priorities. Meanwhile we were leading the cultural change and encouraging high levels of engagement, transparency and participation to enable the changes. As in any organisation, areas of specialism pursue their own interests, are often unaware of the interests of others and frequently act at odds with colleagues. There was a significant risk we would trip each other up and miss the creative opportunities of closer cooperation. The pressure of Mobilisation deadlines and the complexity of the work would make these problems more likely.

At the start of Mobilisation, the HR Director expressed her fears about our planned engagement and preparation process, and me – or anyone – talking with Birmingham staff while they still worked for the public sector. TUPE required release of information in a controlled way within a formal consultation process according to a legally defined timeline. The HR team were concerned that our engagement with staff at the prison contravened the requirements of this process. The challenge was helpful, as it clarified our role and stance to everyone. We did not know any of the detailed future staffing plans and we were not there to represent G4S; therefore, we could not contravene the formal communication processes. We were there to represent the whole system, and I described my stance as being on everyone's side.

We recommended a monthly Alignment Meeting for the heads of the various areas involved in Mobilisation. Each time we met we drew up a timeline for the next six to twelve months across four flip charts, with a section for each person to complete, showing what they would be doing over that period. Additionally, we talked through what had happened, what had been learnt, and what we were going to do. As a result, we could all see the whole picture. Our facilitation encouraged everyone to listen to each other and understand what others were doing and why. The agenda was set collectively according to what anyone noticed and wanted to raise.

We created a *Cultural Risk Register* to track the range of cultural risks that were identified as the Mobilization phase progressed, and the mitigations that were undertaken. While there were so many technical tasks to accomplish, this ensured the whole team was thinking about the culture. The Cultural Risk Register formalised the implicit risk-based approach we had taken from the outset. At our suggestion, our colleague Mark Seneschall from Prison Dialogue was commissioned to record a rich narrative of the process. What was happening was unprecedented and the value of a detailed record was clear.

Always Expect the Unexpected
We had a carefully thought-through, high-level intervention plan that was adapted along the way according to the circumstances we met. A robust container was being established that enabled unexpected challenges to be managed without risking progress. Challenges now occurred within the container; they did not threaten the container. There were so many details to get right in a fixed and tight time period: staff pay, uniforms in the right size and number, policies and procedures to prepare after due-diligence scrutiny, buildings to check. Unexpected issues were continually being uncovered in many areas along the way. By far the most personally challenging was the departure of the Head of the Mobilisation Team and prospective Governor of the prison, following the sudden tragic death of her son.

Becoming G4S

Transition-Eve
On HMP Birmingham's last day as part of the public sector prison estate, at the end of the dayshift, a ceremony took place in the Centre (the hub of the radial Victorian building). The area was crowded with staff, the large prison bell was rung, and the chairman of the POA gave a proud and moving speech. The ceremony gave respect to the history of the prison, as the intervention had done from the outset, and which I believe was part of the success.

Zero Hour – 1st October 2011
G4S took control of HMP Birmingham 00:01 on 1st October 2011. Overnight the reception was painted in G4S colours, the HMPS flag was taken down and the new G4S flag raised, and the keys were counted and handed over.

I was there as many staff arrived early for their morning shift in their new G4S uniform, such was the feeling of excitement and anticipation. Everyone felt that they were part of the success of the day, and the pride that they had managed the transition without any prisoner disturbances. I experienced a genuine sense of camaraderie and kindness as people appeared with bacon rolls and cups of tea for their colleagues. One female officer, whose husband also worked at the prison, told me, "We had a curry last night and got everything ready – I don't know why but it felt like a special occasion, like the first day at a new school". Union representatives were alongside G4S executives and prison senior managers, providing a strong leadership presence. There was no trouble from prisoners, and no resistance from staff. The MD was proud to be able to report to his CEO, waiting anxiously for news I am sure, that the prison had been unlocked as normal and there was an excellent atmosphere in the prison.

Still in the background a Tornado Squad was close by should there be any disturbances. They were not called upon, as inside the prison there was almost a festival atmosphere. Outside the prison this had become *a non-event* but inside it was a significant victory!

What Happened Next?

The Transition period continued until the end of 2011, while new staffing numbers, structures and roles were introduced. I facilitated a reflective *Lessons Learnt* process about Mobilisation, including representatives who managed the process on the government side. In 2015 we also facilitated a session, hosted and convened by Prison Dialogue, to consider learnings from the whole privatisation process.

A two-year Transformation had to be delivered according to the promises of the bid and subsequent contract between G4S and the government. This included technical innovations such as body-worn cameras, 'clocking-in and clocking-out' for staff, touch-screen kiosks for prisoners to manage more of their own affairs, and cost reductions.

Dialogue Associates was contracted to provide consultancy and coaching services during this period. Though I do not intend to describe this phase in detail, it is worth noting that many people were eager to continue working together in the way they had experienced during Mobilisation. Changes in behaviour and attitude introduced through the Mobilisation intervention were sustained in areas. I supported managers leading two major restructures of residential areas, helping them to use a participative Dialogic decision-making approach to include all the stakeholders to work together. As a result, a major move of prisoners in protective custody from one housing unit to another (more challenging that you would imagine), and the opening of a Social Care Unit for elderly and disabled prisoners were delivered successfully. They had received no Dialogue training, but the managers had embraced the principles of ownership and participation. I introduced the simple concept – if you talk about *them*, include *them*. They found it worked. In fact, in 2014 an officer received a national commendation for the development of the Social Care Unit.

Principles of delegation, distributed leadership, accountability, and ownership were taken strongly into the culture in many forms. For example, name badges were introduced for all staff, so they were personally identifiable; senior managers were required to report regularly at a trading review for their department; first-level leaders were responsible for managing the budget for their area. I was providing coaching and consulting for the new prison Director and facilitation of the Transformation Board (the Alignment Meeting).

Staff at HMP Birmingham had a taste of how to do things differently, but not the skill. Without Dialogue skills training and leadership development a Dialogic approach was not embedded nor therefore sustainable. We proposed introducing Dialogic training and development, but because it was not a contract deliverable it did not happen, despite some enthusiasm off the back of the successful Mobilisation.

Closing Reflection on Dialogic Intervention

On reflection, when you work *with* people, rather than doing things *to* them or *for* them, the contribution you make can be overlooked. This is both the power of the work and its downfall. It behoves us as professional practitioners to make our work explicit, so that the skills can be shared and extended. The effectiveness and reliability of those skills, especially in high-stakes situations, attests to the professionalism.

Our intervention in the privatisation of HMP Birmingham, and the Mobilisation phase described here, shows how Professional Dialogue can enable highly conflictual and fragmented organisational situations to work out in a constructive way. The cultural intervention required understanding of organisational power, individual and collective decision-making and risk. We had to appreciate the context and current situation from the perspective of all the known stakeholders and design the intervention in response. As we engaged with new people and heard their point of view, we were able to adapt the intervention design to include them where necessary. We used a range of intervention design skills, including how to work with history and how to think about the future; how to integrate and align organisations and subgroups; when to work with a distinct subgroup and when to mix relevant subgroups (and what that mix should be). Design skills for meetings (the check-in, facilitated exercises, questions etc.) enabled each session to support the live needs of the situation. Convening skills meant I knew who to include and how to get them into the room.

Our intervention practice was based on deepening and extending the container to include more of the people and situation. The container was developed through my use of the Dialogic Practices (Voice, Listening, Respect and Suspension), and activating the Dialogic Practices in others towards each other – through meeting designs, facilitation, engagement and relationship. With the container people were aware of what was happening because all the information was equally available to everyone, they began to see the potential of the situation and they were able to participate, make coherent decisions and take coherent action.

The stance required for the intervention was to engage everyone as an equal, to be on everyone's side, and to act on behalf of the whole system rather than one part of the system. This stance is based on the principle that everything is interconnected, and there is a way in which the situation can unfold constructively for everyone. I believe this case describes how we achieved a constructive unfoldment at HMP Birmingham.

Conference Session Extracts

From a conversation with participants considering the paper with the author

Speaker 1: What I was wondering about is intervention. What is intervention?

Speaker 2: Shall I offer a perspective? My first involvement with dialogue was a piece of work that we did with Bill Isaacs, who was coach to a management team of which I was a part, and I think that was dialogue. Basically he just got us working together as a team more effectively. I think the terminology might label that as dialogue in the room, but I think it's a blurred line about where intervention starts . . . . This was bringing groups together to be more effective, and building containers. So where does that sort of stop and where does intervention start? I just think it's a continuum.

One of the things he did, he just got us to assume the other guy's role. There was an intervention, but it wasn't in pursuit of a specific problem. I think part of what you and Peter do particularly, and what I think is . . . I'm not just saying this . . . what is spectacular about your work, is that you design interventions. So you go beyond "let's just build the container" to "let's do something that is focused on a particular area – to, "What are the ranges of activities that we can implement, which have a sort of dialogic aspect to them that will make a difference?" I think that's the real nugget. You kind of have a sense of what you do, but you don't copy.

So, essentially the client is over *here* and they would like to be *there*, and they often hire a consultant to help them or to partner with them to get from here to there. And then I think it gets really interesting, because then each consultant is left with saying, "We're exploring how we're going to get you from here to there". And that's exciting, because we each would do it differently, and we each have very different ideas on what would work. And either we have something somewhat set, or we are designing in the moment and don't have something set. So that's how I see an intervention.

Speaker 3: I had to find a way to design an agreement with the company for *not* knowing. So, I usually only give them an overview of different kinds of interventions, or points in the process and what it could cost, and then we just go from there. We have some checkpoints on the way where we can see if there is a budget that we have to not exceed. There is a question of whether intervention skills are a gift that you have as a person, or are something that acquirable, that you learn. I have the feeling that you have a skill, a way of understanding the system, a soft approach, a way of being and relating to people. Some people can have these skills naturally.

Speaker 4: So, two quite different things came to mind when you asked your question. One was, when I did my organizational development course, there was this phrase that was often said: When you start, when you have that first conversation, it's already an intervention. It starts with that first phone call, so make sure that the right people are even in the call, and be aware that this is already an intervention. The other picture that comes to mind is . . . about doctors and surgery rooms. When you have surgery you want to be healed, or you're hoping to get healed. Usually intervention is not just something minor, but an intervention in medical terms is something quite major. So it's a major change that's supposed to bring healing in some sort of way. You actually do something more dramatic with a particular objective in a certain time frame, time comes into it, or you accompany people over a longer time. Then there is a design and there is a process behind it that allows you to travel that distance with the system.

Speaker 5: I can sort of recognize everything you say there. This one-time team-building session or workshop . . . I feel the same, it's not satisfying afterwards. It has to be a longer thing where you can actually feel a part of seeing that something actually happens.

Speaker 6: I'm a struggling a bit with the word, because *intervention* relates for me "to intervene". For me that's kind of to interrupt. So you interrupt some sort of processes, which will became unconscious and just carried out without knowing. If you want to change patterns which are unconscious, you need a lot of effort, because you'll not only have to stop patterns but create new ones as well. So you have to do it over and over again until the new patterns are unconscious too. So, short-term interventions are almost a paradox.

Speaker 1: For me, intervention is about trying to change the course, using the skills quite deliberately to change something. Something working out in a way that you believe is unhelpful, otherwise you wouldn't intervene. If you see this is going well, why intervene? I knew there was a way that things could work out that people wouldn't get hurt, and that everybody could be better off. And that we needed to provide the opportunity for that to happen. It wasn't that it's got to be x, y and z, but there is a way in which it can work out constructively and we'll find out how that is.

Speaker 7: I want to thank you. I am very touched by what you've done and how you've presented it. I think that a lot of what you have accomplished comes to who you are, your ethics, your sensitivity, your intelligence. Of course, what you know is useful as well. But I think what counts the most is what you are. Because you invite cooperation just by your vocabulary, by how you present. And this invitation to cooperate – not everybody has it.

Speaker 1: In my own development as a dialogue practitioner, I started with dialogue in the room, and then I found, well, that's not enough – we need to intervene. And then

I did interventions, so I go, "Well that failed, so I need systemic work . . ." There is a natural path. As you work on intervention you realize how much better you need to be as a practitioner in the room, and how much you need to grow. Every step you need to grow as a person to be able to encompass the work you're doing. So I think it always comes back to that.

Postscript

The author's reflections, written some months after the conference

I posed the question "What is intervention?" to colleagues at the conference session, after they had heard about my work at HMP Birmingham. This question helpfully changed the dynamic from *learning from me* to *learning together*. People noticed and shared their own ideas about intervention, prompted by my work. The more precise question I meant was "What is dialogic intervention?" The perspectives that came up led me to think about this in more depth.

Some people's words seemed to imply that dialogic intervention is simply communication or 'sorting things out by talking about them'. I see it as more than this. My paper describes some of the skills and patterns that are needed, that practitioners can learn. However, I have been thinking about what else is needed for dialogic intervention. What is the subtle discernment that leads to intervention decisions, such as with whom to engage, about what and when? This seems to require appreciation of the context, history, subcultures, power differences and dynamics; time and timing; and taking a perspective that includes the past, present and future – the whole system and the individual. Such dialogic discernment is difficult to describe.

During our conference session this discernment was named, variously, 'magic', 'a personal quality' or 'genius' (which I particularly liked!). While such descriptions may be flattering, there is an important underlying question posed rhetorically by one participant – are intervention skills a gift or acquirable? I stated in the paper my belief that intervention skill or capability is acquirable, and anyone can acquire that capability. Yet, I am not able to clearly name and describe the generic skill of dialogic discernment for intervention. This skill is not yet explicit, it is tacit – difficult to verbalize and therefore to transfer.

I had always attributed this lack of expression to not wanting to shout about my achievements (a characteristic from childhood), and that as long as the outcome was successful it did not matter if anyone knew what I did. However, I am now thinking I lack the awareness and articulacy – I find myself needing to say, this is not to "blow my own trumpet" – to be able to verbalise and transfer the skill. That may be true of the profession.

Professional Dialogue as a Research Methodology

Peter Garrett

I began using the term *Dialogue as a Research Methodology* in 2014, although my business associate and colleague Jane Ball and I had been using Professional Dialogue for research purposes for many years prior to that. The first published research drawing on this methodology was undertaken by us for the UK Ministry of Justice in 2015. Before introducing the Research Methodology, it would probably help to say what I mean by Professional Dialogue. The word *dialogue* is used widely in the media to mean many different things, from the spoken text of a play or a movie, to a discussion or a negotiation between protagonists. This has led me and some of my colleagues to use the term *Professional Dialogue* to distinguish what we are doing from the meaning attributed by others to the word *dialogue*. Here is my description of how Professional Dialogue plays out in my own practice:

Dialogue is a skilful way of talking and thinking together that establishes a common flow of meaning amongst a group of people. The spirit of Dialogue is to understand rather than to convince, and the unfolding process of Dialogue changes the ground and context out of which the various relationships arise. Professional Dialogue is a transparent way of learning together and humanising an organisation or community. Through Professional Dialogue, organisations and communities are able to engage the collective intelligence of the participants to make better decisions, and to realise the creative opportunities inherent in any problem. The ongoing practice of Professional Dialogue at a systemic level generates sustainable strategic and operational change. In a Dialogic Organisation or a Dialogic Community this is underwritten by the ongoing regeneration of its culture, including shifting historically stuck patterns of behaviour, for the constructive benefit of the whole.

The emergence of dialogue as a profession took some 35 years, having been conceived within a modest meeting of 46 people for a weekend with David Bohm in a hotel in the English Cotswold Hills, and eventually being incorporated as the Academy of Professional Dialogue in 2016. During this period I was in position to make significant contributions to the practical and theoretical development of Professional Dialogue: first as a social entrepreneur (bringing theoretical physicist David Bohm together with a wide range of people in experimental, private Weekend Dialogues in various countries across Europe and Israel); then as a facilitator of Dialogues within organisations where I worked in prisons and in the community within the criminal justice system for 10 years; as an organisational consultant (in small- and medium-sized enterprises and in a series of four different multinationals, each for four or five years at a time); as a systemic change consultant (in six different US statewide correctional systems, the most transformational one taking six years, and to a UN-related multinational and multi-stakeholder organisation); and then chairing the international Academy of Professional Dialogue and leading its Professional Standards and Accreditation Board 18 months' consultation to establish profession-wide standards.

During this extensive career I have learnt through practice, not through books, and as much from the mistakes as the successes. Few if any books want to teach you mistakes, yet without making mistakes you cannot become masterful at what you do. For many years I have used a form of Action Learning with Jane within Dialogue Associates, where we design meetings (within our interventions, and within our overarching systemic change processes), plan, undertake work, record what happened, reflect and learn from each step of our work together. In the process we have generated thousands of images of flip-chart workings that document our progress. This learning pattern has enabled us to codify the Implicate Change Model, derived empirically from our organisational and community change work. This model, or pattern, is a way of sequencing a series of Dialogues, each with a different emphasis, in order to achieve a common understanding and meaning amongst a seemingly disparate group of people, and hence cultural change. The key to its success is that it addresses collective thought, held within subgroupings of like-minded people, that tends to sustain incoherent views despite contrary evidence and logic. The support and challenge between different subgroupings is what shifts the ground or context of relationships between them all. We have proven its application in small-group initiatives and short-term interventions, as well as its value in bringing about effective organisational change amongst thousands of people in large organisations. The Implicate Change Model is just one key part of a multifaceted and integrated model we have developed for Professional Dialogue. I will say more about it though, because it gives a feel for the spirit and method of our work, and it relates directly to research.

The graphic that follows depicts the changing focus of attention and 'work to be done' in a sequence of group conversations to bring about coherent change in multiple stakeholder organisational or community systems. We use seven phases (*identify, name, discover, gather, get-it-together, commit* and *design*) within each cycle of engagement, engaged in sequence until all are active. These are not mechanistic steps to be 'applied' to a situation, or building blocks to be set in stone before moving on. Once activated, each one continues to remain live and influential, so whilst concentrating on later phases, where the emphasis may be on, say, *gathering* or *committing*, more may still be learnt and understood about the need or opportunity in the initial *identifying* phase.

Some think of Dialogue as a generative space where new insights emerge freely of their own accord. Although there is some truth in this, the belief that a self-organising approach might bring this about in a reliable way is rather simplistic. My long and varied experience reveals there is a rigour required. It involves the skill, practices and a dialogic disposition that

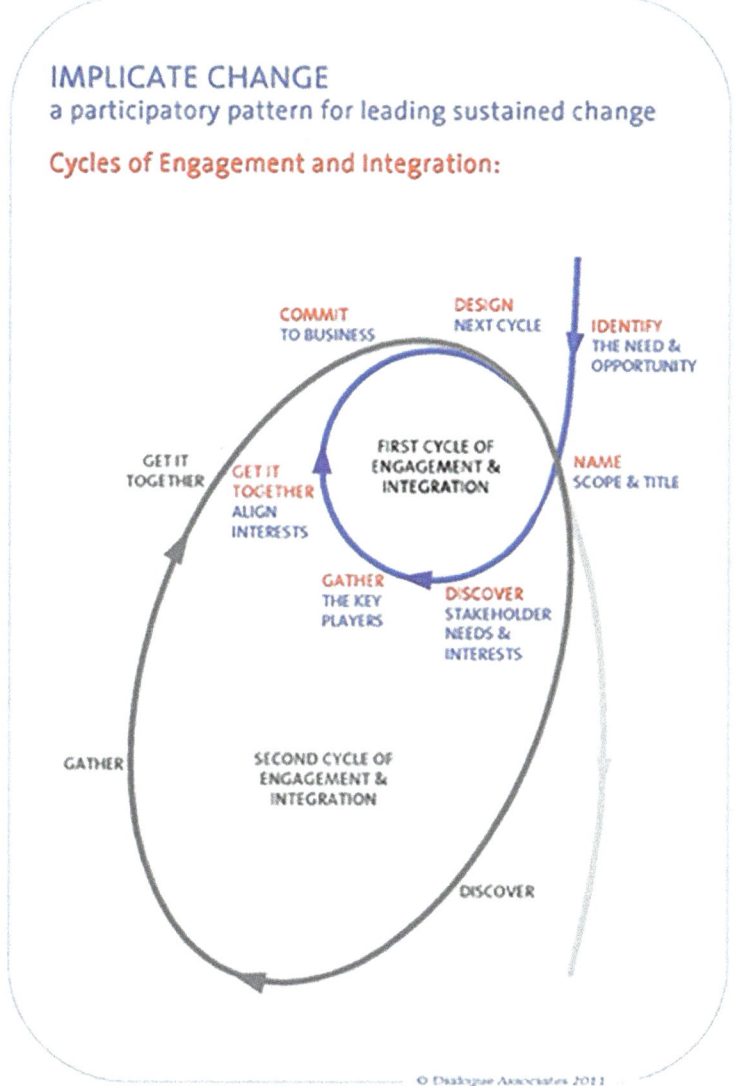

are embodied in Professional Dialogue. Along with that, the Implicate Change Model can guide the process by which generative change emerges in a fragmented system:

- *Identifying* the existing need or opportunity provides the starting point, and the start of determining if it is worth doing.
- *Naming* the work defines the scope and is the basis of the contracting with participants, providing focus and realism.
- *Discovery* involves understanding the systemic situation and finding who is involved or affected by the change. If each of their needs and opportunities are evident and may be met, then they will participate in the generative change process.

- *Gathering* is the bringing together of the subcultural groupings, or representatives of them in one conversation. Those gathered need to represent the resistant as well as the willing, because for a resilient and sustainable change things have to be thought through thoroughly and understood from multiple perspectives.
- *Getting-it-together*, which has a deliberate double meaning, refers to establishing a common meaning. (This is not a matter of persuasion, voting or consensus, but deliberate inclusion to achieve a common understanding. You may question whether that is always possible, but in my experience it invariably is. The reason is evident in the nature of reality, where everything is already internally and externally connected, as well displayed in David Bohm's Implicate Order ontology – hence the name Implicate Change Model).
- *Commitment* is the witnessed intention to act on the basis of the common understanding and meaning that has been created together. This is necessary because of the inevitable regression, caused by memory, when participants are no longer together looking forwards, but are back in their old world where nothing seems to have changed. Systemic change requires others participating as well, and doubts that they will do so cast their subtle shadows.
- *Design* extends the change process to include the next wave of participants, who will need to move through a similar process rather than being told the answer. Are people resistant to change? Only if they are told what they have to do, and are given the fixed answer determined by someone else. People who participate in the process with others enjoy change!

So that is the context for Dialogic Research.

Dialogic Research and the Implicate Change Model

In 1995 I first encountered researchers in organisations where I was working, and I have encountered many more over the years. Some were modest master's degree students and later reappeared as senior professors and heads of university departments. I watched how they worked and how they were viewed by the staff or community members whom they were researching. I began to form a view about their profession, based on my assumption that I knew little about research myself. Then it dawned on me that I too used research, and in a professional way. It is integral to the Implicate Change Model I just outlined, but Dialogic research is different from the research I saw being undertaken by others. The difference began to take more form when I heard a conference speaker say something to the effect that taking another person's words for one's own is called plagiarism, but taking the words of many other people for one's own is called research. That is what really did not sit well with me about the researchers I encountered, and I started to reflect on why and how my own approach differed.

The Dialogue work I began with David Bohm in 1984, and continued to his death in 1992, was based on the fundamental recognition of pervasive fragmentation in human society, which is the root cause of extensive pain and suffering. This fragmentation takes the form of conflicting identities and interests between nations, religions, ethnic groupings and all sorts of subcultural divides such as right- and left-wing, rich and poor, old and young, male and female, and so on. After David's death, when I began introducing Dialogue into different organisations, it became evident to me that the inherent structure of an organisation – and organisation is itself fragmentary. Role specialisation, which is fundamental to developing a good career, means people know more and more about their own area and less and less about other areas. For example, the computer programmer, the legal counsel, the shop floor worker and the senior executive are rarely interchangeable roles. Of course organisational size and location are key factors, and in a small organisation of 20 people working in one location there may be significant overlap and common understanding. But if that is expanded to hundreds or thousands of employees who operate from different physical locations, then fragmentation quickly becomes evident. Few have an understanding of the whole operation.

Communication flows (and can falter) up and down (hierarchically) and side to side (between different departments, functions and various working locations). This is the common experience in every large organisation. It is a result of the decision-making power structure inherent in organisations, and I have discovered how to address this fragmented and silo mentality through Professional Dialogue. First, one has to understand the situation by engaging it, and that process of understanding is *research*.

As I understand it, research typically starts with the formulation of a research question. Dialogic Research, on the other hand, starts with identifying a *need* or an *opportunity*. Either you see something you don't need, or you don't see something you need. Typically people will tell you what they *want* (or don't want) rather than what they *need*. So *discovery* is required in order to understand the situation more clearly. Things are the way they are for a particular reason, and understanding that is a precursor to designing any meaningful change. But people cannot always tell you why the systemic situation is like it is, not least because they have only a partial picture, based on their role and specialisation within the organisation. So we talk and think with groups of people, generally 15 to 30 people in one conversation, or several hundred people, depending on the situation. The aim is that nobody is speaking behind another person's back, so as we progress we are no longer talking about 'them' because they are present in the room to answer for themselves. We have now begun to diverge from most other research approaches in a fundamental way. The Dialogic Research is not partisan. It is wholistic, holds multiple perspectives even if they are seemingly contradictory, and develops a common meaning amongst the group, including the researchers. So the researcher is not an objective observer who privately records and owns the information, collected for later publication in their name to further their academic career. Instead, the understanding is held and owned as common knowledge by all the participants, including the researcher, who makes a valuable contribution. What emerges is first-hand knowledge and collective insights about the common situation and what might be done about it.

Clearly I am making some ethical statements about the nature and purpose of this kind of research. In Dialogic Research the intended beneficiary is the whole rather than one or other of the parts. This is because concentrating on the interests of just one of the parts leads to fragmenting it from the whole. By analogy, the forest may be seen as an essential part of the overall ecology that includes flora and fauna. Separating trees out, and seeing them as lumber to be converted into money, could lead to indiscriminate felling of trees that may be profitable to the land owner but damaging to the larger ecology. Similarly, landowners drilling for water in areas suffering drought may get temporary benefit but lower the water table for everyone around. The aim, therefore, is to have all the different voices and interests represented in the room so that informed decisions can be made by and for the whole. In this way the Dialogic Research sets the context for systemic decision-making. It has the spirit of a commonwealth rather than befitting those who commission the research, potentially to the detriment of others.

Case Study One: Uncovering a Complex Truth

It is also the case that Dialogic Research can arrive at different outcomes from other forms of research. Let me give an example. Jane and I were embarking on an interesting piece of work on culture change in a juvenile correctional system when those who commissioned our work discovered they had misunderstood the terms of their grant. It had to be applied specifically to the Prison Rape Elimination Act (PREA) rather than more generally to cultural change (which they anticipated would in turn affect their PREA monitoring scores). The grant would be withdrawn at the end of the month, and a sudden change was required. We agreed to a new one-week research contract specifically regarding sexual harassment and abuse in their prisons as defined by PREA. Given we had just five days in total on-site to complete the work and report the outcomes, we had a challenge. A typical research approach might have been to monitor the statistical trends in the available data, and search online for best-practice options that could be implemented by the agency, making some recommendations based on the available data. We had the benefit of already knowing some of the staff members in the two prisons involved, and opted for Dialogic Research instead.

There were more than 500 members of staff involved, along with a larger number of prisoners, so we needed some careful logistical planning during the two weeks available before we arrived on-site. We telephone-interviewed a small selection of informed senior staff and, given what we heard, created an initial theory of what may be happening in the two juvenile prisons involved. It seems that abuse by juveniles of staff had been occurring for many years and perhaps had become institutionalised. We drew a graphic depiction that displayed our naive thinking at the outset of the research. Since we were not independent and objective observers, but a part of the research system, we wanted to make our thinking available and to be just as open as we were inviting others to be.

We arrived on Monday and finished on Friday of the same week. It was an action-packed and revelatory week. Prisons are hierarchical command-and-control institutions where permission is needed in advance of any activity, so we opted to start at the top. On Monday morning we met with the Executive group at their headquarters building, along with those responsible for collating and distributing their research statistics. Their figures showed a steady decrease in incidents of harassment and abuse, as one might expect given the organisational and cultural changes under way. We wondered if we were wasting our time, with our services being used to confirm their good work; the problem would soon be completely eliminated! We asked about the history of the situation, and heard that levels of abuse varied significantly according to the leadership style in use and the measures adopted, but it had continued for many years. As they talked and considered the history of the situation, we recorded notes openly on a flip chart, encouraging the group to make corrections as appropriate. Then we explained our own preliminary thinking about how such a problem might have become systemically institutionalised, based on what we had heard in our telephone interviews. Lastly we confirmed the series of meetings we had already agreed and planned, thereby reminding them of what we would be doing before we met them again at the end of the week.

As they knew, our next round of meetings would be with the Wardens and Leadership Teams at each of their two prisons. In these two separate meetings, one in each prison, we displayed the record of our initial Executive meeting and ran through their version of the history. We gave these groups the chance to agree or amend (in a different colour pen) the version we had heard from their seniors. They did have different views and, not unsurprisingly, they were harsher on the executive responsibility for the problem than the executives had been on themselves and their predecessors in that role. One or two had personal experiences of abuse by prisoners, and were deeply affected recounting what had happened to them. The incidents ranged from prisoners exposing themselves through to assault, and we heard about an attempted rape. They felt some options for remedial action had been incorrectly dismissed, and some opportunities had been half-heartedly rather than fully implemented. They did, however, agree with the official statistics. When we questioned their confidence in these figures, we were told by security staff that anyone who did not report an incident risked losing their job if found out, so they could guarantee the accuracy of the numbers. We ran through the graphic of our theory about the institutionalisation of the problem, inviting feedback, and then described the subsequent meetings we would be having.

And so we proceeded with each successive grouping down through the two prisons in much the same way. We revealed our own changing thinking, and ran through what we had heard from all the previous groupings, invited additions to the history and current levels of harassment and abuse in the facilities. Each grouping knew what we had previously been told. We were not the experts, but the gatherers of the various versions and experiences, conveying them to others. The middle management was less reassuring. Many of them had experiences of harassment, both past and recent, and some had been deeply affected by incidents at work in the prison. They recounted different tactics to either avoid or address the individuals responsible. The uniformed staff varied in their views more than others. Some raised the question of how incarcerated juveniles might be expected to mature sexually in such difficult circumstances. It became evident from failed prosecutions that whatever juveniles did in their cells was considered to have occurred 'at home', and was treated differently from what took place in public places. Otherwise the courts would have been overloaded with prosecutions, presumably. There was a responsible professional caution on the part of prison staff about putting youngsters onto a Sex Offenders Register that would affect their status and reputation for the rest of their lives.

By the time we reached the medical and treatment staff, we could have been in a different world from the downtown executive offices. They literally burst out laughing when they saw the statistics in use by management, claiming the real figures were at least tenfold greater than those we had. The laughter was short-lived, however, as they recited incident after incident in painful, personal detail. They were subject to daily harassment with minimal support from uniformed staff members, who apparently often turned a blind eye to the situation rather than addressing it. Asked why they did not record the incidents, they explained that if they did, they would have to spend all day writing reports. It was gruelling to hear the levels of anger and trauma amongst the group, and I found myself wondering why none had taken legal action against their employers. It was a similar situation with the Education Department, where the teachers suffered frequent exposure during lessons and at times feared for their safety. Some showed visible signs of retained trauma and ill health that they related directly to this continual sexual harassment. Perhaps 80% of the teachers described first-hand experiences both with male juveniles exposing themselves to female teachers, and female juveniles stripping off their clothing before male teachers, thereby ensuring they could not be manhandled.

Then we engaged the youngsters themselves. A progressive Student Council had been established, comprised of the most responsible juveniles, and we explained to them why we were meeting with people in the two prisons. They agreed there were high levels of harassment and abuse in the prisons. We gave one of the participants the flipchart and pen, and he solicited the views of his colleagues as to where most incidents occurred: in line waiting to move between different parts of the prison; in the classroom; the shower; the swimming pool and so on. They put the typical number of weekly incidents against each location and seemed better informed collectively than the staff. They did not condone the behaviour of their colleagues and were keen to participate in its ending. We arranged a second meeting with them when we would ask how they thought this might be done.

Finally we met some of the high-repeat offenders themselves. Only one individual volunteered to meet with us from one prison, so Jane and I talked with him for half an hour. Three volunteered from the second prison. We asked to meet them together as a group, and we were advised quite categorically that none of them would choose to speak unless we spoke with them individually. We persisted, however, and the three of them were brought into the room with their hands manacled behind their backs, to meet the two of us, and two uniformed staff members that were there for security purposes. We introduced ourselves and the purpose of meeting to them, namely to understand move about the PREA situation in the prison. As a check-in I asked each of them, if they could recall it, to describe the first time they sexually harassed a member of staff. In each case it was deliberate exposure, and they had prepared meticulously for the occasion. Their memories were impeccable and the excitement of the occasion came through in the accounts of their vicarious experiences. They quite thoughtfully also addressed our enquiries and challenges to what they had done. They were clearly addicted to their behaviour and it would take a serious intervention to shift what had in each case only started after they entered the prison. One had been placed on an intervention programme that had been designed by a psychiatrist in the prison for small numbers of participants to be treated in depth, but the prisoner had been thrown off the course when he was found to have repeated the offence whilst under treatment.

That completed the downward journey of our discovery process through the prisons, meeting representative groupings hierarchically from the top to the bottom. We had heard perhaps 150 accounts first-hand and had shared our changing appreciation with all the staff about what was happening and why. Next we worked our way back up the different levels, considering what could be done to improve things. Our aim was to have some generally agreed and coherent options that could be taken up by the diverse-membership Working Group we discovered had been set for that purpose.

Two of the high-repeat juvenile offenders said they believed their behaviour was situational and would simply stop on release, so nothing was required. They may have proved to be right, but it seemed unlikely to me and Jane and we said so to them. The Student Council was more forthcoming with their ideas of what could be done. We met with them for a couple of hours on the Thursday morning so that they could prepare their ideas in advance of a meeting with a wide range of staff members, including all members of the Working Group. Jane and I then coached them how to do a good monologue, so that they could present their ideas well. Our advice included looking at someone at the back of the room and talking to them personally so that they could hear and understand them, then gradually picking up other interested people until everyone is attentive – that kind of thing. We practiced it with them, and when the time came they did brilliantly, far better than the staff members! There were perhaps 30 people in the room, of whom 12 were juvenile prisoners from the Student Council. We had the staff members and the Student Council members alternate in making proposals, which they had written earlier on sticky notes, and they stuck them onto the wall for everyone to see. Done this way, ideas followed on from earlier ones and progressively built up an intervention picture. There was a surprising level of commonality in the ideas, including the proposed 'island' isolation of all repeat offenders, segregated as a group, to provide carrot-and-stick incentives for change. There were at least 15 distinct proposals, including mentoring and other roles that the students proposed they could themselves provide for their colleagues – more than enough to make a substantial start.

We heard proposals from almost all the other groupings we had previously met, although listening to all of them in the time allotted was a huge constraint. We displayed their ideas on the wall for support and challenge and to stimulate further thinking, and showed them what others had come up with in meetings before theirs. Then we compiled all the proposals we had, as recorded with the groupings involved. We met with the Working Group, made up of more senior and accountable staff members from all the different parts of the two prisons, to consider the whole set of proposals with them. They were surprised by the high level of harassment and abuse, although some had suspected it. For example, one said he often heard about incidents in staff training sessions that did not appear in the weekly reports. So some were genuinely surprised when they heard what had been described, whilst others knew but had turned a blind eye to the situation. They agreed with the weight of proposals to address the situation and were clear they had substantial ways to proceed to address the situation. At the same time, they did not seem confident that the Executive would proceed with the resourcing of a robust intervention to try to solve the problem. When I pressed harder, it became evident that they believed the Director had many other priorities and he might be slow to prioritise this one. I took note of this openly and in writing.

Finally we re-met with the Executive group, with whom we had started our week-long journey, and walked through our busy week of Dialogic Research. We displayed the flip charts, starting with their own from the Monday morning meeting, showing the adjustments and additions made by subsequent groupings, and then displaying the additional sheets in sequence. We showed our final version of the institutionalisation of sexual harassment and abuse in that Department. They were attentive and disturbed by the evidence they were seeing from their staff and from some of the juvenile offenders. They had never taken the time to speak directly with the offenders involved in the enquiring way we had done, and were learning things they had never previously considered. We walked through the Working Group options, and since the lead for that group was himself an executive, he was present in the room to hear our closing report. I included the fact that that group did not have full confidence the Director would prioritise the resourcing of the proposal they had endorsed. This opened the possibility of them having that difficult conversation there and then, or after Jane and I had departed. In closing I said we would put our Dialogic Research findings to them in writing.

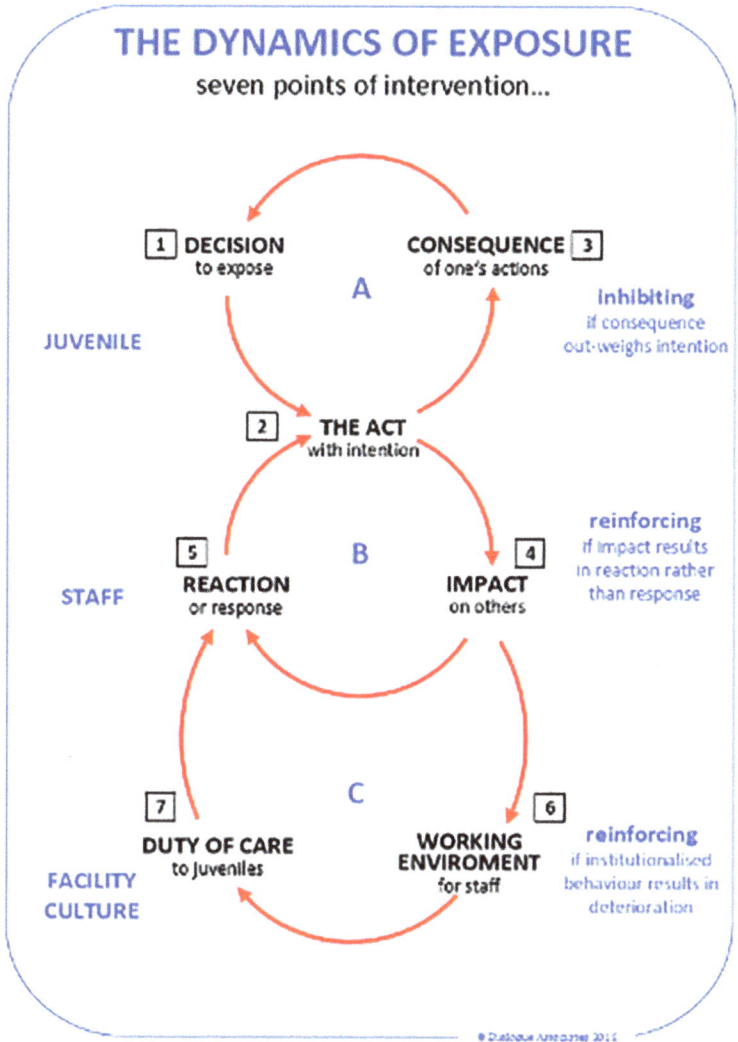

The Director was appalled with the situation and expressed the depth of his concerns, and his appreciation for our uncovering their actual situation. The team quietly digested their collective failure of duty of care to their staff and the juveniles in their care. We heard no immediate statement of action by the Executive collectively, and the lead of the Working Group registered his disappointment. On our return to the UK we compiled a full report and sent it to the entire Executive and Working Team. I reminded the Director that because of our research methodology, there was nothing in the report that had not been openly considered with him, his Executive and his staff, both in terms of the need to address sexual harassment and abuse, and the innovative and generally accepted ways of addressing it that had been collectively compiled.

You may recognise various key features of our Dialogic research methodology from this short case study. Firstly, we found a different result from the other methods of research that had been relied on and trusted in use in that Department. One might say that was simply due to poor communication between staff members, but it is often the case that good communication within and across organisations is lacking. This often happens because the information sought and reported means different things to different people. At an executive level the figures they had showed they were doing their duty in tracking and addressing a challenging problem, which added to their credibility. It was a matter of upward communication to the politicians who control the budget allocations and are concerned about public reputation. The middle managers suffered the typical middle-manager's dilemma of wanting to please their seniors, and being uncertain how to manage their duty of care to the staff who report to them. The uniformed staff saw the entrenched pattern of sexual violations as normal business in a prison. It goes with the job, they assumed, and so they did whatever their colleagues did. The teachers, medical and treatment staff (largely females working with a predominantly male juvenile population) had the least power or effective voice in the situation, and suffered the most. The juveniles themselves, who learnt this pattern of behaviour after entering the prisons, came from largely dysfunctional families. Many of them had hardly developed as adults, but were living in much the same incarceration conditions as experienced by adult prisoners. So it is not surprising that communication up and down and across the organisation was fractured. It is worth saying that essentially this is not untypical of any organisation, including financial, religious, academic and political institutions, to name a few. Dialogic Research opens the way for a different kind of collaborative input into policy and decision-making.

You may also have noted that Dialogic Research is an ethical and principled approach to research. It starts with respect, based on the assumptions that things are the way they are for some good reason. Enquiring without judgement, in order to understand, starts with the researchers, and is deliberately extended to those participating in the research to encourage them to encounter one another in a different way. This does not mean that they condone one another's behaviour, but rather that they stand in the other person's shoes to look at it from their point of view. The researcher listens in a way that encouraging people to be genuine and authentic, and to explain their thoughts and feelings carefully. The deliberate use of Dialogic Practices (Voice, Listening, Respect and Suspension) creates an ambiance or atmosphere of open learning in which anything can be considered. Some would call this an agenda-free conversation, but it is more than that. There is a very deliberate purpose or agenda all along, based on the need or opportunity identified – in this case the PREA-defined measures of sexual harassment and abuse. But there is not an agenda to persuade people to think or act in a particular way. Rather, there is an effort to discover how they do think and feel. You cannot fix something if you do not understand what it is, and the underlying causes of it being that way. Then, as the complex of systemic dynamics reveal themselves to everyone involved, ways to proceed start to become evident.

In this approach the researchers are participants, as well as facilitators of a particular kind of dialogic group-work. They support and challenge their own and others' views in service of taking the conversation to a deeper level. They reveal their own thoughts and feelings to make them transparently available, so that they are not inadvertently or covertly affecting the research process. Recordings are made publicly within the organisation as a common data resource, wherever possible using the original speaker's own words as a link back to the feeling or idea expressed. The Dialogic Researcher is not privately accumulating information for later selected reporting. The information and learning is held as commonly as possible. Everyone is affected by the situation and should have the best opportunity to contribute intelligently to its resolution. This is the creation of a common meaning amongst a group of people for the benefit of all. The researcher has ownership too, and can make respectful use of the learning, as I am doing now by writing this paper and making the methodology available to others.

Case Study Two: Dialogic Research and Cultural Regeneration
A second case study may give more perspective to how I have been using Dialogic Research as a part of my whole-system change work. This is also in the field of criminal justice, and took place a few years later than the first case study. Jane and I were approached by the Commissioner of a US State Correctional Department that had suffered rioting and the tragic murder of one of the uniformed security staff members. The Commissioner approached us a week after the incident, but it took almost a year to raise the funds to engage our services. It was apparent from the outset that culture change was required, and initially we contracted to look into the situation to see how best to proceed. We arranged two, one-week visits, one month apart. Then we telephone interviewed a handful of senior people to hear their description of the situation we would be encountering. Our interest was also to ensure we established a degree of understanding and agreement about how we might partner with them to regenerate the culture.

We wondered what level of emotional disturbance would be present in the system almost a year after the tragic event. Our research design was a similar pattern to the previous case I described, beginning at the top and working our way hierarchically down through the organisation – but in this case we had twice the amount of time, and could anticipate working on the subsequent intervention so we could be more thorough. We started with the top 20 or so statewide executive staff members, and explored the history of the Department by dividing it into chapters – one chapter for each Commissioner in its history. Then we heard stories to bring this history to life. We found a recurrence of extreme violence. The preceding incident, perhaps five or six years before, involved the rape of a staff member. The attacking adult prisoner was shot dead. Despite this, there seemed to be some emotional distance between the executive officers and the prison where the riot had occurred a year previously. There was not the urgency we had anticipated, although people had clearly been hard at work introducing new initiatives based on the governor's report on the incident and its recommendations and requirements. They knew culture change was required but seemed not to know how to address it.

Our second meeting was with the leadership team of the large and complex prison where the rioting and death had occurred a year previously. At that meeting we encountered something that was the case with each of the staff groupings we met thereafter – a reluctance to talk about the incident, and then a relief for having done so. Once we had all introduced ourselves to each other, we asked each person to describe their experience of the day of the riot. There were soul-searching descriptions, questions that could not be answered by those present, and things said that had never been spoken before to their close working colleagues. There were strong emotions and tears shed. There had been limited take-up of counselling offered to these staff members, and our session with them proved to be cathartic. Not all were at work on that fateful day, but everyone was affected by what proved to be a protracted hostage-taking. It had been tracked live in the media for all to follow, and many hours had elapsed before the eventual decision was taken to storm the building and rescue the staff held there. In a command-and-control situation like this, it is necessary to wait for an order before proceeding, but there were confused views about how decisions had been made, and in the recounting a deep remembrance of the impotency to act in protection of colleagues who were in danger of losing their lives.

Thereafter we met with captains and staff lieutenants, then lieutenants, corporals and sergeants and on down to the basic-grade correctional officers (COs). These COs comprise the large majority of the staff members, so we met in three separate groupings, rather than one, with between 10 and 15 staff members in the room each time. In every session there were intense emotions and tears shed by a number of participants. We had heard over 100 testimonies by the time we reached the prisoner groupings. Again, because of their large numbers, we met them in three separate groupings also. They were disturbed by the incident and candid, saying they had never anticipated a death, but they shed no tears. Each grouping had different ideas about the cause of the incident and what should be done. Some pointed to the legislative changes that reduced the more restricted detention of difficult prisoners and placed them in general-location housing without having earned that right. Others saw the housing of out-of-state serious offenders as the root cause. Some attributed the incident to variations in strictness of rule enforcement by different shifts of security officers, whilst yet others criticised leadership's apparent disregard for local requests to rehouse difficult prisoners. Tellingly, every group agreed that the riot was predictable, but nobody succeeded in intervening to prevent it. This revealed to everyone who participated that the communication disconnections were up, down and across the organisation.

What about the existing traditional research? All the internal and external investigation reports were made available to us, but we chose not to read them. Criminal charges were still being processed and we did not want to get embroiled in legal issues. We were interested in what people thought and felt about their situation. How they talked about each other would collectively define the identity and culture of the organisation, and that is what we wanted to understand. During every session we made flip-chart records in response to a number of questions we raised with every group. These included the predictability of the riot, the current levels of safety compared to those at the time of the riot, what could be done in the short-term, and so on. At each step we shared the responses of other groups to increase the common understanding. People were fascinated and sometimes incredulous about the responses they were shown from other groups. This strengthened our view that the culture and communication were fragmented hierarchically. Time did not permit us to meet with the medical, treatment and educational staff until our return the following month but, as we anticipated, there were similar fractures across the organisation between these various departments and between each of them and security staff. We had heard so much we almost felt like witnesses ourselves. We had listened to first-hand accounts from officers in assault gear who stood ready outside for hour after hour through an icy cold night, waiting for the order to storm the building; from staff who refused to go home until the situation was resolved; from those who directed the emergency services gathering in the car park; from those who prepared assault vehicles to batter down the door; from staff who inspected the arrested prisoners after the storming of the building; from those in the shift control room; from those who had tried to make advance warnings; and from those whose family members tried to stop them going back to work. These people who worked in the prison were a strangely close-knit, committed yet complaining body of people, broken into many different subcultural groupings – each open within their own group and privately making strongly negative attributions about others.

Jane and I digested what we had heard and made additional notes to retain important details that might inform our later work, and gave a verbal report to the Commissioner and a few of his colleagues by telephone. Then a month later we returned to make the journey back up through the organisation, from the prisoners and then correctional officers through the ranks to the executive. The first round of meetings had been emotional and cathartic. It is hard for people to think clearly when they are emotionally disturbed, so we needed to check what we believed they had meant. With each group we re-presented their flip charts and asked them to confirm, amend add to or delete the various points to give a better picture of their collective view. They knew this would be seen by others, so there was some consideration of what was prudent to report, but the safety and anonymity of being part of a group reinforced their desire to be genuine and heard accurately. The resulting sheets confirmed the key points: every group predicted the likelihood of an incident; groups believed they had reported this concern but had not been heard or responded to; nobody intervened to prevent the incident; there had been no effective review and redefining of procedures to ensure this could not happen again; most felt the prison was as dangerous as it had been a year previously, if not worse; and communication across the organisation remained ineffective. Back at the executive level, they took our reporting on the chin, saying it was what they feared but expected. In that meeting we were encouraged by the Commissioner to report all this in just the same manner the following day to the members of the House of Representatives and the Senate who might fund the whole-system culture change work. We took his advice and, in the presence of many of the Executive staff, we met the two members along with the

Commissioner and his Deputy, and helped the Department secure the necessary commitment for funding to enable us to work with them for a number of years.

You could say this marked the end of the Dialogic Research phase and the start of the whole-system change work, but of course there is more to be learnt every day. As a piece of Dialogic Research it was very effective in informing our design. We devised a Dialogue Skills Training to be delivered to mixed staff groupings of various ranks and from security, non-security and treatment departments. This was to help form relationships and improve communication up, down and across the organisation. We took a similarly mixed group of staff volunteers (many of whom we had met during the two weeks of Dialogic Research), and trained them to deliver this one-day session, off-site, to every member of staff in groups of 14 to 20 at a time. It was designed as a fully participatory experience based on exploring the Dialogue Practices and other skills in familiar working situations. It included, for example, a hierarchical line-up of the chain of command, to enable an enquiry into how information and requests move up and down the line. We backed this up with two-hour, Skill-Build sessions delivered in the prison to reinforce the use of the skills in daily work. Then we added a Dialogic Coaching Training for every supervisor to secure accountability. Awareness had not been the problem, because every grouping believed the incident was predictable. It was accountability that had not been exercised for people to act effectively on what they knew. We then adapted the Implicate Change Model into a Working Dialogue for broad 'across-the-prison' collective action. It involved the identification of a real need or opportunity, the naming of an initiative to address it, an invitation for relevant input from any person working or living in the prison, and then a structured process to design and implement the change effectively. This is aimed at replacing the impotency of that tragic night of rioting, and the waiting hour after hour, with collective and constructive activities where everyone can play a part by contributing their thinking and understanding to the successful outcome. It is hard to imagine we could have made such a well-informed design without the preceding Dialogic Research.

Some other features may be more evident from reading this second case study. In Dialogic Research we are aiming to build the authentic voice of each subcultural grouping, to ensure it is heard and understood. We are putting the organisation into conversation with itself. The Dialogic Research is itself an intervention that changes things whilst it is being undertaken – in this case one feature was catharsis, another was the discovery of a surprising level of common awareness combined with ineffectual communication. Next we are looking for the Dialogic Research to lead to material and constructive change. In contrast, some traditional research may simply report on the situation as seen by the researchers, and leave people to do whatever they think is best. Investigations may do something similar whilst also defining what has to be done – generally in the form of a long list of required actions. In Dialogic Research we are looking to set the context for collective decision-making, resulting in the formulation of action that makes sense to those involved because they contributed to the formulation of the understanding.

The Challenge

I believe, as I have described through two case studies, that Professional Dialogue is a significant new approach to social research. It gets different results because it reduces the distance between the decision-makers and the impacts of the decisions. I call it a methodology rather than a tool or skill, because it is based on a different ontology, and consequently there may be differences in the conception, intention, theory and practice from other forms of research. In combination, these present something of an inherent challenge to the intention and methodology of the various more traditional forms of research that I have encountered. To underline my point, let me bring out the features of Dialogic Research and make some contrasts with some other approaches to research:

The Researcher and the Research
- *The starting point is to identify an existing need or opportunity in the situation* – rather than starting with a research question and finding a situation in which to research that question
- *The intended outcome is a material benefit for the organisation or community, and participants involved* – not the generation of knowledge per se, or publication material for the benefit the researcher
- *The researchers see themselves as facilitators and skilled participants* – not independent and 'objective' observers

Data and Information Gathering
- *The research takes the interests of multiple stakeholders into account and is systemic or wholistic* – not partisan or for the benefit of one particular client or grouping
- *Data is collected publicly with participants, and later reviewed with them to ensure it represents their views* – not privately, without their knowledge and without their revision
- *Much of the thinking is done together in groups (often of between 15 and 30 participants) to explore collectively held views* – not via expert observation, or focus groups, questionnaires and interviews that analyse multiple individual opinions

Researching with Respect
- *The existing situation, including aspects of incoherence and lack of awareness or participation, are enquired into with respect. There are underlying reasons that things are the way they are, and the research leads participants to reveal these reasons to everyone involved*

Ownership
- *The research is owned by all the participants* – not solely by the researcher and the commissioning client

A Common Understanding
- *Researching dialogically is itself an intervention, as the various sub-cultural groupings participate in a systemwide conversation to establish collective understanding, learning and better ways of working together or relating to each other* – not a detached set of observations or private analysis about the situation
- *This creates the context for collective decision-making, and the formulation of constructive ways to proceed that are generally understood to be of value* – not private data collection for detached analysis and decision-making

One significant limitation of Professional Dialogue as a research methodology is that it requires professional researchers. By that I mean people who are sufficiently conversant with dialogic skills and practices to enable them to think with people, rather than making private observations or simply recording then analysing what people have said. Also, these researchers need to be mature enough and humble enough to meet all the participants as peers, whatever their hierarchical level. In the two cases I cited, this means relating to both the 'executive' and the 'prisoner' as peers. Developing such researchers is a small price to pay if it moves the whole field of research beyond partisan and self-serving enquiries. Those who know less about research methods give great credence to the research outcomes for their policy-making, so a development in the methodology seems essential and long overdue.

Conference Session Extracts

From a conversation with participants considering the paper with the author

Speaker 1: For me, an interesting question is, who is research for? Is it for someone who has commissioned the research and is paying for it? Is it research for those subjects who were being researched for their understanding? That also brings up the question of what forms of results that we want. Because if the forms of results are simply healing of the system, how do we prove that? How do we document that? It brings up all kinds of questions.

Speaker 2: I come from another side with it. What if people ask: "What is the distinction between this and a good piece of process consulting?" I suppose I am asking what your identity was when you were there.

Speaker 3: My impression from your presentation is that you want change on the individual level, how people understand themselves and their connection to other people, but you also talk about the system in this business, if I can call it that. Your practice is connected to change in all these levels. So, it's not a question of quality or quantity, but it's a question of, does your change work?

Speaker 4: I think in this paper Peter's been attempting to get at something that would produce results at a lot of different levels. I think you didn't go into the wider narrative of how in the first place does a system like this produce a mess like the one you had to intervene in, but that implication is there I think it's really worth trying to harvest the distinct research bits out of this.

Speaker 5: I believe this approach is in the interest of the whole system, whether or not the commissioner might like it.

Speaker 4: I think at the bottom of all this is your ontology. I don't know if I have that ontology or not, but you're saying it's critical. It's at the basis of your work.

Speaker 5: So, I explained it in a way with my views about respect, and that everything's the way it is for a good reason. I don't believe there are any bad people. There may be people who behave badly at times, but generally we all do what we try to do. Even when I screw up, I didn't intend to hurt people, though I do sometimes. If you take that assumption about everybody in a system, it's the way it is for a very good reason. Now we find we have to do it differently and how do we do it? It is a systemic answer in my view. If we assume that it's organised the way it is for good reasons and there are bits we don't know about, if we can understand them and reveal them, we can start to act intelligently together. I think that's the source of what I mean by the ontology. Everything is unfolding from one common Implicate source — it is not unfolding from a large number of different incoherent sources. The Implicate is already coherent, but it's fragmented in a human consciousness, it's broken up, and then we're acting within what we've got, which is a mess.

Speaker 2: The system understands, yes. That's the more critical piece, that the system understands the unintended consequences. I don't know what the right words are, but a more engaged, participatory and dialogic approach generates a different core of knowledge. I think it's worth articulating what that is. There's extractive knowledge and then there's engaged knowledge. It's not that people aren't nosing around this territory. What's distinct about this is that it takes a fairly high level of maturity and skill. And courage, because the dominant pattern of research — forget the systems we are intervening in — don't want this to happen. They're designed so it can't happen. Seriously.

Speaker 4: Yeah, they're skilfully sustaining the very fragmentation that they're complaining about. But what you're saying is that the research is for the whole-system understanding, as opposed to research for the researcher's understanding. If we built up a picture of what was different about this kind of pattern of research, that would be a really powerful outcome of this conversation.

Speaker 6: You made another distinction, which is that the system understands it. This is a second layer of difference, because if you go with the assumption it wants to understand something, you act differently.

Speaker 4: Yeah, but it's resistant. There's a taboo on understanding.

Speaker 7: This is really threatening stuff to the powers that be, and I'm thinking now in terms of my experience in academia. We construct academics based on good research, right? We know some things, and then we can teach it, and that's the truth. If we start to come at our research, and at what we teach, from a completely different ontological model, then a lot of existing knowledge is questioned, and people don't like that. That's very threatening. If we are to grow as a Professional Dialogue academy, we're going to have to be aware of just how threatening we are. This approach would step on the heels of many disciplines, like action research. In other words, they would feel threatened, that there isn't enough difference. Actually, there's a profound difference, but they would feel threatened by years and years, decades and decades of what they teach in terms of participatory research, action research, and so on. They don't want to have to rethink how they do things. We used to think in OD that there were states of being in organizations. And so, what we were paid to do as consultants was to go in and say, "Okay, we're going to freeze right now and research where this organization is. And then we're going to show what a better state would be". Unfreeze it and do something, and then freeze it again, right? Everything's frozen. Whereas in our ontology, everything's in process and flow, and we are part of the system. We're not just going to study it and then walk away.

Speaker 5: Well, we weren't just getting awareness, we're getting understanding of the work and the cultural regeneration required from a culturally damaged system. We proposed doing work, and said it was going to take five years, not less. So then we had to go and present what we found to the Senate and House of Representatives in order to get funding. So then, what do you tell that group? Do you tell them what you really found? Or do you tell them something else? I'm going to tell them exactly what I found, right? It's not different. That's quite threatening for the guy in charge of it sitting next to me, when I tell them, "This is a highly damaged system", and I'm talking to people way more senior than him. It's the transparency of it that's dangerous in a way.

Postscript

The author's reflections, written some months after the conference

Before writing this paper I had a keen interest to explore my dialogic experience of social research. I loosely defined this as a methodical enquiry that led to substantiated views about what was happening in a situation. I had seen researchers come in and out of prisons where I was running weekly Dialogue Groups, and I could see the caution with which they were viewed, and the constrained access they had to the people living and working there. In comparison I was in the flow of the thinking amongst the prisoners, staff and management.

On writing the paper I became quite clear that I and my colleague Jane had been doing good professional research, and that we approached it in a very different way from the researchers we met. When I had described our research to others they thought I meant qualitative rather than quantitative research, but I believe both are necessary. Others thought I meant participatory rather than objective research, yet again both are needed. So I had to start to explore our methodology more deeply, and the ontology on which it is based. I found that we used a transparent and systemic thinking owned by everyone and aimed to be of benefit to all. This led me to emphasise the inherent challenge we represented to more traditional forms of research that sought to understand the perspective of a particular sector (such as Muslim radicalisation, or the traits of good security officers).

During the conference I was delighted with the level of support and challenge offered by the respected academics present. Some did not even recognise what we had done as research. That began to reveal how radically different it is. Essentially, our research methodology has been facilitating the common and transparent development of local knowledge that forms the systemic common-sense basis for beneficial change.

My co-editor Cliff Penwell questioned the degree to which I was presenting the paper as a challenge to other forms of research as against explaining my own, something that already concerned me, and so instead I tried to deepen the understanding of my own methodology. The inherent challenge remains, and I have retained a contrast of the features of our methodology vs others, but placed this at the end rather than the start of the paper.

And writing this Postscript confirms my pleasure in extending the whole field of Professional Dialogue, and the uplift it can provide to the role and reputation of research in complex local situations.

Putting Dialogue to Work in the Virginia Department of Corrections

Harold Clarke and Whitney Barton

[Note: *For useful context and background about how the Virginia Department of Corrections uses Dialogue as a central part of its approach to creating a healing environment within the criminal justice system of Virginia, please see the next chapter, "Dialogue and a Healing Environment in the Virginia Department of Corrections." It is reprinted from last year's published conference papers.*]

Dialogue in the Room

The Virginia Department of Corrections (VADOC) began its Dialogue journey in 2010, and has continued to evolve under the leadership of Director Harold Clarke. Prior to coming to the Virginia Department of Corrections, Director Clarke had already been introduced to Dialogue by Peter Garrett and William Isaacs. Director Clarke realized that Dialogue was the vehicle that could give substance the Healing Environment concept in the VADOC. In order to effect change and create a healing environment across the VADOC, Dialogue would have to permeate the culture of the Department.

The first step to achieving this was to introduce and teach employees at all levels within the VADOC basic Dialogue skills. As part of the planning for this, the Dialogue Practitioner Development Program (DPDP) began. This program provided training and development to selected individuals so that they could effectively work as Dialogue Practitioners in the VADOC. Once trained, these Dialogue Practitioners returned to the field where they trained all employees in Dialogue Skills. Today these skills are practiced and reinforced in the Department's Learning Teams. Dialogue Skills Training has become required for any new employee who comes into the VADOC. By doing this, the VADOC ensures that every employee learns the foundation of Dialogue. Since the beginning of the DPDP, the number of Dialogue Practitioners in the VADOC has grown from 24 to approximately 275!

As the initiative continued to evolve, a decision was made that it was necessary to reach a deeper level of understanding of Dialogue. The focus for the next phase of training would become the management staff within the VADOC. They now had the basic skills for talking and thinking together, but as managers there was room for them to continue to improve how they provided support and promoted accountability with their staff members. As with the Dialogue Skills Training, the Dialogue Practitioners in the DPDP were trained in Dialogue Coaching so that they could provide the same training to management staff in the field. Dialogue Coaching Training provided management with the concepts of Dialogue, Coaching, and Progressive Accountability, which would in turn enhance their leadership skills. This training allowed management to learn and practice how to effectively coach their staff, reinforcing effective ways to talk with, engage, support, and train them. It also allowed Dialogue Practitioners to learn and practice the Coaching skills to assist each other in their own development. Just as the Dialogue Skills training became a part of required training for new employees, the Dialogue Coaching training became a requirement for all management staff.

Putting Dialogue to Work

One of the most significant ways that the VADOC began to use Dialogue as an intervention process was by implementing the Offender Resettlement Journey (ORJ). In 2014, three ORJs were piloted in the Department with significant success. More ORJs have followed with equal success and impact. This process examines the offender journey from beginning to successful transition back to their community, at which point they are free from any involvement with the criminal justice system. Careful consideration is given to those who are chosen to return to the VADOC and symbolically "walk" through their journey. The VADOC seeks individuals with a high level of responsibility to ensure and reinforce credibility of the information shared during this process. The ORJs reinforce Dialogue skills and enhance engagement between employees and returning citizens. The ORJ process provides firsthand views from offenders about what helped and hindered their progress. As a learning organization, the VADOC is constantly evaluating areas for potential improvement. The ORJ has provided a new perspective about how the Department can improve.

In mid-2016 the VADOC was ready to advance the Dialogue initiative further. The Department was eager to use Dialogue to design and bring about effective, long-lasting change. It was important that employees engaging in Dialogue see the value of contributing their voice and ideas, and not just see it as "all talk."

Following conversations between Director Clarke and his Executive staff members, work began to convene a diverse group of Dialogue Practitioners to dialogue about ways the Department could move this initiative forward and make it more meaningful and practical. The group worked closely with consultation from Peter Garrett and Jane Ball. As this group continued to meet, they talked and thought about ways in which they could achieve their goal. From the sessions, Peter Garrett and Jane Ball were inspired to create the Working

Dialogue model, which would bring structure to the way Dialogues were facilitated and add an action-planning portion. In this model, the Dialogue skills are used to explore needs or opportunities, enhance processes, problem-solve, and make effective decisions. The key to doing this is to ensure that all staff members affected by the change have a voice. The Working Dialogue model includes five phases, with each one being followed by a set of "gate" questions. In order to proceed to the next phase the "gate" questions have to be answered by all participants in the Working Dialogue.

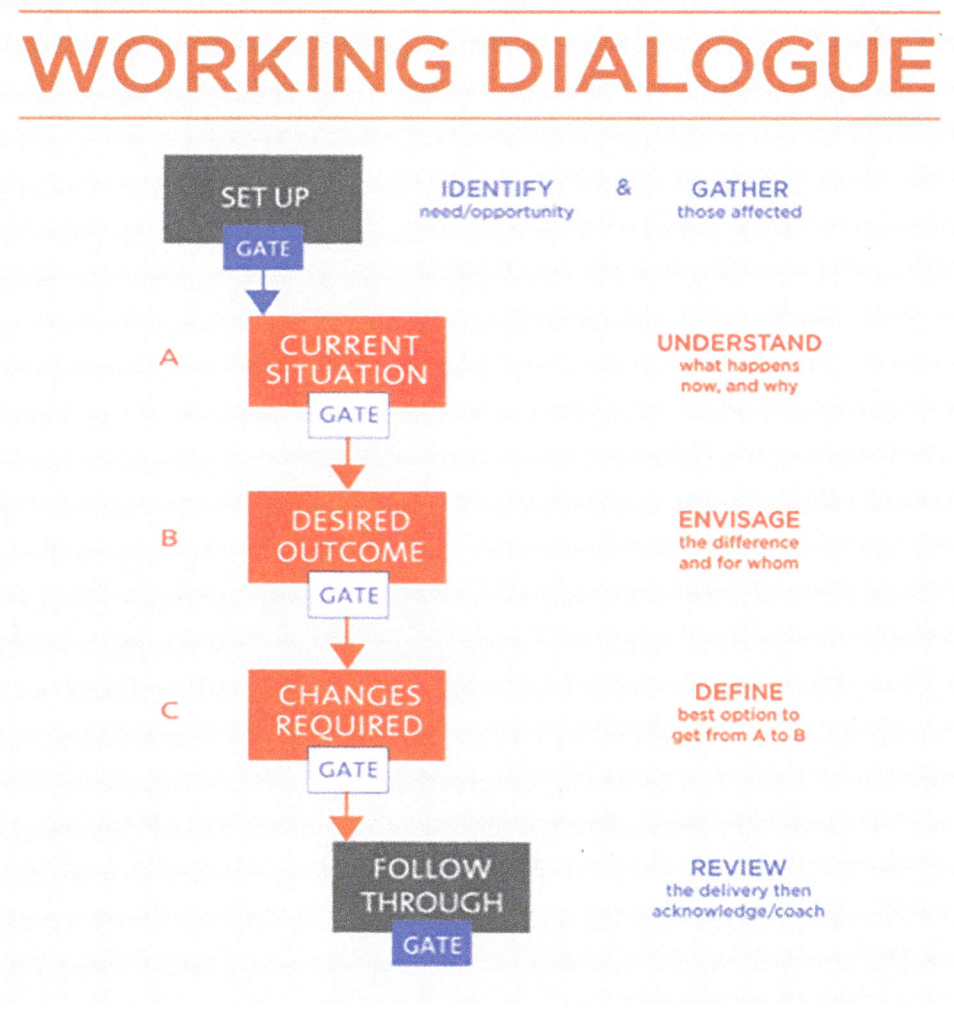

The Working Dialogue model was introduced on a regional basis. Peter Garrett and Jane Ball met with regional leadership and Dialogue Practitioners, along with statewide leadership, to explain the Working Dialogue model and to clarify expectations of how it would be used in every business unit (prison, community center, and central function) in the agency. As part of this introduction, Peter and Jane laid out a process for the development of additional Working Dialogue Practitioners to facilitate. Peter and Jane also developed six Working Dialogue Practitioner skill-builds. These were a structured set of learning plans which included material about Dialogue skills, Dialogue coaching, and Working Dialogue. Each skill-build involved learning new skills and then reinforcing those skills through practice, both in the classroom and in the field. This learning initiative provided a deeper level of training for Dialogue Practitioners to prepare them to be effective facilitators. In addition, a new wave of Dialogue Practitioners was selected to specialize in Working Dialogues. Over the course of several months, Dialogue Practitioners around the state participated in and completed a weeklong training, at which they engaged in all six skill-build lessons. The skill-builds continue to be utilized as a refresher and to train new Dialogue Practitioners.

While Working Dialogue training was being provided across the state, the VADOC was beginning to pilot Working Dialogues in some individual units. One of the Dialogues took place at Dillwyn Correctional Center (DWCC), about 70 miles west of Richmond, Virginia. The purpose of the DWCC Working Dialogue was to look more closely at the need for reducing contraband inside the facility. Early on, it was recognized that not all voices, specifically those of K9 Officers and night shift officers, were present in the Working Dialogue. As a result, the Working Dialogue was paused and reconvened once the opportunity was given for those missing voices to be brought into the process. To ensure that the Working Dialogues continued, the Executive Leadership of the VADOC set an expectation that all units would have at least two Working Dialogues each quarter. The following illustration shows the Working Dialogue model created for and used in the VADOC. When asked to reflect on the impact of Working Dialogue, Regional Operations Chief of the Eastern Region, Mr. Gregory Holloway, stated, "When conducted by definition, designed specifically for the VADOC, Working Dialogue incorporates basic dialogue skills to make it easier to address ideas, opportunities and issues with stakeholders, departments, and those who are affected by the outcome. The business practice has a significant and positive impact on the Department both procedurally and for policy amendments."

As the VADOC continues to embrace and recognize Working Dialogue as an intervention tool, many opportunities and needs have been successfully addressed. Regional Operations Chief of the Western Region, Mr. Henry Ponton, shared, "I believe that Working Dialogue is a great tool that is assisting the units. They are a good way to include all voices in the decision-making process. We improve culture by including everyone in the process." The case studies below represent Working Dialogues that have done just that within the VADOC. These examples come from each region within the VADOC and reflect needs and opportunities from the facility and community side of Corrections.

Case Study #1: Balancing Probation Officer Workloads

Set-up

In early 2019, District 23 Probation and Parole had experienced the departure of several Probation Officers who specialized in supervision of offenders and report-writing. Because these departures were occurring simultaneously, the challenge of balancing workloads in the office increased exponentially. The Probation Officers providing supervision of offenders were identified as the group most affected by staff departures. Some of these Officers were left with caseloads surpassing 140 offenders, and although there were some newly hired Officers, little relief could be provided because they were not being fully trained. This need was brought forward by District 23's Chief Probation Officer, who became the sponsor for the Working Dialogue. Consideration was given as to whether addressing the need would result in some material benefit, whether those affected were being included in the Working Dialogue, and whether the Working Dialogue had a clearly stated purpose. Once the Dialogue Practitioners and the Chief Probation Officer agreed that all considerations had been met, they were able to proceed through the first gate.

Current Situation

The identified group of individuals convened to begin this next step of the Working Dialogue Process. The importance of this phase was to look at what was currently happening in District 23. The following statements were included as a description of the current situation:

- Supervision Officers' loads are in excess of 140 cases
- Newly hired Probation Officers are not able to carry caseloads
- Officers are specialized, either as Investigators or Supervision Officers
- Investigators are assigned approximately 10-15 Pre-sentence Investigations (PSIs) per month
- Current numbers do not support five dedicated PSI writers

All participants of the Working Dialogue considered whether anyone had been left out, if everyone's perspective had been heard, and if there was an agreed understanding of the current situation as reflected on the flip chart. The group was then able to pass successfully through the second gate.

Desired Outcomes Phase

The group would now begin to work towards what they wanted and needed moving forward, sharing their vision and ideas. The following desired outcomes were expressed:

- Maximize officer caseloads (reduce caseload with current staff)
- Increase the number of staff who can supervise cases

- Cap the number of Pre-Sentence Reports for the remaining Investigators
- Determine which Pre-Sentence Report writers' duties can be dispersed equably
- Have current staff complete two to three Pre-Sentence Investigations per year (or as assigned)
- Have all staff trained to write Pre-Sentence Reports
- Train current Pre-Sentence Investigation Writers in general supervision of caseloads
- Have a practical plan and commence executing the plan by this Summer (2019)
- Have a meeting with all staff to advise of expected changes

Once all voices had been heard, all participants considered whether the outcomes would be the best for all, if there were any real benefits, and if the outcomes were worth doing. The group then was able to successfully pass through the third gate.

Changes Required
The group was now at the point where they could begin to develop their action plan of how to get from their current situation to their desired outcome. The following action plan was established:

- The Chief Probation Officer will meet with the Pre-Sentence Investigation Team to discuss expectations in broad terms and timeframes
- All staff will be advised of the Pre-Sentence Investigation change at Staff Meeting
- Senior Probation Officer and Identified Peer Trainers will train Pre-Sentence Investigation Writers on general supervision expectations using the Basic Skills Worksheet
- Pre-Sentence Investigation Writers and Supervisors will train Supervision Officers to prepare Pre-Sentence Investigations
- All staff will be trained in Introduction to Sentencing Guidelines through training provided by the Virginia Sentencing Commission

After developing the action plan, the participants considered whether it was clear who was responsible for doing what and when, if predictable risks had been addressed, and if the plan was an achievable route of getting from the current situation to the desired outcome. At this point, the group was able to successfully pass through the fourth gate and set the action plan into motion. A follow-through date was scheduled for Fall of 2019.

Case Study #2: Color Code

Set-Up
In August 2019, the question arose whether District 12 would benefit from implementing a color-code drug testing system. The purpose of implementing a color-code system was

discussed, and it was determined that this would be a good topic about which to convene a Working Dialogue. The unit's Dialogue Practitioner, Working Dialogue sponsor, and Unit Head agreed that the Working Dialogue should involve treatment staff, security staff, probation officers, and management team members. The group considered whether the Working Dialogue would be worth doing, if all individuals had been identified to participate, and whether the Working Dialogue was well named. Once agreed, the first gate was passed through successfully.

Current Situation
The identified individuals met to dialogue about what was currently happening in District 12. The following items points were expressed during this phase:

- The District 12 office treats every positive screen as a new use (THC stays in the system)
- There is no policy implemented for color coding
- There's no set way to follow through in a positive drug screen in a particular color-code status
- Probationers are given a short orientation about the process
- District 12 has a 58% average noncompliance rate
- Color code caters only to a controlled population
- There is not enough funding to support need
- Color code is only being used as a pilot program
- There is not enough staff to utilize the program
- District 12 is down one surveillance officer
- There is only one female surveillance officer to fulfill urine screens
- There are a large number of clients with substance use with no signs of improvement
- There are no flexible schedules given
- There is only one morning testing slot available, which conflicts with many probationers' need for transportation, etc.
- Some probationers have no cell phone service
- There is not enough notice being given to surveillance officers if the probationer's phone is no longer working, etc.

Once all voices were heard, the group considered whether anyone had been left out, if everyone's perspective had been heard, and if there was an agreed understanding. Without any difficulty, the group passed through the second gate.

Desired Outcomes
The group then proceeded into the next phase to discuss what they wanted for District 12. It was easily agreed that the District desired a standard color-code practice be established, vacant positions be filled, and that an increase in the budget be received. The Working

Dialogue participants further agreed that the outcome was the best for all involved, and that it was worth doing because it would provide real benefits to the District.

Changes Required
Participants next would work on identifying changes needed and develop an action plan to carry out the changes. The District 12 action plan included the following:

- A Color-Code Matrix will be developed to clearly define color-code status, frequency of testing in each phase, how to move within each category, and when it is appropriate to staff a case with a supervisor for a potential violation.
- Request consideration from Regional Administrator for a roving tech position for District 12
- Disseminate a new Color-Code Matrix to the District 12 staff to be implemented into practice

After completing the action plan, the Working Dialogue group considered the appropriate gate questions for the Changes Required phase. Once satisfied that all conditions had been completely met, the group set a follow-through date. Because of this Working Dialogue, the District was able to develop and implement a new tool and practice that could be used by staff.

Case Study #3: Offender Movement Optimization

Set-Up
In October 2018, the Central Virginia Correctional Unit for Women identified a need to improve and optimize offender movement within the facility. Recognizing that many people would be impacted by a change in this area, the Unit Head and Dialogue Practitioner identified participants from many different areas to invite, including security, medical, VCE, business office, treatment, mental health, DCE, religious services, education, work supervisor, and food services. To prepare to move to the next phase, the gate questions were considered. It was determined that a Working Dialogue was worth doing, that everyone had been included, and that there was a clear purpose.

Current Situation
All identified participants came to the table to discuss what was currently happening with offender movement. Through talking and thinking together, the following was documented as the current situation:

- Master Pass List inconsistencies. This involves scheduling (balancing work, programs, and school), outside work, and input/removal of the Master Pass List

- Training regarding the use of the Master Pass with *all* staff, including the shortage of staff (for example unmanned post-basements)
- Offender movement
- Lack of communication with notifications

All participants were asked to consider and respond to the current situation gate questions. The group was able to successfully move on to the next phase after agreeing that no one was left out, everyone's perspective had been heard, and there was an agreed understanding of the current situation.

Desired Outcomes
The group then moved forward to thinking about what they needed in terms of offender movement. This gave them all an opportunity to brainstorm about how movement could be improved. The following desired outcomes were stated:

- Consistency with the 24-hour-clock and controlled movement
- Utilization of appointments in lieu of calling for offenders
- Training on how to use the Master Pass List (for example, utilization and movement)
- Non-security personnel conducting visits to avoid using trip passes
- More coaching to officers by supervisors
- More staff and FTOs being hired
- Staff accountability for knowing location of offenders
- Open communication with all staff on notifications
- Supervisors following the chain of command when needing assistance (specifically outside work supervisors)

As with each phase, the group was again asked a set of gate questions to determine whether the process could move forward. The participants were able to agree that the desired outcome would be the best outcome for all, there was real benefit, and the desired outcome was worth doing.

Changes Required
After thinking and talking through the current situation and desired outcomes, the participants now began to identify what action was needed to achieve their outcomes. By doing this, the group developed the following action plan:

- Explain the 24-hour-clock to all staff
- Have a copy of the Master pass visible at all posts
- Non-security staff will receive a copy
- Executive staff will review and implement 24-hour-clock

- Timeframe: Address at Lieutenant's meeting on October 30, 2018
- Go over utilization of Master Pass List in briefing each day
- Continue on-the-job training for staff
- All medical personnel and the Chaplain will receive a copy of the completed Master Pass List each day
- The Master Pass List will also be added to the supervisor's daily report
- Immediate supervisors are responsible for setting the tone for staff
- Supervisors are responsible for training their staff in each day's briefing
- Supervisors will also begin on-the-job coaching immediately
- Field Training Officers (FTO's) will be sent to school
- New staff need to be hired
- Standards of Conduct will be used to address staff accountability immediately
- A chain of command list will be created by the Department Heads

To work through this entire process, the group met on two separate dates. This allowed them to put adequate time into developing an action plan that would get them from their current situation to where they desired to be. After developing an action plan, the participants identified a follow-through date to review the Working Dialogue, and to determine if any further action would be needed. To be able to set the action plan into motion, the group considered whether it was clear who would do what and when, if the predictable risks had been addressed, and if the plan would get the unit from their current situation to their desired outcomes. All participants agreed that it would. This Working Dialogue allowed the unit to look at their current processes for offender movement and make them better.

Sustaining a Dialogic Organization

The expectation that all units complete at least two Working Dialogues per quarter remains today. As units continue to experience the positive impact and results of Working Dialogues, the number of Working Dialogues completed rises. In this year alone, there have been over 200 Working Dialogues completed and reported throughout the VADOC. Dialogue is no longer an initiative but is now the way VADOC does business. It is a practice that is used every single day to enhance the healing environment of the VADOC. As George Hinkle, Operations Chief for the Central Region stated,

> *Working Dialogue is an excellent model, meshing dialogue practices (core communication processes) in the management of real-world (often everyday) challenges, achieving better outcomes while honing dialogue skills, enhancing relationships, generating better thought. The integration of working dialogue brings a practical sensibility and outcome-driven texture to our dialogue processes*

drawing upon our "leading energies" while near-seamlessly meshing with [our decision-making model] promoted by VADOC, as well as project management approaches in practice.

In 2019 the VADOC established a new position to further support sustaining Dialogue within the Department. The new Dialogue and Business Practices Administrator was carefully selected to provide leadership, direction, and organization for the development and implementation of effective cultural changes, communication strategies and decision-making through Dialogue to support re-entry and the public safety mission.

The VADOC is recognized as a Dialogic Organization, but at times it seems as though the journey is just beginning. In an effort to be sustainable, the VADOC immerses its employees with Dialogue through Dialogue Skills training, Dialogue Coaching training, Offender Resettlement Journeys and Working Dialogues. The VADOC continues to explore ways it can take Dialogue to the next level. Committed leadership is necessary to create a sustainable dialogic organization. We believe having an ongoing focus on learning and the basics of Dialogue, simultaneously, will help our Organization realize its goals.

Conference Session Extracts

From a conversation with participants considering the paper with the authors

Speaker 1: Somebody said yesterday that they are hearing a lot about the really great work we're doing with dialogue [at the VADOC], but there are challenges. There are people who are more comfortable with the command-and-control system, where they don't have a voice. They would rather just be told. . . . That's what they're comfortable with, and they prefer that. So it's still challenging to get them on board, to really embrace that and use their voice in the process. One of our biggest challenges is that we're dialogic and we want to permeate to where every single person in the department is a part of dialogue, not only feels that we are dialogic, but is a part of it.

Speaker 2: One of the other things that Whitney does is she makes sure that we have a sufficient number of people who train us. Dialogue practitioners, positioned across the agency, who can provide the support and training divisions that are necessary in the prisons, because we're scattered across the entire state geographically. So we have people positioned, deliberately, in all the regions and all the locations. She makes sure that training is ongoing, and we are always looking for opportunities to deploy those resources, to be useful within the organization. One time it was considered to be an initiative. We are now in the phase of making this a business practice. To make it alive and keep that alive, we are putting the practices into policy. This is going into policy as the way in which we make decisions.

Speaker 3: I have a question on efficiency, because I have a traditional business school background. I think it's amazing what you're doing – creating this learning situation is amazing – but the immediate thing that might come to mind is cost. It sounds great, and I'm sure you can do it in a public institution, but we are trying to run a company here, and what about the cost of having everybody talking so much? We may need more people because we are spending so much time on all this talk! Have you been able to see or measure in any effective way the efficiency of actually having this inclusive approach to running your business?

Speaker 2: Anecdotally we can talk about better outcomes from all of this, because the staff will tell you that there are good outcomes. And the regional directors and the wardens, and everybody that's been involved in these will tell you they have better outcomes. And that it's getting their people working better together, so therefore the environments become better places in which to work. But also you can take a look at some of the data that we're getting, that we talked about earlier. Now, today, for the third consecutive year we have the lowest rate of recidivism in the

United States in our institutions. We have a level of violence that has just plummeted in our institutions, inmate on inmate, staff on staff. All these are measures that are used regularly, and everything that we do is causing these changes to occur within the system.

Speaker 4: What was striking me is that you have really transformed the culture of your organization. Effectively, and through policies, you're continuing to just change the DNA of your organization. And you've been very strategic on many levels, including the placement of dialogue practitioners, not just randomly dispersed, but they're specifically, purposefully dispersed. So I have a question. Is there a pattern in a large, complex organization, where one could anticipate hotspots? In other words, is there a critical spot in the organization where the resourcing of the dialogic approach is particularly important for the whole system?

Speaker 5: I think that is the most important factor behind this success story. It's so interesting. . . . My experience is that Harold's management role is essential. We work in a similar way in Sweden with our projects, but it very seldom happens that we have this strong support from the highest leadership level. We can engage people on the middle level, in small units, but to do this in this huge organization demands this very strong belief from top management that this is the way to go forward, and it's risking his or her political life to convince leadership close to me, because they can kill you anytime if they want to.

Speaker 2: I think dialogue is the best way to go, because with dialogue you're enlisting others to go along the journey with you. You are not telling them what to do, you are telling them who they are and how, together, you can accomplish certain things using the dialogue skills and using the dialogue practices and actions, because interacting human beings are communicating, and this is an improved way of communicating.

Speaker 5: I think the strength with dialogue, compared to total quality management and stuff like that, goes back to David Bohm. He was very much focused about our awareness, the way we think, the fragmentation and suspension. And that's something very unique for dialogue. The theme for this afternoon is intervention. I don't think David Bohm had any ideas about intervention whatsoever, and he had no ideas about team development whatsoever. But he taught us the importance of giving attention to our thinking process, and that's the most basic thing that can take us anywhere. David Bohm didn't care about results. He cared about the thinking process as such, and what we have to do is develop ideas like this that you have now. All the skeptical people will want results, so we have to try to understand why we should measure, and what we should measure so we are true to the basic idea behind dialogue.

Speaker 1: One of the things we have been considering with the staff is power, coercive power over, power with, and power from within. A lot of what we're doing is taking the power over, to bring it to power from within, and power with. They have been very uncomfortable with their power, and so they are trying to be more comfortable, owning their power, facing hierarchy, being okay with hierarchy in that it serves a purpose. But thinking about power in a different way, and how they're sharing with each other, and how they're empowering each other. There are parts of their system where they can shift to having more dialogic types of experiences with each other.

Speaker 6: I think there is a natural order of things. It's not always evident when things are jarring and feeling disruptive. Then it's a pretty clear sign that we're moving away from the natural order of things. And I think Harold, and Whitney, your example, is of an organization that's getting pretty close to a natural order of things.

Postscript

The authors' reflections, written some months after the conference

With over 13,000 staff responsible for approximately 37,000 incarcerated persons as well as about 68,000 individuals on probation and parole, our agency's investment in becoming a dialogic organization has been a major commitment. We have deeply experienced the ways dialogue helps the VADOC stay true to its mission.

That is why the title of our paper, "Putting Dialogue to Work in the Virginia Department of Corrections" has been—and still is—relevant. We have put Dialogue to work changing the way we engage, helping us to learn helping us to make decisions. This continues to impact our culture.

We were not sure how our paper would be received by those in attendance at the conference. We have heard many opine that Dialogue is not about decision-making, but in the VADOC we have developed a concept of Working Dialogue that serves us well. Working Dialogues are intended to help staff recognize needs and opportunities within their work units and organization, and to work together collectively to make decisions using Dialogue skills.

What we found at the conference was a lot of interest and inquiry about what we were doing, and how we were using Dialogue as an intervention tool. To be able to share our work and experience in writing before the conference, verbally at the conference, and now in reflection after the conference has been rewarding. As we presented our work we were prepared to answer questions and be challenged by those who have long studied the work of David Bohm. We responded to challenges and questions as best as we could, sharing our success and the positive evolution of our organizational culture as a result of Dialogic work.

Because of our experience with Dialogue we no longer need to operate under a "command and control" culture. Rather, we operate as a dialogic organization, where every individual within our Department – both staff and offenders – offer a valued voice and contribution to everything we do. Our motto is "we are in the business of helping people to be better," and that includes our staff as well. We are able to have greater impact by taking advantage of our diversity; we make it our strength through the use of Dialogue. We found writing the paper and addressing it with others at the conference to be encouraging.

Dialogue and a Healing Environment in the Virginia Department of Corrections

Harold Clarke and Susan Williams

[Note: *This paper is reprinted from the 2018 edition of* The World Needs Dialogue! *and is a companion to the paper in the chapter before this one.*]

Personal Background for Susan

I am the Organizational Development Manager for the Virginia Department of Corrections (VADOC). In this role, I am responsible for the implementation, coordination, and management of the initiatives that enable the Department to achieve its strategic goals. I lead the business practice of Dialogue for the Department but have not always been in this position. I started with the VADOC in January 2008 as the Mental Health Supervisor for Probation and Parole. I supervised the transition of individuals with mental health needs from incarceration onto probation, ensured their linkage to services in the community, and assisted probation officers with managing their cases. Along with my direct reports, I served as the liaison between institutions, including prisons and jails, probation, psychiatric hospitals, and community mental health providers. I also provided training across the Department on various topics including mental health and mental illness, stress management, leadership, and evidence-based practices. Although the VADOC Dialogue story began in 2010, I didn't enter the Dialogue scene until later.

So begins our story . . .

Creating the Conditions

In 2010, the Virginia Department of Corrections (VADOC) was in transition. The goal of the newly elected Governor was to enhance public safety with a focus on reducing victimization, improving the outcomes for offenders returning to their communities, and reducing recidivism by strengthening re-entry programs. Thus the Virginia Adult Re-Entry Initiative was established. The Governor searched for a new Director for the Department to further that mission. The question for the appointed Director, Harold Clarke, then became "How could the Department best enhance the programs and services that are working and eliminate those that aren't, while motivating employees and engaging external stakeholders towards a common purpose of effective reintegration of offenders into the community?" Having previously been the Director in Massachusetts, Washington State and Nebraska, Harold Clarke had an idea of what would help move the Department forward.

When Director Clarke was newly appointed in Nebraska, he reflected upon what the Department needed. At the time he thought, "The best way to create lasting systemic change is through the culture." With the assistance of the National Institute of Corrections (NIC), the Department conducted a Future Search Conference. Over the course of 2½ days, over 80 stakeholders representing the Department and the community engaged in Dialogue to find meaning and common ground to envision a better reality for everyone. Out of that conference, Director Clarke thought about having a "clean, clear, sanitary, healing environment, just like a hospital."

By the time he was Director in Massachusetts, while still working with NIC, the idea of a Healing Environment was formed. As described in the book *Healing Corrections: The Future of Imprisonment*, the NIC Norval Morris Project was established to create a more "just, effective and humane Criminal Justice System." (Chris Innes, 2015, pp 14-15) The project participants, including Director Clarke, wondered how they could "transform correctional leadership and the workforce in ways that would empower staff to reduce recidivism and promote prevention." There, the concept of the Healing Environment expanded from just the physical aspects to include the cultural aspects: a place and an atmosphere where staff could engage with one another to address issues and impediments in order to become better performers. That, in turn, would impact the inmates, thus benefitting the whole organization.

Around the same time as he was pondering on the creation of a Healing Environment in Nebraska, Director Clarke was introduced to the concept of Dialogue through one of the pioneers of Dialogue work, Peter Garrett. As the agency was exploring the idea of the Healing Environment, he realized it could do so dialogically. This would mean that all employees could use their voice, which would bring about a better understanding and more staff support. As he experimented with Dialogue and the Healing Environment, Director Clarke saw that results included a stronger culture and employee engagement focusing on offender re-entry and reduced recidivism. After the Director left Nebraska, he shared the Healing Environment concept in Washington State with similar tangible results and then again in Massachusetts before heading to Virginia. With Peter Garrett, he introduced in each state the concept of Dialogue as the foundation to build the Healing Environment. He believed that all initiatives were better when Dialogue was used to pull them together. Dialogue creates a foundation and a format for better understanding and communication. Director Clarke did not force leaders to conform to the concept. One of his aims was to change the "command-and-control" culture and mindset. Therefore, he didn't command people to follow the principles. He nurtured those leaders who were interested as well as next-level supervisors who desired the changes and tapped them to model the way and inspire others.

By the time Harold Clarke arrived in Virginia, its Department of Corrections had already begun work in moving toward a re-entry-focused agency through the Virginia Adult Re-Entry Initiative Strategic Plan. Many programs and projects were being piloted and introduced. Additionally, the VADOC aimed to be a learning organization and more effective agency through the use of evidence-based practices and programs, and the introduction of Learning Teams. (Learning Teams are small groups of employees that meet regularly to communicate, learn together, practice skills, grow professionally, and continually develop the organizational culture to better achieve its mission.)

The Director realized the VADOC needed a vision and mission to pull the various initiatives and strategies together in a manner that could be understood by every employee, offender and stakeholder. Creating a Healing Environment was the perfect solution. The VADOC began to purposefully establish a culture where everyone – employees, offenders, and stakeholders – would be treated with dignity and respect; they would create together an organizational culture that would prioritize helping people be better through support and accountability. He realized that, more than ever before, the vehicle for the expression of the Healing Environment had to be Dialogue.

Dialogue was the foundation that supported the cultural change. Dialogue has been key in aligning goals, breaking down silos, integrating separate pieces, and creating common expectations. Dialogue became the means of bringing people together to talk, think, and learn. Dialogue introduced a common language and specific skills which allowed people to engage with one another with less misunderstanding and increased participation amongst all levels of employees. Dialogue created the atmosphere where voices could be heard and new ideas could emerge.

Laying the Foundation

The introduction of Dialogue at the VADOC occurred in a top-down fashion. After discussing it with his Deputies, the Director introduced the topic through his reading list. All of the Executive Team members and Unit Heads (wardens, superintendents of facilities, and probation chiefs) received the book *Dialogue and the Art of Thinking Together* by William Isaacs. In it, Isaacs emphasizes the power of a Dialogue to open possibilities and see new options by speaking in a way that contributes one to the other.

Following the assignment of the reading, Dialogue Associates Founders Peter Garrett and Jane Ball were brought in to train the Executive Team members in some basic Dialogue skills. They began by looking at the history of the organization and having the leaders think about the culture of the Department at the time they began. David Robinson, the Chief of

Corrections Operations, serving directly under the Director, viewed the session as an opportunity for growth. He observed that by reflecting on the history, and learning to think together, the agency would be propelled forward like an arrow from a bow. Following a period of transition and uncertainty, there would be growth, movement forward, and the rise of new leaders.

The first dialogic skills introduced were "check-ins" to learn how to get everyone in the meeting attentive, participating and focused. Executive Team members and Unit Heads were tasked with going back to their staff meetings and using check-ins and then come back together to reflect on the results. For those familiar with Dialogic skills, this will seem like a basic task. However, at the time, it was the first hint of a cultural shift. The VADOC culture did not value hearing everyone's voice, and many meetings were held in a monologue fashion. In fact, many participants were so unaccustomed to speaking in meetings that they resisted participating in the check-ins initially. Deputy Director Cookie Scott recalled appreciating this change the most. She reflected that this was a different way of interacting; it provided the opportunity to sit within the Executive Team in a better way. The meetings were less directive and there was more conversation. The team members were able to learn about one another, hear one another's authentic voices, and get a sense about not only what other people were thinking, but about who each individual was as a person and as a leader.

Meanwhile, Chris Innes was continuing with the Norval Morris Project and working on his book, *Healing Corrections* and Dialogue Associates was developing a plan to bring the Dialogue skills across the entire Department.

In 2012, Dialogue Associates began meeting with the Executive Team and Unit Heads on a quarterly basis. They taught them Dialogue skills for talking and thinking together and engaged them in thinking about and developing visions and initiatives for the Healing Environment in each of their Units. What would each institution, facility, probation office, and administrative department do to create a Healing Environment for their offenders and staff members? Greensville Correctional Center, for example, is the largest prison in Virginia and houses over 3,000 offenders. Greensville is the site of separate residential treatment programs, including mental health, medical, sex offender, and a veterans' unit. Additionally, Greensville includes a work center and a death chamber. With there being so many different functions and employees at Greensville, they needed a Healing Environment Initiative to bring them together. Greensville felt like several different institutions, with different goals, each with distinct staffs, who happened to be working on the same 1000-acre compound. They were working in "silos" with limited communication or cooperation. They chose the motto "One Team, One Mission" as their Healing Environment Initiative. This made it clear to everyone that although Greensville was made up of a lot of components, they were all one team working towards the same goals.

Some Unit Heads struggled with the idea of working with their employees to develop Healing Environment Initiatives. They were still confused about the concept and not used to hearing the voices of their staff members when making decisions. However, over the course of the year, all of the Units managed to develop something that contributed to the Healing Environment. The impact was immediate in many areas. Employees had been allowed to contribute their thoughts and ideas to a major Department Initiative. Many were hopeful and enthusiastic about having been allowed to share their voice, and even more excited about the possibility of the Unit making the changes necessary to attain the Healing Environment goals. Many people expressed cautious optimism for the development of a respectful and supportive environment.

In 2012, Dialogue Associates also recognized the need to introduce Dialogue skills to all of the nearly 12,000 employees in the VADOC system. They began a Dialogue Practitioner Development Program (DPDP). The DPDP would start with the training of 24 individuals from across the Department to learn Dialogue Skills and then train and introduce these skills to others in the agency. I received an email saying I had been selected to be part of this group of trainers. I was excited to learn the new skills. I had heard the word *Dialogue*, but other than that had very little understanding what it was about. I also had been conducting many trainings around the Department and didn't mind adding another one. Little did I know that Dialogue was going to be something completely different than what I had been doing and would ultimately change my world!

As our training as Dialogue Practitioners progressed over three days, our understanding of the concepts increased. We could see the value in the skills, especially the practices. We practiced with one another and learned how to deliver the Dialogue skills in the seven-hour standardized format of the Dialogue Skills Training. Despite understanding the importance of the subject, our ability to use the skills and our image of ourselves and our roles was limited. We believed ourselves to be "trainers" and focused on the definitions and explanations of the skills and, in some regards, more than their use. Along with my fellow 23 colleagues, we began systematically and enthusiastically training each and every person in the VADOC on the basic Dialogue Skills – with a focus on getting the trainings completed. Within a couple of months, many of the Dialogue Practitioners began to run into difficulties. Their supervisors did not want them being away from their positions for days or even weeks at a time, and they were finding it difficult to juggle their regular work with their Dialogue duties. Some Dialogue Practitioners were running into strong resistance at the Assistant Unit Head and Middle Manager levels. Nevertheless, the Director and his Deputies were not swayed from the goal. They continued to engage with the Unit Heads on the importance of the Dialogue skills. The Dialogue Skills Trainings were conducted at every institution, facility and probation office; on average about 24 participants were taught at a time until all employees had taken the training. Additionally, the Dialogue Skills Training was incorporated into the Basic Skills Training for new officers and employees.

The Dialogue Skills Training focuses on interaction through check-in/check-out and the modes of engagement. Awareness of the modes of engagement helps determine how the conversation will proceed; the right mode should be selected according to the goals of the conversation. If, for example, the purpose is to only convey brief information and not engage the participants in any exchange, then a monologue may be the correct mode. If the aim is to hear people's thoughts and have input from different perspectives, then Dialogue would be the preferred mode. The training also emphasizes how to have functional conversations using the actions as well as quality conversations having the practices in place. The Dialogic practices of "Voice," "Listen," "Respect" and "Suspension" set the tone for quality conversations. Through these practices, an environment where people feel comfortable sharing and learning is developed. People feel safe to share their thoughts, and genuine exchange of ideas can happen.

The reaction to the Dialogue Skills Training was overwhelmingly positive, especially amongst the frontline employees. It was really the first time a concept was introduced that emphasized the value of their opinions or even the ability to provide their thoughts on a subject. As one Correctional Officer stated, "The Dialogue Skills Training explained that I am allowed to have a voice and my opinion should at least be respected even if it's not the final decision." The more often employees were exposed to the concepts, the more deeply established the skills became. Understanding was deepened in several ways. The initial introduction was accompanied by Dialogue posters that were placed in every Unit. There were separate posters for each skill set to help keep things simple. At a glance, a person could see the types of skills and a word that helped define each.

While the initial Dialogue Skills Trainings were being conducted, Peter Garrett began writing articles about Dialogue for the monthly newsletter that is electronically distributed to every employee. The articles explained the dialogic skills and principles in more depth than when introduced in the Dialogue Skills Training. They offered staff members the opportunity to read at their leisure and understand the larger purpose of the initiative. The first article was "What is Dialogue?" Here is an excerpt:

> *There are times when clear instructions need to be given in a command-and-control mode, particularly in times of crisis and with issues concerning security. There are other situations in which it is more helpful to think things through with others before reaching a decision, particularly when making changes that affect other people. The simple principle here is to include people who are affected by the change in the decision-making process, and this is where Dialogue is needed. In Dialogue people are encouraged to contribute their thoughts, experience and understanding in order to improve the quality of decisions.*
>
> –Peter Garrett, Around Corrections: Vol 1. Issue 3 – Feb. 2013

Another way in which the Dialogue skills were reinforced was through the Learning Teams. Learning Teams are small groups of 10-15 employees that meet regularly to communicate, learn together, grow professionally, and continually develop the organizational culture to better achieve its mission. At that time, Learning Teams were established within the Probation and Parole Districts, where they mainly focused on teaching the officers skills in motivational interviewing and effective communication with their probationers. A few of the institutions also had Learning Teams which focused on effective communication and case studies/scenario reviews. That is, within the Learning Team, the members would discuss a real-life situation that had occurred to examine what went well and what could or should have been done differently.

Learning Teams were scheduled to meet for an hour, twice a month. Those Learning Teams were efficient in teaching and practicing certain skills, including reflective listening, asking open-ended questions, using affirmation, and conducting "change talk." However, those skills alone could not address a deeper level of effective communication, especially amongst colleagues. Dialogue holds the practices that set the climate, and changes the way people treat one another, respect one another. It opens their minds to new perspectives. Those are the added elements of more effective communication. It was imperative that all employees received these skills.

Dialogue Associates continued to work in separate sessions with the Executive Team, the Unit Heads, and Dialogue Practitioners on their development. Then they also began to work with selected staff members from those various groups to strengthen and expand the Learning Teams. The group developed a series of seven Dialogue Learning Plans. The purpose of the Learning Plans was to reinforce and practice the Dialogue skills within the Learning Team to support the use of Dialogue throughout the Department. More impressively, the group developed a comprehensive plan to systematically introduce Learning Teams across the Department in the Units that did not have them, develop and train facilitators known as Subject Matter Specialists (SMS), and conduct the Dialogue Learning Plans and assess the knowledge gained at the end of the seven Learning Plans.

The plan started with six pilot sites. Those sites were allowed to develop their own system for assigning employees to Learning Teams, scheduling Learning Teams, training their facilitators (SMSs), and conducting the Learning Plans. Some lessons could be completed in one session and other lessons needed two sessions to be completed, but it was at the discretion of the Units and the Specialists. After the pilot sites began, the workgroup continued to convene and examine which aspects were most effective and which were least effective, and to make recommendations and develop guidelines accordingly. The rest of the Department, with over 40 institutions and facilities and over 40 probation and parole offices, were incorporated into a 15-month Dialogue and Learning Team rollout with Units being brought in each quarter. Everyone in the Department was assigned – and new employees continue to be assigned – to Learning Teams. Revised Learning Team vision, mission, and policy were

created. The Learning Team Model, a visual representation of the agency's values, practices, initiatives, and purpose of the Learning Teams was created so that every employee would know that the VADOC is a learning organization and the Learning Teams are the mechanism to create and sustain a safe environment for staff to learn together in a way that fosters positive change and growth.

After the first year of training, it was clear that more Dialogue Practitioners would be needed to assist in getting the entire Department trained. An additional 60+ Dialogue Practitioners were brought into the Dialogue Practitioner Development Program (DPDP) while the first group of Dialogue Practitioners earned certificates as Dialogue Practitioner Trainers. Over the years, the DPDP has continued to grow as Dialogue Practitioner cohorts have been systematically brought in across the State and trained in the basic Dialogue skills at the same time as the more experienced Dialogue Practitioners, who have continued to grow in using their skills, gaining more knowledge about Dialogue and learning new skills. It was clear to the first cohort after the first year that they were more than trainers. They realized the impact of Dialogue and how they were change agents for the Department. Presently there are approximately 275 active Dialogue Practitioners in the Department. The Practitioners span across levels from Correctional and Probation Officers to Wardens, Probation Chiefs, and Regional Administrators. They come from diverse fields such as Education, Food Service, Medical, Agribusiness (agricultural operations), Environmental Services (chemical, industrial, and waste management), Research, Technology, Treatment, Security, and more. Every Unit has at least one Dialogue Practitioner and some larger Units have six or seven. We will continue to examine the activities of the Dialogue Practitioners and, later, the impact of their work.

Following the large wave of introducing and reinforcing the basic Dialogue skills through the Dialogue Skills Training, the introduction of Dialogue Learning Plans in the Learning Teams, and the articles written in the newsletter, the Department was ready for the next level of skills. Dialogue was not only a way to communicate and engage, but also a way of developing accountability. As Peter Garrett noted, Dialogue provides a forum to think through together the consequences of our collective actions and to shift our expectations of one another. It was time to move the Department from learning and talking about the skills into using the skills. This meant using the skills for better communication and quality interactions, and even more so to further the mission of the agency. It was especially incumbent upon the leaders in the Department to establish initiatives that serve a purpose and for employees to understand that purpose.

Thus, the idea of *"Serving the Commonwealth of Virginia"* was created. Dialogue Associates designed a poster which captured the essence of all of the activities of the Department and placed each of them into one of four categories. Every activity or decision of the Department should support at least one of these categories: Fiscal accountability, Operational accountability (incarceration), Community accountability (re-entry and probation), and Moral accountability (doing the right thing as well as the things that help individuals become better citizens). Over time and with new research and knowledge, the actual activities or initiatives may and should change, but the overall goal of reducing recidivism remains the same under the umbrella of serving the Commonwealth (Virginia is called a Commonwealth instead of a State as a largely symbolic term).

Just as it was important for employees to understand not only what they were expected to do but also why, it was also important for leaders to be accountable in how they lead. A good manager manages things and processes and meets the set requirements. A good leader leads people by the way he or she talks to and guides them to determine the way forward while accomplishing the tasks required. The VADOC had excellent managers. They had worked hard to develop safe and secure facilities. There was a very clear command-and-control

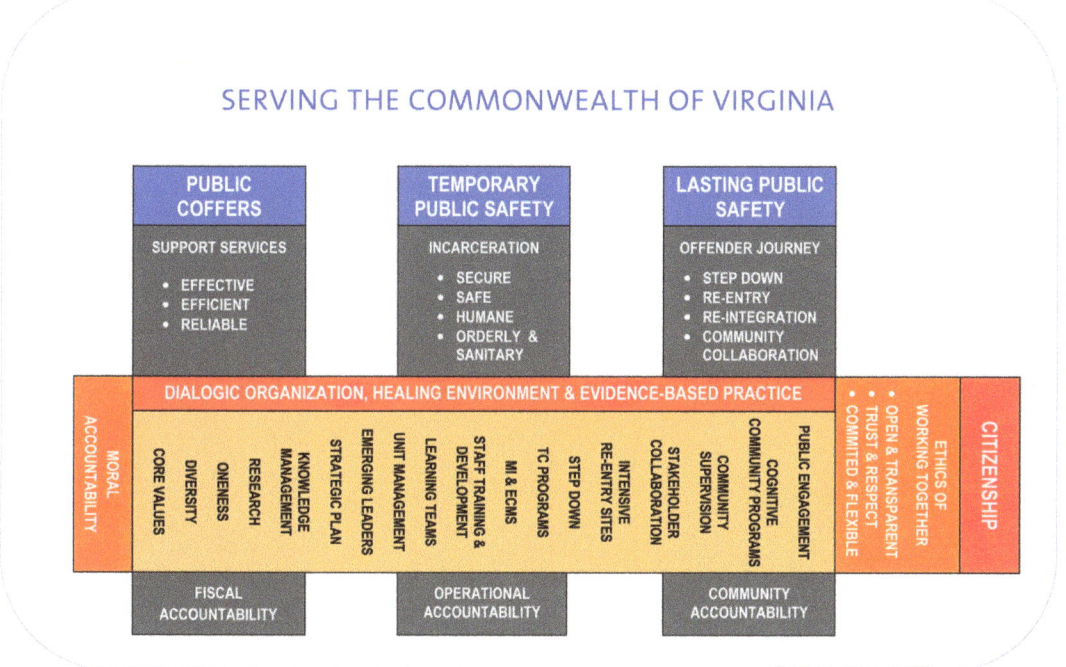

structure in place. Yet even before Harold Clarke came to the Department, there was movement in developing the culture to be even better. It was certain that the leaders of the future would need to evolve. The next phase of Dialogue helped shape those nebulous ideas into structured, easy-to-understand principles. The Dialogue Coaching Training brought the concepts of Dialogue, accountability, coaching and leadership needs together in a seven-hour training. The idea of Dialogue and accountability was based on the premise that proactive support and challenge was more effective in shaping behavior than reactive disciplinary action.

The structure incorporates four levels of accountability actions: Dialogue, Coach, Hold to Account, and Discipline. The aim was for Unit Heads and supervisors to start building the foundation of the communication with Dialogue in their Units. Dialogue would be the mode for co-creating and taking ownership for ideas together, and for engaging with, supporting and challenging the day-to-day with each other. However, the coaching does not stop there. Supervisors needed to take the time to individually coach employees to improve their performance and support their individual development. Coaching is a matter of both support and challenge for actions, behaviors, and impacts. Even with coaching, sometimes people make mistakes, take shortcuts, or disobey directions and the supervisor has to respond. Even so, when the supervisor approaches the situation and engages the employee in a skillful conversation while using the Dialogue skills (e.g., listening with the intent to understand and respecting the person's perspective, keeping an open mind, authentically voicing their expectations), the result is more likely to be favorable. And finally, discipline may be necessary when certain policies or laws are violated.

The Dialogue Practitioners were trained in the principles of coaching and then sent to facilitate the Dialogue Coaching Training with the management teams of each Unit as well as the Executive Team and the supervisors at headquarters. During the Dialogue Coaching Training, the supervisors had the opportunity to practice the skills of coaching an employee and holding an employee to account by doing role plays in groups of four. The groups consisted of one person playing the role of being the supervisor, one playing the role of the employee, one person supporting the supervisor and coaching him or her if her or she became stuck or veered off track, and the fourth as the bystander, providing observations of the entire role play at the end. Each training included several Dialogue Practitioners so that each small group could also have a Dialogue Practitioner sitting in. The Dialogue Practitioner for each group served as a facilitator keeping everyone in role, coaching and bystanding.

During every training session, inevitably there would be supervisors, oftentimes many, who would express dismay at the thought of doing role plays. Many were reluctant participants. However, afterwards participants offered overwhelmingly positive feedback and support for that aspect of the training. The supervisors were excited to learn and practice strategies to effectively support, encourage, and hold their employees accountable. Many participants even had "light bulb" moments when they realized their role in the problematic behavior, either through lack of coaching, unclear expectations, or other reasons. One sergeant expressed his epiphany as "I realize that I am contributing to the problem of our turnover. I do not get involved individually with the new hires. I tell them what they need to know and then I wait to see what they're going to do. I do not make any investment in them until I know they're going to stay. Now I see that I need to make an investment in them and that is what may help them transition better and remain employed with us. I am going to work on coaching someone every day."

Another aspect of the Dialogue Coaching Training that helped the supervisors to think differently about coaching was the introduction of the Leading Energies. The Leading Energies give purposeful and productive direction to the coaching conversations. All of the Leading Energies are necessary for a successful outcome. Dialogue Associates defined the four Leading Energies as Visionary Energy, Performance Energy, Citizen Energy, and Wisdom Energy, and each has a distinct purpose. The Visionary Energy is thinking about the future. It is dreaming about what the future could hold and being able to see the big picture. Coaching with

Visionary Energy asks questions such as "Where do you see yourself a year from now?" or "How do you envision your department?" Performance Energy is about getting the work done as expected. Performance Energy wants the numbers, data, and results. The positive use of the Performance Energy in coaching is setting targets and deadlines, checking in with the employee on the status of their progress or showing them how to track the data.

It only takes Visionary and Performance Energy to accomplish a task; set the direction (Visionary) and get it done (Performance). However, the other two Energies bring quality to the work. Citizen Energy involves being interested in the people, getting them participating, and making sure the right people are in the right positions, Citizen Energy coaching acknowledges the contributions of others, and provides them with the training or support needed for their success. Wisdom Energy brings perspective and reflection, as well as awareness, organization, and balance. The Wisdom Energy coach lives by the motto "Work smarter, not harder."

The VADOC, as many organizations, had a tendency to overuse Performance Energy and underutilize the other Energies. There were many things to get accomplished and many priorities. Therefore, the majority of the supervisors tended to fall into Performance-based coaching. It was all about the numbers and meeting target expectations. With that being the case, when an individual wasn't performing up to expectation, the supervisor naturally fell into reinforcing the targets and deadlines and using disciplinary actions if they were not met. The progression of the disciplinary process often consisted of a warning, a write-up, and then a disciplinary action. Supervisors who didn't want to be overly punitive sometimes went too far in the other direction and made several verbal warnings but did not offer any other consequence or coaching. The structured nature of the coaching practice using the Leading Energies within the Dialogue Coaching Training offered supervisors new ways of thinking about interacting with their employees and approaching issues. Using the Dialogue skills also helped them think about what was behind the behavior. Was it a training issue? Did the person need more support and guidance? Did the person not understand the importance of the task in the big picture? Did the supervisor need to set the expectations more clearly and follow up? It was clear after the trainings that the majority of the supervisors began to think about their roles and approaches to coaching in a different manner.

The goal of teaching the Dialogue Practitioners about coaching was to help them as trainers and leaders become proactive and to help the leadership in the Department learn to be more proactive as well. The Dialogue Coaching Training was specifically designed to reinforce how supervisors talk to, engage with, support, and train employees to attract and retain quality people to accomplish the mission. Additionally, through coaching, employees are better able to make good decisions on their own and bring creativity and innovation to the workplace by sharing their ideas. These important qualities are not prominent in a command-and-control culture. The VADOC is seeing gains from becoming a coaching culture. Employees are being recognized for establishing innovative programs and practices.

The Dialogue Coaching Training became a standard day of the Basic Skills for New Supervisors Training and remains so to this day.

Dialogue in Action

Most of the employees of the VADOC either embraced or accepted the use of the Dialogue skills as part of the way business is done in the Department. However, even though they were participating in Dialogues, there was a disconnect about how to obtain results from the Dialogues. People were not putting the ideas and information into practice. Some were becoming frustrated with the Dialogues, claiming that they were "all talk"; some made statements such as "They are good for hearing all of the voices, but they don't get any real work done." It was clear that people would need more guidance in conducting Dialogues that were meant to solve problems and make decisions. Thus, Peter Garrett and Jane Ball designed the Working Dialogue with input from a small but diverse working group. The Working Dialogue is a structured method that uses the skills within a Dialogue to explore opportunities, enhance processes, solve problems, or make decisions by including those affected by the change.

The Unit Head conducts the set-up with the Dialogue Practitioner who will be facilitating the Working Dialogue. They review the purpose and focus, who should be invited and the event details. Then they send out invitations to the participants. The actual Working Dialogue consists of three phases including a) current situation, b) desired outcome, and c) changes required to get from the current situation to the desired outcome. The current situation highlights what is presently happening regarding the situation. All of the participants share their thoughts and the DP facilitator notes them on a flip chart. By the end of the session, the DP will summarize the points reflecting the common understanding of the group. At the end of the session, there is a "gate" before moving to the desired outcome. The gate consists of questions to make sure all considerations have been made before progressing. The questions include 1) Has anyone been left out? 2) Have we heard everyone's perspective? and 3) Do we have an agreed understanding? Each participant answers the questions on a scale from one to ten, giving the facilitator an opportunity to examine the issues further and possibly reconvene if key voices are missing or if there are scores below an eight. Alternately, they know they are clear to move forward if there is no issue.

The second phase of the Working Dialogue, the desired outcome, has the goal of thinking about new ways of working together to benefit the Department. The participants generate ideas of what they'd like to see happen or how things could ideally become. They tangibly describe what it would be like. The end of the session is then also closed by another set of gate questions. The third phase consists of looking at the changes required. The participants brainstorm as many different options as they can think of to achieve the desired outcome. Then they examine the risks and benefits of the options and make their selection. Once they have made their selections, they create an action plan detailing who in the room is responsible for doing what and by when. The session ends with another set of gate questions. The final aspect of the Working Dialogue is for the Unit Head and the DP to meet again to complete the follow-through by reviewing the process and the action plan to determine its effectiveness.

The response to the Working Dialogue was predominantly positive. As previously mentioned, a sizeable number of the employees of the VADOC are structured, performance-oriented individuals. Therefore, the structure of the Working Dialogue and the action plan, generated to monitor performance, fit with their personalities. They were able to see the tangible results of the Dialogue and felt a sense of accomplishment versus when they felt they were "wasting time" sitting in a regular Dialogue. All of the Units were charged with having at least two Working Dialogues going every quarter. This mandate was met with displeasure. Unit Heads who supported the process felt resentment at being forced to use it. It required the use of Visionary Energy to get them on board. They had to understand the big picture that new habits require practice to become ingrained. Any new process that isn't reinforced will be lost.

It was also pointed out that the Dialogue Coaching Training was provided to the Management teams. Then the Management Teams were expected to take it back to their middle managers and first-line supervisors. Because it wasn't required, only a few of the Units actually exposed all of their supervisors to the concepts. Then it had to be incorporated in the middle managers' and supervisors' annual training for a year to make sure that every supervisor had been introduced to the concepts. Furthermore, Management Teams did not use or reinforce the coaching and Leading Energy concepts amongst themselves and thus forgot some of the skills. Most Unit Heads accepted the rationale and attempted to use the Working Dialogue as a standard practice as much, if not more than, what was required.

At this time, Wisdom Energy has guided the Units in that they understand the Working Dialogue and it has become a business practice within the Department. They use it as needed and as appropriate. Several Units, especially Probation and Parole, are even using the Working Dialogue to address issues with external stakeholders and partners. However, this is not limited to Probation. Even institutions have used Working Dialogues with external agencies to accomplish joint ventures and goals. For example, one facility used a Working Dialogue with the Department of Transportation to plan how to use the offender roadcrew workforce in conjunction with the work to be done by the Department of Transportation. The results of the Working Dialogues have demonstrated a commitment by the staff for continuous improvement. People want to fulfill the mission of the Department and want their work to be meaningful. The future direction includes gathering the results of the Working Dialogues to share in a forum so that others can benefit by hearing ideas and information shared in other Unit Working Dialogues.

One of the most powerful interventions to affect systemic change is the Offender Resettlement Journey (ORJ). The experience an offender has from the time of arrest, through incarceration, then probation and until they are no longer supervised and out living as a productive citizen is their journey. To be resettled means to be successfully living in the community, free of involvement in the Criminal Justice System. A key event of the ORJ is to have one or more offenders recount their own personal journey in front of an audience of staff members, external stakeholders and partners and family members. They symbolically walk through their journey while answering questions from a facilitator. The DP facilitator asks questions about their experience, their emotions, and what helped or hindered them along the way. In this way, the audience connects to the person as a human being with feelings and an inside perspective. The audience gains insight into the pivotal moments, experiences, and conversations that impacted these peoples' lives and how they can work better for the people who are still under their care or supervision.

Dialogue Associates partnered with the National Institute of Corrections to pilot three ORJs in 2014. Those events focused on a) specific aspects of re-entry issues from a high-security prison as well as re-entry issues for offenders who were difficult to program, as they were moved around institutions because of their misbehavior; b) offender re-entry into probation to eventual successful community living; and c) intake issues for offenders when they first enter into the VADOC. All of them were considered to be successful even though success was measured in different ways for each. What made them successful was that staff members and community stakeholders heard the stories and thought differently about their systems and what was working and what was not. They created lasting changes as a result of the events. For example, in one community, they restarted a Council comprised of various community stakeholders including VADOC, local law enforcement, Department of Social Services, Community Mental Health Treatment, and more to collectively address offender re-entry issues and work together on the most difficult cases requiring multiple points of intervention. In one of the institutions they realized that a lot of time was spent sending the personal property of the new intakes back to their homes. However, if they could communicate that to the jails before they brought the offenders, then the offenders could give the property directly to their families before leaving the jail and heading to prison.

In January 2018, Dialogue Associates returned to conduct four more ORJs with a focus on intensive re-entry and examining the slice of the offender journey between the last year of incarceration, which focuses almost exclusively on re-entry programming, and the first year of probation, which focuses on getting the offender settled into the community. Since the regions of Virginia are quite different from each other, sites were selected to represent those geographical areas as well as a women's prison which serves offenders from across the Commonwealth. At the conclusion of each of those ORJs, the participants were placed into small groups to reflect upon the stories and generate topics or issues to be explored in more depth. Out of those groups, nearly 20 topics were brought up that needed to be examined. An ORJ Steering Committee determined that seven of those topics were universally applicable and should be examined from a statewide perspective. Working Dialogues were convened on the local level to address the site-specific topics. Working Dialogues also were convened with participants from across the Department for the seven universal topics. And as momentum works, those Working Dialogues prompted more issues to be addressed and more Working Dialogues, which are currently ongoing. For example, after a group discussed the need for enhanced peer support, increasing the use of external mental health peer supporters became a topic for a Working Dialogue. As a result of that Working Dialogue it was noted that peer support for substance abuse treatment is not substantially different from mental health peer support. Peer support is now recognized as a certified profession in Virginia. Therefore, a new group is working on developing the peer support requirements for certification of our offenders so they can have marketable skills upon discharge. This is just one example of the material benefits of the ORJ. There are many more tangible outcomes that improve the lives of the people under our custody and supervision.

Reaping the Benefits

There has been no other initiative that has penetrated through this organization at all levels as Dialogue has. Dialogue has taken root within the VADOC and has influenced every employee from every department as a true business practice that supports every other initiative. Dialogue has purpose and meaning for each employee, and has truly created an environment that encourages and enables each and every worker to know their role in working towards the mission.

Life in the Department has changed for all levels of employees. Everyone is encouraged to share their voice. Ideas and programs have been implemented because an employee – who may have previously kept quiet – was able to share their thoughts openly. Skillful conversations and Dialogues are happening at all levels, with people trying to gain common understanding and goals. By communicating more regularly and using Dialogue skills, people are more connected and willing to work together to resolve issues. There is a greater feeling of "oneness" that we are all in this together and have a shared vision towards which we are working.

Working Dialogues are happening every day across the VADOC to continually improve processes and procedures. The Department continues to be recognized as an outstanding leader and innovator in many different areas, including the response to the Prison Rape Elimination Act, reduced use of restrictive housing, Step-down (an incentive-based program for high-security inmates to progress within the system) and re-entry programming at maximum security prisons, Effective Practices in Community Supervision, Opioid addiction treatment, developing recycling centers (which have financially benefited the Department as well as produced marketable skills for offenders), focused mental health treatment while incarcerated and while on probation, and more.

All of the initiatives of the VADOC, beginning with the Healing Environment as the milieu and Dialogue as the mechanism, come together in service of the mission. The lead-in to the Strategic Plan quotes Director Harold Clarke: "We are in the business of helping people to be better." That is the mission condensed into one easy-to-understand sentence. And the Department must be doing something right. For the second year in a row, the VADOC has led the United States with the lowest recidivism level in the Nation at 22.4%, and it continues to decline. Other state agencies, Departments of Corrections from other states, and even other nations are looking to Virginia for guidance. The Secretary of Public Safety and Homeland Security for Virginia, Brian Moran, stated:

> In 2011, under the leadership of Director Harold W. Clarke, the Virginia Department of Corrections initiated a multiyear transformation and has since undergone a wholesale culture change. The department consistently seeks opportunities to enhance existing practices. Now, other states and countries visit regularly to observe our practices and to understand how we have achieved success. The State Department has even partnered with the Virginia Department of Corrections to train other countries' correctional leaders . . . Clarke has created a healing environment within the Virginia Department of Corrections by instilling a culture in staff and offenders alike that motivates them to create and foster positive and progressive changes. He operates from the principle that how we treat and engage offenders on the inside affects our communities on the outside; it affects the victims and their families, families of offenders and the men and women in our care, 92 percent of whom will one day be our neighbors.
>
> — Brian J. Moran, *Bristol Herald Courier* via AP, June 15, 2018

However, as compelling as the story is from the Director, his supervisor and his employees, the most powerful testimony comes from the offenders under our care and supervision. A former offender who participated in the ORJs has formed his own business to help other formerly incarcerated individuals. He wrote an editorial to the paper about how the VADOC changed his life, excerpted below.

> When I first arrived at DOC [Department of Corrections], I had no idea if I would make it out alive. With "life" hanging over my head, my incarceration started filled with darkness, despair, and hopelessness. This was during a time when the governor and director of DOC seemed to care nothing about our rehabilitation or our well-being, and there was no real access to programs.
>
> Then in 2012, Gov. Bob McDonnell appointed Harold Clarke as the director of the DOC, and Director Clarke changed everything about my experience in the DOC. From that point, he emphasized that re-entry begins on day one and began implementing programs to help inmates to think differently and acquire employable skills.
>
> I could immediately feel Mr. Clarke's presence throughout the system, especially in the re-entry department. Even if an offender had not accomplished anything during his or her entire incarceration, there was now a director who said, "I'm still going to give them an opportunity to succeed in their last six to 12 months, and have a chance to make it in society."

The re-entry program also helped inmates get D.M.V. identification cards, which can be difficult to obtain. This made renting an apartment or applying for jobs possible upon release. These seemingly simple tasks can be huge barriers for incarcerated people.

While incarcerated, I co-facilitated multiple treatment programs in re-entry, such as Thinking for a Change, Victim's Impact, and numerous other programs. I can relay countless stories of success by the men who participated, including me. When I was released from prison, I felt over-qualified to re-join society. I was armed with pro-social concepts and definitions, and the tools necessary to succeed.

– Paul Taylor, "Preparing for Life after Prison in Virginia,"
Richmond Times Dispatch, June 2, 2018

Vision of the Future

The VADOC journey with Dialogue continues. To review up to this point, Dialogue Skills Trainings are conducted for new employees and Dialogue Coaching Trainings are conducted in every new supervisor's class. Dialogues are conducted on the different shifts to hear the voices of the correctional officers, during annual in-service trainings to have input from front-line officers, first-line supervisors, and middle managers, at monthly Unit Heads' meetings for leadership to think and grow together, and across the Units. Dialogues have been conducted with visitors to better understand their concerns. Working Dialogues have become a business practice and are conducted internally as well as with external stakeholders. The skills have become part of the culture. There is still room for improvement in the culture change from command and control to direction and support as well as moving decision-making to the lowest possible level and making sure that all of the voices of the people who will be impacted by decisions are represented in the process.

Two developments currently in process include bringing offenders preparing for release (known as Returning Citizens) into the Dialogue fold and equipping them with the skills and knowledge of Dialogue in the final two years before their release. They will learn how to have more productive communication and better engagement. Over time, the skills could be introduced to the other offenders and even at intake so that they can have positive, quality conversations from the start. There are already instances of offender engagement in Dialogues with staff members, and teaching them the skills will only enhance those Dialogues. There is even potential for the "Elders" (higher functioning offenders charged with responsibility of encouraging, engaging, and guiding other offenders in the therapeutic program) to become Dialogue Practitioner trainers and coaches.

The other development is the evolution of the ORJ. The ORJ has been revised to reflect the goals of the VADOC. Now known as the Reentry, Reintegration and Reflection Experience (R3E), the enhanced purpose is discovering from the experiences, thoughts, and feelings of participants to reflect upon and learn current practices with the intent of gaining insight and understanding that will drive action for change, new areas of development, and overall improvement. The Department will continue to learn from the intensely personal experiences of the individuals under our care and supervision, and will delve deeper into areas in need of improvement.

References

Garrett, P. (2013). "What is Dialogue?" *Around Corrections*, publication of Virginia Department of Corrections. Vol. 1, Issue 3, retrieved from http://www.prisondialogue.org/files/files/What%20is%20Dialogue%20by%20Peter%20Garrett.pdf.

Innes, C. (2015). *Healing Corrections: The Future of Imprisonment*. Boston: Northeastern University Press.

Isaacs, W. (1999). *Dialogue and the Art of Thinking Together: A Pioneering Approach to Communicating in Business and in Life*. New York: Currency/Doubleday.

Section Three

Systemic Dialogue

The third level of work is Systemic Dialogue, in which the circle is drawn yet again larger to encompass the whole system. This requires a change in perspective for the practitioner, as one must now look from the vantage of the whole rather than from the part or the fragment. The aim of Systemic Dialogue is for the organisational system to evolve into what could be called an adaptive Dialogic Organisation. Each Systemic Dialogue is unique, but for success the Professional Dialogue Practitioner will have to assume the stance of an architect rather than that of a facilitator or consultant, and stand alongside each participant as a peer, whatever their status. The practitioner must also include all the elements that have previously been excluded and reduce the distance between the decision-making and those impacted by the decisions, while at the same time engendering wholistic images, metaphors, processes and thinking that reveal deeper alignment than had previously been apparent. Finally, the Systemic Dialogue practitioner must generate a collectively held, integrated and evolving vision along with the wisdom to work with people and how they relate to one another to realise this vision.

– P.G.

Trim-Tab Dialogues: Transformative Vision and Action in South Asia

William Isaacs

From 2011 to 2016, the South Asia Champions Dialogue Process (SACDP) engaged dozens of officials, leaders and development organizations to create a series of innovative conversations that would catalyze several billion dollars of investment. Sponsored by the World Bank and the Department of International Development (DFID), this activity brought about honest exchanges among senior leaders and officials across South Asia in the management of Energy, Water, Climate, Ecosystem and Trade.

This group achieved unprecedented results. Among other achievements, they:

- stimulated the design and commissioning of the first-ever India-Pakistan energy transmission line;
- catalyzed trade through river dredging of inland waterways between India and Bangladesh;
- supported the expansion of a first-ever regional energy grid between Bangladesh and India;
- helped defuse a border conflict between India and Nepal;
- set up unprecedented, sustained cross-national dialogues among officials from different sectors; and
- produced an actionable strategic vision for developing South Asia, now being pursued, that had not previously emerged in 30 years of sustained effort.

However, none of these outcomes were envisioned or would have been considered possible at the outset. Shyam Saran, a participant in the process and former Foreign Secretary of India, writes that the SACDP was born out of the realization that "despite the compelling and often self-evident rationale for regional economic integration, South Asia had remained at the margins of the global trend towards such integration." Even with considerable efforts by The Asian Development Bank, the World Bank and by South Asian leaders themselves through Summit-level declarations and the creation of the South Asia Association for

Regional Cooperation (SAARC), "there has been only limited and halting progress in advancing regional economic integration in South Asia."*

Shared Challenges Demanded Regional Cooperation

South Asia is one of the least-integrated trading regions in the world, with only 5% intra-regional trade, as compared to 22% in sub-Saharan Africa and 50% in East Asia.† It is also one of the poorest regions, and its populations are among the most vulnerable to climate change. As it became evident to the participants through this process, South Asia's most critical challenges could not be solved except through regional cooperation. The shared ecological crisis required a joint response that transcends political differences.

For example, the region's energy limitations could be easily met by taking advantage of the complementarities of energy supply across the region and stimulating cross-border electricity trade.‡ The ability to eliminate poverty would be greatly enhanced by trading together instead of sustaining the fragmentation of the region. The World Bank estimates that intraregional trade was $23 billion in 2015, only about one third of the potential of $67 billion.§

The project set out to close two gaps. Together these created a pressured context in which inaction would become ever more problematic: 1) The wide discrepancy between the evident promise of regional cooperation and the notable absence of action ("aim low, shoot even lower," noted one participant), and 2) The realization that while this was the "Asian Century," South Asia ran the risk of being left out by failing to participate in the global economy.

Breaking Through Constraints: The South Asia Champions

From its inception the SACDP was envisioned as a cross-regional conversation among a group of preeminent leaders to address the fragmentation in the region by exploring directly the causes of difficulties and their potential solutions.

At the core of this process was a sustained, multi-year candid dialogue at which a core

---

* Shyam, S. (2015). "The South Asia championing and visioning process—Reflections and next steps." Internal White Paper for the World Bank.

† Kathuria, S. (Ed.). (2018). "A glass half full: The promise of regional trade in South Asia. South Asia Development Forum." Washington, DC: World Bank.

‡ "The potential gain from regional electricity trade in South Asia," World Bank Blog, March 16, 2017, https://blogs.worldbank.org/developmenttalk/potential-gain-regional-electricity-trade-south-asia

§ Kathuria, p. 36

group of participants that the core team called "Champions"—a term that describes the leadership required to deliver an innovation breakthrough within a constrained context—engaged together to surface the true causes of difficulty, create a new narrative for South Asia, and stimulate a new level of action.* They came from all eight South Asian countries: India, Pakistan, Nepal, Sri Lanka, Maldives, Bhutan, Bangladesh, and Afghanistan. The Champions met in 10 primary sessions over a period of about five years, with a series of design and development conversations and activities that supported and enhanced the impact of the effort.

The invitation was extended to leaders who had been intimately involved in these issues, held positions of prominence and authority in their countries, and who could engage the highest levels of their respective political systems to address and begin to remove the obstacles to new understanding and insight. These people understood the complexities involved in promoting regional engagement. In many cases the leaders we engaged had known each other for many years and had interacted formally through their official positions. Our process deliberately "formalized informality" by removing some of the barriers and trappings of engagement and enabling people to speak honestly and off the record, out of the direct sight of both their home institutions and the media. This off-the-record, protected quality of engagement was one of the more critical features of the process.

Five Core Components

At its core this process brought a small group of people together with the aim of having an impact on a much larger system, an effect visionary thinker Buckminster Fuller once referred to as a "trim tab." A trim tab is a small surface attached to the edge of the rudder of a ship that makes it possible for the rudder to turn more easily. We sought to create a dialogic trim tab, intending to address the fragmentation in the macrocosm by transforming it in a microcosm that contained the diverse factors with which we were concerned. The intention was to impact not only the steering mechanism, but the direction of the larger ship of regional economic cooperation. Five deliberate interventions during the Champions Dialogue characterized this innovative approach:

1) **Shifting the Identity Narrative** – To have an impact on the system, we needed to shift the underlying identity narratives carried by people. That included, but was not limited to, the mindsets of the most senior leaders in the respective countries with which we were concerned. To the degree that people held rigidly to national or political identities, an expansive spirit of cooperation stalled. Ultimately the process became an inquiry into identity itself, made possible by the fact of the

---

* See Schon, D.A. (1963). "Champions for radical new inventions." *Harvard Business Review*, 77-86.

relatively secure and established democracies in the region. As one participant put it, "We're moving into a genuinely postcolonial moment. We are now confident about our individual identities; nations are confident about their nationhood. . . . [Now] we're wrestling with questions about identity in the context of globalization —if our identities are becoming more expansive in terms of how we engage globally, we cannot get away from the need to take the neighborhood with us on that journey."*

2) **Reframing Meaning** – We allowed traditional and familiar conflicts to surface and get reframed in ways that surprised and energized the participants. These conversations went beyond merely being candid.

For example, at the first gathering in 2011, a conversation between a Nepalese senior official and an Indian leader explored the question of why India at the time threatened to charge an extra tax on electricity sold to Nepal. The mistrust between India and Nepal on this score had scuttled many potential deals to develop and sell Nepal's hydropower to India, its obvious and primary market. This mistrust had led to the failure in Nepal to develop its vast hydropower potential (estimated at between 80 and 100GW – enough to power much of South Asia) for decades. Nepalis believed that India had harmed them in the past and would do so again; the Indians tended not to notice that their scale and economic size was seen as a threat and barrier to increased trade negotiations.

"We would never have enforced those provisions," said the Indian official. "Then why did you put them in there in the first place?!" asked the exasperated Nepali.

In a brief instant during the conversation, the historical momentum that had generated a pattern of mistrust, and a sustained blind spot, began to show itself and to shift and so this could be openly discussed. An offshoot of this dialogue carried on in a series of conversations in Nepal, with the assistance of several of the Champions in this group. This opened the way for a Power Trading agreement for the sale of electricity from India to Nepal that would end decades of power shortages in Nepal. Together with the efforts of many others, the leaders signed an agreement within a few years, leading to several major hydropower projects that will in time greatly transform the energy infrastructure of Nepal and the region.

By surfacing these factors, we began to get beyond mutual suspicions. As one participant noted:

At the initial stages, it was not easy to construct a shared narrative among participants which would avoid arousing nationalist sentiments but identify at least some common perspectives which could be built upon. Through the process of honestly and forthrightly confronting and talking through some of the political and psychological barriers that divide South Asian countries, it became possible to

---

* Champions Meeting Notes, Delhi November 2014.

reduce the level of suspicion and distrust and explore commonalities on which one could build a more forward-looking approach to regional cooperation.*

3) **Moving Beyond Problem-Solving** – The focus of our dialogues went beyond a "problem-solving" orientation; that is, we engaged the underlying emotional and intellectual complexities that have guided the region's political and economic policy-making for decades. We sought to make these discussable, and to discern what new actions could begin to transform them. This immediately differentiated our shared dialogue from traditional policy conversations.

   The aim here was not initially to "solve problems" or create action plans, but to understand and transform the conditions out of which the problems had arisen and been sustained. It was also to find a way to address these problems which, as will be outlined below, began to emerge in powerful and organic ways. But we began with the premise that seeking to change conditions with the same frame of mind that created these mindsets in the first place would not work.

   Summarizing the first session, one observer wrote:

Participants were invited to speak from experience, to take a step back, to see and speak from a wider perspective than our familiar roles, acknowledging that these will be part of the equation. The challenge for the gathering would be to surface contradictions and to hold them, to invite fresh and original thinking together such that those present could be capable of determining the right next steps, beyond currently held views and approaches.†

4) **Evoking a Dream** – A formative factor in any dialogue is the dream people carry about its potential. We found that there was a profound, latent dream and sense of potential held by many people in the region—that of a unified South Asia. The success (however dubiously regarded) of regional integration in the EU was a model many South Asians looked to. But what lay below the surface was something much larger. While divided for more than 75 years through wars and interventions, many still held the memory and experience of a whole South Asian identity. There are many markers of this, ranging from a common obsession with the same kinds of films, music and cultural icons, to shared memories of families who now live divided and in different countries, to a sense of history where, for many thousands of years, South Asia shared a common context and sense of belonging.

As one participant put it, our challenge was "to translate our shared history into a shared destiny." One of the characteristics of the process was that it became safe to articulate this

---

* Saran, Ibid. p. 13
† Meeting notes, Pattaya Champions Session World Bank Meeting Notes, 2011

dream, despite many pressures and political realities that spoke against this. "One South Asia" became the label that participants recalled and brought to mind—to the point of creating a Twitter account with that name. It took some years to build momentum, and the drafting of a vision document, to bring participants to a common sense of the future. By 2015 in Colombo, Sri Lanka, one of the participants put it this way: "I spell SouthAsia as one word—I dream of South Asia as un-fractured." Another added, "What we're trying to do right now is dream a dream, one that should excite and appeal to everyone. What does a South Asian community dream of? That's the dream we will appeal to."*

A collective output of the process was the development of a vision paper intended to articulate this dream, shift the narrative and outline a strategic approach to change. Developed through a series of dialogue sessions, the paper spoke directly to the Champions' collective assessment that one of the causes of the lack of progress was the absence of an articulated vision. As one participant noted:

The premise of this project is that one of the reasons there is relatively little excitement around the idea of regional cooperation is this: there is no vision behind the current articulations of the idea. They remain largely bureaucratic exercises, often entailing a series of projects, but with no real passion behind them. On the other hand, those outside government who are passionate advocates of regional cooperation have often not developed a coherent framework that generates excitement. South Asian Cooperation seems once again to drift between a present that cannot long endure and a future that is hard to envision. There has been no framework developed by South Asians collectively, where the creation of a framework is itself an example of working together. This project is an attempt to provide such a framework.†

This participant's words stemmed from the commitment described here, and the actions of these leaders followed suit and continue today.

5) **Creating a Shared Path to Action** – Another vital element that characterized this project was the development of actionable projects and a wide series of investments and results that could not have been envisioned at the outset. This is particularly interesting, given the fact that the focus initially was precisely on *not* generating new projects, but on surfacing, understanding, and transforming social, economic and political "fault lines."

One of the challenges of conversations like these, sometimes labelled "Track II diplomacy"—talks among national leaders acting outside of official channels—is integrating the insights generated in these settings back into the mainstream policy contexts. This is often more generally the case in dialogue, where insight does not seem to lead to any obvious action, and people can begin to lose interest in continuing.

---

* Meeting notes, Colombo Champions Session World Bank Meeting Notes, 2015
† Meta, P. South Asia Vision Project, 2016.

We bridged this gap in two ways: each of the Champions stayed in touch with the senior political leaders of their respective countries—some through informal channels, some as direct advisors to their prime ministers. We would also frequently meet informally with government leaders before and after these sessions. This quickly allowed ideas that had been generated to find fertile ground in action. In addition, the World Bank brought to bear its convening power and its project finance and project generation expertise in support of this effort, producing a delivery mechanism that was closely integrated into the dialogue from the beginning.

The World Bank leaders themselves had been trained in dialogue techniques and understood the value of engaging in a reflective manner. They participated in the conversations, but the Champions themselves were the primary participants. At the same time, these leaders were able to quickly translate the ideas of the Champions into action. This happened many times over the years of the project, to the point that the dialogues generated an ongoing stream of work that the Bank and other agencies worked on, while the Champions acted as advisors and at times intervenors to help senior officials understand the value of and support these activities. They acted, in other words, as Champions in two senses: generating new insights and supporting their delivery in partnership with the World Bank.

To take an example, at the first meeting of the Champions group the participants noted that the Punjab part of Pakistan often experienced "load shedding"—managed shortages of electricity for many hours at a time—and that the Punjab part of India had excess power that it could sell to Pakistan, something that had never before occurred. As the group spoke, the idea emerged for India to sell power to Pakistan. Several of the participating Champions were at the time involved in the conception and development of the first-ever Bangladesh India power line, progressing at the time, and one for which the Champions process would eventually provide a major boost. The unlikely nature of a project like the one between Pakistan and India loomed. "Do we really need to rehearse the reasons against it in this room?" one person asked. "Why not explore it?" someone else offered. Within three months, there were conversations in the prime minister's offices of both Pakistan and India, agreeing to commission a joint technical team to explore the feasibility of building a 500-megawatt transmission line between the two countries. By 2013 the line was commissioned. During this period were many instances where the Champions intervened to help facilitate the progress of this effort, which was first envisioned in this gathering.

How the Process Unfolded

Inception
All creative processes begin with particular people in immediate, concrete situations. The narrative of how this process began is instrumental to its unfoldment, something which is always the case. As it turns out, the participants in the dialogue process itself also were listening for a story from the very start.

In March of 2011 I was sitting with a small group of World Bank Directors from South Asia at a resort called Chewton Glen in England. They were attending a leadership program run by my firm and were interested in exploring how we could collaborate to apply the concepts and experience they were having in this program to the challenges they saw in the world and in their client base. One of this group, Salman Zaheer, had grown up in India and was the son of one of the country's most senior military officials. He had married a woman from a Brahmin family in Bangladesh and felt a strong sense of responsibility to the region, and to its development. He had spent his career working on energy challenges in the region and was now the Director responsible for regional integration for the World Bank.

In this conversation we initially explored the question of how dialogue could be applied to the challenges of rivers and water stewardship in the region. And then we asked, why be limited to that? Why not find a way to engage the leadership of South Asia as a whole in a strategic dialogue about the future and potential of the region? We imagined we might start with a layer or two away from the prime ministers, but then create a mechanism by which all the prime ministers could engage fruitfully together. We envisioned assembling a group of eminent leaders from each of the South Asia countries to explore what might be possible.

Salman took initial responsibility with several others to identify leaders in the region who could participate in an off-the-record dialogue on these matters. We agreed to maintain a spirit of informality, to invite people carefully and to maintain as much diversity of thought and perspective as possible. We invited several currently serving and recently retired senior political officials, as well as several prominent leaders of think tanks in India and Bangladesh. Included in this number were a former foreign minister, foreign secretaries, a finance secretary, a power secretary, and foreign affairs advisors to a prime minister. We also invited a group of World Bank Directors and staff from the region.

Setting the Field

The nature and quality of the invitation for any dialogue deeply determines the subsequent experience people have. The way the context is set enormously influences what people expect, the attitudes they bring, the quality of imagination and openness with which they enter the conversation, and ultimately the experience they have. We think of this quality of experience as the "field" of creative possibility and experience in which people participate.

Kurt Lewin defined a *field* as a set of factors in the life space or psychological arena.* David Bohm spoke about a pool of common meaning.† Building on these ideas, I define a field as the living environments created by the quality of relationship, thought, and energy actually experienced by the people concerned. A field is an energetic context in which a pool of

---

* See Lewin, K. (1951). *Field Theory in Social Science: Selected Theoretical Papers*. New York: Harper & Row.
† Bohm, D. & Nichol, L. (2003). *On Dialogue*. New York: Routledge.

common meaning may emerge. This experience can be transmitted from one person to the next, is held in the symbols and artifacts of the shared experience and is subsequently conveyed in the stories and narratives told by those who participate in it.

Research on fields, and the expansion of understanding of this term, is an important component in the development of dialogue as defined here. This idea has immediate practical implications. Because fields are "upstream" of the experience of thinking and action, they provide a high-leverage avenue with which to influence social and action outcomes. These fields can be directly and precisely influenced through the quality of tone and interaction expressed and exchanged by human beings.

In the case of the South Asian Champions Dialogue, we worked very carefully to set a field for the dialogue in which the participants would bring a quality of exchange that was markedly different from the one that they had known in their professional roles—often with each other—in diplomatic and governmental contexts. We sought participants who we felt could both bring stature and authority to the challenges of regional cooperation, but who also had the openness and humility to engage in a manner that would expand and intensify the quality of the field of exchange. This would make it possible to form a new pool of common meaning together and, from that, to allow fundamentally different social and economic actions and arrangements to emerge.

The setting of the field has many concrete implications. We sought for our first meeting a place that all participants would see as neutral. We had to consider the asymmetrical power of India relative to all the other smaller South Asia countries. Holding the first meeting in India would have immediately been seen as a biased step by many participants. Geography and place played a critical part in the strategy we pursued. We held the first session in Pattaya, Thailand, completely outside of the region. Air travel across the region, as with all trade, is quite restricted. Thailand was one of the few places most people could get to fairly easily, and it did not have excessive emotional baggage attached to it.

We also held careful interviews with each potential participant, during which we expressed the intention of the dialogue. We made it clear that we wanted simply to create an initial inquiry together about the potential of South Asian economic regional cooperation. We asked in the invitation that each participant to come prepared to make a brief (five-minute) introductory talk on the possibilities of regional cooperation in the 21st century. We asked each candidate to be brief and to "evoke the future without censorship . . .to offer your true ambitions for the region . . . and to be challenging and innovative." We asked them to state their dream, and not to hold back.

Informal conversations circulated among the participants on the content of the dialogue as well, including the agreement that regional economic cooperation needed to be conducted within the context of cross-national exchange. Shyam Saran noted of the time that "there was a need to acknowledge and deal with the often-unspoken but nevertheless powerful mindsets which retard and prevent the realization of opportunities for collaborative action, incrementally chip away at these roadblocks, and eventually construct an alternate but shared narrative conducive to change in the right direction."*

Initial Session

The first Champions gathering in Pattaya was characterized by, as one participant put it "a remarkable candor." A positive mood and exchange formed very quickly, as well as a direct and open acknowledgement of the history of conflict and difficulties in the region. Within a few hours the participants began naming others that they felt ought to attend gatherings of this sort—prominent leaders from across the region, people they felt could bring vision and add to the fresh perspective emerging in the room. We reflected on the range of new activities already emerging, such as building a transmission line (CASA 1000) that traversed four Central Asian countries, including Afghanistan and Pakistan and a cross-border power exchange between India and Bangladesh. The existence of breakthrough activities such as these encouraged the group to imagine other possibilities. The pattern that emerged in this meeting set out a path of action for subsequent ones. These included mapping the stakeholders who needed to be included, identifying "owners" who had a strong stake in making regional cooperation succeed, including and transforming opponents into allies, identifying ways to help achieve breakthroughs and progress through new potential activities and projects, and building strategies for progressively expanding popular and political consensus.

Summarizing his experience, one participant said this about the first meeting: "This is the best meeting in over a decade. We are speaking true . . .I feel invigorated by our conversation. It is emboldening and I sense the potential and opportunity coming through in our dialogue. There is a deeper understanding of the need to come together now . . . . We are at an inflection point." †

Threads of the Conversation

We held ten sessions over a five-year period from 2011 to 2016, along with a wide number of spin-off projects and events. Two distinct concentration areas began to emerge in our discussions.

1) **The exploration and crafting of an alternative narrative for regional economic integration.**

    This began with the recognition of the need to shift from the use of the word *integration* to *cooperation*. We explored the underlying fears and assumptions people

---

* Saran, Ibid, p.3
† Champions Process Meeting Notes, Pattaya 2011.

held, and the unspoken but problematic attitudes and beliefs that had characterized regional engagement over many years.

Champions Dialogue Meetings

	Location	Focus	Date
1	Pattaya, Thailand	Champions Meeting	November, 2011
2	Thimpu, Bhutan	Champions Meeting	July, 2012
3	Dubai, UAE	Champions Meeting	June, 2013
4	Delhi, India	Visioning Session	October, 2013
5	Delhi, India	Champions Meeting	January, 2014
6	Kathmandu, Nepal	Visioning Session	June, 2014
7	Kathmandu, Nepal	Champions Meeting	June, 2014
8	Delhi, India	Visioning Session	November, 2014
9	Colombo, Sri Lanka	Visioning Session	March, 2015
10	Islamabad, Pakistan	Champions Meeting	February, 2016

South Asia is a complex community, one that feels itself to be a singular place and, at the same time, highly fragmented. Said one participant, "We have an enormous capacity in South Asia to be deeply schizophrenic. The common cultural experience and the trust deficit coexist. This is a fault line running through most of us, which could be triggered at different points. It's not the party of peace versus the party of war, because we all succumb to one or the other. Is there a way of addressing this ambivalence?" Another noted the self-defeating quality that seems to pervade South Asia, saying that "In South Asia we've always found a way to trump economic rationalism." But through these explorations, a positive tone continued to emerge: "Once we dream of freedom, all these fears—of economic and cultural hegemony—vanish."* We named and openly reflected upon this underlying psychological complexity in the region.

Participants recognized that the forces of integration that had led to the EU and other region economic exchanges—and the forces of tribalism and fragmentation that had produced nationalistic battles over many decades—coexisted in the very conversations we were having. We were not merely talking about these forces; we were experiencing and exploring them directly. And we continued to find ways to create breakthroughs and insights.

This thread of the conversation led to the recognition that the absence of a compelling vision for South Asia had directly contributed to the failures to act: "We're perpetually suspended in the space that the current paradigms don't work,

---

★ Champions Meeting Notes, March 2015

but there's no articulation of what the current project is, the new language." A subset of the Champions group took it upon themselves to craft a document which the larger group iteratively reflected upon over a series of gatherings. This resulted in a rich statement that had the full backing of the group, and included not only a frank analysis of some of the causes of the difficulties, but a strategic framework for platforms for collaboration, which generated a wide range of action and continues to be used today. The group spent several sessions developing and reflecting on this vision statement.

2) **The identification and discussion of concrete projects and activities the group could catalyze.**
The seed of the India Pakistan transmission line became a subject of reflection and review at several sessions as technical work between the two countries progressed. The group explored the breakthrough in the supply of power from India to Bangladesh and considered how that could become the basis of a subregional energy grid, much of which has now begun to emerge. The group also considered and backed the development of a Nepal India transmission line.

New possibilities not previously imagined emerged from the group. For instance, at the Dubai meeting there was a debate about the challenges of building road infrastructures to facilitate trade. Trade as a whole is greatly restricted in the region, partly as a result of tariffs and the failure to permit free trade, and partly due to limitations in infrastructure. "It takes too long to build roads," someone remarked. "Then why don't we dredge the rivers?" asked another. The realization that inland waterways in the Eastern part of the region could provide a greatly accelerated avenue for trade energized the group. Within six months this became a World Bank project with substantial investment to expand river channels and rebuild ports and jetties. Bangladesh and India formed a new trade agreement, allowing the project to be implemented. The Champions dialogues also stimulated the idea of the co-location of border checkpoints, something that authorities in India have embraced and implemented.

Challenges and Breakthroughs

The dialogue process was not merely an exchange *about* the region but was itself the emergence of a new microcosm of coherence *within* the region. Eventually a core group of seven Champions informally but authoritatively held a concentrated focus such that any and all of them could facilitate and guide the exchanges. Interestingly enough, there was never explicit education about dialogue or the process. All the learning was experiential.

Several thresholds and challenges did emerge, however, the navigation of which enabled the experience of coherence and shared meaning to deepen over time. For instance, we had a deliberate policy of not having anyone join the gathering without first having been interviewed and briefed by one of the participants. The nature of the conversations was sufficiently different from what people had experienced before that we felt the need to induct them into the process consciously and deliberately.

Historic Memory Creates Initial Resistance
Somehow, despite our careful induction process, a very senior Pakistani official—a former foreign secretary and ambassador to the US among other places—arrived at the second session without preparation or formal invitation. It was not entirely clear to anyone how this had occurred. This gentleman was used to commanding a significant audience wherever he went, and with some justification given his accomplishments. He quickly objected to the format of the conversation, which consisted of a circle of chairs and informal exchange. He had advice to the organizers and wanted to be heard. It took some time to understand his concerns, but eventually they became clear. He told us that we were engaging in a manner that did not require people to speak as experts, or from their formal positions, but from their experience and internal reflections. It came clear that he was concerned he would not be able to contribute in the manner he was used to and would feel left out of the conversation. He gradually discovered that he could relax and support the inquiry, which had already begun to foster some radical innovative ideas, including one from another of his senior Pakistani colleagues who brought out the idea of raising a $1bn regional cooperation fund to stimulate the activities we were considering. This gentleman realized that he was welcome and began to contribute generously and enthusiastically.

Another challenge emerged when some of the deeper issues between the countries surfaced. For instance, the lingering fear that this was an India-directed dialogue came out through the Pakistani participants. We feared that they might decide not to attend. Eventually through a series of offline conversations it was agreed that we would send one of our number, a former ambassador from Bangladesh to India, to Pakistan to have a series of conversations with participants and potential players to uncover the real concerns. This trip enabled people to surface their misgivings about their own government's willingness to engage and sustain a commitment, their reluctance to lose the relative comfort of their situations if their actions towards cooperation were misread, and their skepticism about India. This effort to reach out led to some offline frank exchange, honesty from the Pakistanis about their own anxieties, and a stated willingness to engage.

The next meeting, held in Colombo Sri Lanka, found us hosting a new group of five Pakistanis, including Ambassadors, a prominent CEO and a former Finance Secretary. Some of the existing group wanted to alter the focus of the meeting, which was to concentrate on reviewing the newly crafted vision paper, to accommodate these new guests. On the morning of the first day we saw all five of the Pakistanis having breakfast together. Although we were concerned that they might object or issue some kind of challenge statement to the group, we did not alter the plan and process of the dialogue. Within two hours the exchange was free-flowing and rich; there was no sense of divide among the participants. The focus turned to the vision paper which had been fully drafted by this time and was seen as "a true reflection of how far the group has come." Said one participant, "this exercise is a means to an end and the end itself as well. The end: there is something called South Asia which is a positive thing. We have a vision for it which is prosperous and poverty free. So it's an end and a means to that end."*

Initial Skepticism Leads to Learning

Most remarkable was that as the conversations progressed the Pakistanis became ever more engaged, to the point that they began openly asking how we could deepen backchannel exchange with India to finally and seriously address some of the underlying difficulties. They made a frank acknowledgement that, while they publicly claim India is the cause of their difficulties, they felt that they themselves are more to blame, and wish to find a way to shift the situation. We discussed and opened a more deliberate mechanism and process of business-to-business discussions across the countries as a result of this conversation. These exchanges astonished several experienced hands in the room, who noted that they had never heard conversations of this kind so openly before.

Perhaps the strongest indicator of a shift here was what came next. The Pakistanis were keen to host the next meeting. This took place in February of 2016 in Islamabad, and a very wide group of visitors and participants attended some of the sessions. For a variety of reasons holding a meeting of a group of officials from all South Asian countries in Pakistan is itself no small achievement. There had been no impetus to navigate these complexities until the Colombo meeting. Attendance in Islamabad was robust. Many Pakistanis wanted to attend.

At one point a guest from the World Health Organization, invited by the Pakistanis, began to speak. She had not been briefed as to how the dialogue process worked. She did what is somewhat typical in these kinds of forums: she began to make a brief speech, making her three points, one after the other. She carried the assumption that she needed to advocate her view, rather than participating in a live and unscripted conversation. Her comments did not fit the spirit of the conversation and that was quite evident to many. Later, in the lobby of the hotel where we were staying, one of the senior Pakistanis who was present for the first Colombo meeting took me aside and said, "we really need to brief people before they come. That lady really had no idea what we are trying to do." It had become clear that we had generated a process where the spirit of dialogue could be transmitted and shared without any explicit attempt to do so.

At another point in this same dialogue, some tension began to arise between a senior Pakistani leader and an Indian. The Pakistani wanted to argue for a different kind of trade

---

* Champions Process meeting notes, Colombo, March 2015.

arrangement between India and Pakistan. The conversation became somewhat heated. What was striking was that one of the senior Indian participants facilitated this exchange, noting that the intention of the conversation was to explore the hidden assumptions that had built years of mistrust and difficulty, rather than to bring back to India a new trade proposal. The goal, he noted, was to develop a new shared understanding and to shift the pattern of the constant arising of tensions like these. The group had begun to reflect on and teach to each other the dialogic approach and a new way to engage together.

A Generative Process

There are huge issues about identity. How does one start? What does one do to take away the old identity and replace it with the regional identity that already exists as well? How does one work towards creating multiple identities and diluting this one national state identity, which is exploited to create differences in people?

Why is integration *such a sensitive word? The problem is that we read too much in-between the lines. So, there would be people who would start reading between the lines and asking: "What does integration mean?" It is an identity issue. Therefore, you want to get into a different narrative to enable the breaking up of walls and a softening to occur.*

– Visioning Session Participants Delhi, 2014

At the core of the Champions process was an inquiry into identity. The quest underlying conversations about a shared narrative was focused on uncovering an experience of identity that transcended the polarizations and divisiveness that has characterized this region for many decades. The process that unfolded allowed the emergence of a level of connection and exchange that the participants stated they had not experienced before, and would not beforehand have believed possible.

What allowed the Champions dialogue process to produce substantial results in different ways from its inception in 2011—not only in terms of a shifting in the experience of identity and meaning, but also in a wide and impactful series of results on the ground?

Deliberate Initial Focus on Not Taking Action

There is a paradox here that is vital to understanding the answer to this question. The process produced a wide array of outcomes, but was not focused primarily on results. The Champions process was in this sense "generative," meaning it created a set of outcomes, and followed a set of creative steps that fostered a deep and serious inquiry. The outcomes were not envisioned at the outset and yet what occurred went beyond expected limits. This happened because people maintained a flexibility, resilience and deep inquiry into the underlying meanings they were making. This is in contrast to a sequential or "blueprint" process, where the outcomes and intentions are relatively clearly defined, and where the ambition is to follow a disciplined set of steps, in a particular sequence, to achieve a predicted and desired outcome. In this case neither the steps nor the outcome were known at the outset of the process, yet the components of the process unfolded organically, each setting the stage for the next development.

The process had two impacts: for the Champions, it created a collegial spirit where greater reflection could occur. However, it also emboldened the typically cautious development experts at the World Bank, who tend to see all the limitations and complexities of the political economy in the systems in which they try to work. They are often caught up in, and give voice to, the expert skepticism that says producing change is very difficult. World Bank staff often found themselves surprised and energized by what occurred:

> *The most important take-away I want to leave this group with is that for us [the World Bank] together with DFID and the International Finance Corporation, what has really changed in the last 12 months, instead of talking about "could we? can we? should we," we have really moved on to the realm of: "How can we make this happen?" How do we get power projects to happen, to let the cream come up to the top, so all of us can put really intensive resources to make several projects happen?**

The development organization's players' internal doubts began to shift from why things can't happen to how to make them happen. The dialogue process freed up energy and enabled a creative outcome to emerge.

The group's initial focus on hosting inquiry that would provide advice to some of the leaders in the World Bank evolved into a conversation among the Champions themselves, which I facilitated, but with the Bank explicitly playing a support-only role. This let the Champions lead the process and create their own momentum. The focus on reflection and a deepening inquiry challenged people to suspend their focus on solving problems and bring their attention to the question of understanding just what the problem really was, what was behind it, and what it would take to shift it. This approach seemed to naturally and quickly lead to action, but of a very different kind than would have emerged if a group of experts had analyzed the problems and recommended a solution. Many of the issues the group took up had in fact been discussed and analyzed through policy papers and statements at SAARC for years. There was not a dearth of expert opinion and formal institutional suggestions about any of these matters; nevertheless there had not been much substantial progress.

First-Person Inquiry

One of the vital differences here was that the diagnosis of the challenges and the articulation of the vision came from the participants themselves, based on their own long firsthand experience as leaders. They were able to surface some of their assumptions and fears, and

---

* Champions Process Meeting Notes, Dubai, 2013.

come to new understandings of the possibilities for action. Having the goal focused on this led to the realization that there was a different way to address complex challenges—an approach in which the seeds of a new understanding could emerge without being limited by the emotional anxieties and potential reactions of others, but one in which those very anxieties became a legitimate part of the inquiry itself.

The Power of the "Trim Tab"

The Champions dialogue process engaged a relatively small group of people who nevertheless had a broad impact on the thinking and actions of a region. The impacts here were due to the generative nature of the conversation, one that enabled a microcosm of prominent leaders to shift their underlying identity narratve, and to openly explore long-held assumptions and historically divisive positions. A process of this kind has a "trim tab" effect. The term "trim tab," as mentioned earlier, was first introduced in 1972 by Buckminster Fuller, a remarkable inventor and visionary. He says:

> *Something hit me very hard once, thinking about what one little man could do. Think of the Queen Elizabeth—the whole ship goes by and then comes the rudder. And there's a tiny thing at the edge of the rudder called a trim tab. It's a miniature rudder. Just moving the little trim tab builds a low pressure that pulls the rudder around. Takes almost no effort at all . . . .the truth is that you get the low pressure to do things, rather than getting on the other side and trying to push the bow of the ship around. And you build that low pressure by getting rid of a little nonsense, getting rid of things that don't work and aren't true until you start to get that trim-tab motion. That's the grand strategy you're going for . . . To be a real trim tab, you've got to start with yourself, and soon you'll feel that low pressure, and suddenly things begin to work in a beautiful way."* *

The Champions process evoked a level of coherence and reflection that cascaded into many different contexts—not only into in each champion's home country, and the associated international development organizations, but also into networks and associations of business and government leaders with whom we interacted.

Design Implications

The process described here could potentially be beneficial if applied in other contexts. Several important design considerations follow:

The integration from the outset of a dialogue process and a delivery mechanism is a

---

* Quoted in *Brain Pickings*, https://www.brainpickings.org/2015/08/21/buckminster-fuller-trim-tab/

critical design feature that should be built into the process. This is a subtle matter, because the logic of delivery tends to be focused on precise execution. It must not, however, interrupt the initial discovery process, which needs to be focused on developing a pool of common understanding and is therefore more oriented in inquiry and in challenging preexisting assumptions. It is very easy for people to get impatient in this process, or for the two logics to compete. It takes a combination of people who have experience with the generative nature of dialogue, but who also have different kinds of expertise, to sit together for a process like this to be effective.

There were many times when some of the more operationally oriented participants from the World Bank and from within the Champions group had to slow down and acknowledge that what was emerging was different from what they expected, and beyond what they alone might have achieved. Achieving a balance in this way opens many possibilities for development organizations and others.

As Secretary Shyam notes in reflecting on the Champions dialogue:

> *This process is different from other efforts to promote regional economic cooperation. The Bank's conventional approach to its developmental role is to peg its action on the basis of economic and technical feasibility of a project proposal. If a project is attractive on the basis of such due diligence, then the case for its implementation is assumed to be self-evident. In reality this does not always happen in a single country situation and even less in bilateral and plurilateral situations . . . . What the process has attempted to do quite successfully is to link the traditional project-based approach to a larger and more persuasive narrative on regional cooperation generated through structured but open conversations among different constituencies in the countries of the region, led by the Champions which identify the deeper political, psychological, social and cultural factors which influence perceptions regarding such cooperation.*[*]

The integration of these two logics created a trim tab effect in the region that continues today. It has allowed cross-national challenges to be explored and, in many cases, transformed, leading to practical action of a kind that could not have previously been acted upon.

The pedagogy and learning is embedded in the process itself, making it more likely to spread. We did not make an explicit effort to educate people about dialogue. We simply engaged together, and gradually people came to understand the nature of the process and the potential it held. This said, the process was carefully designed and supported by a small core group of the people who had been educated in the spirit and methods of dialogue. Eventually the Champions themselves had internalized the spirit and methods of the dialogue, which they observed and experienced, to the point of being willing to support their intro-

---

* Saran, p.23

duction into a dominant culture that did not initially understand or comprehend them. This took courage as well as skill. It also took a considerable amount of effort to continue to keep more distant World Bank leaders engaged, since it did not fit neatly into a single country-level focus, which is the dominant organizing structure of the Bank. As it became evident that the Champions themselves were deeply engaged and concerned to protect the process from intrusions and to sustain it, support continued.

There is wide potential application for this process. The process as it unfolded here could be a template for engagement around a variety of other issues, both for development organizations like the World Bank, but more generally for any national-level engagement process where the transformation of the core narrative is essential for any real innovation to be made.

References
Bohm, D. and Nichol, L. (2003). *On Dialogue*. New York: Routledge.
"Brain Pickings," with reference to Buckminster Fuller's Trim Tab perspective,
    https://www.brainpickings.org/2015/08/21/buckminster-fuller-trim-tab/
Champions Dialogue Process Notes, World Bank Meeting Notes 2011-2016.
Kathuria, S. (Ed.). (2018). "A glass half full: The promise of regional trade in South Asia." *South Asia Development Forum, Washington*, DC: World Bank.
Lewin, K. (1951). *Field Theory in Social Science: Selected Theoretical Papers*. New York: Harper & Row.
Meta, P. (2016). "The South Asia vision process." Unpublished draft.
Schon, D.A. (1963). "Champions for radical new inventions." *Harvard Business Review*, 77-86.
Saran, S. (2015). "The South Asia championing and visioning process: Reflections and next steps." Internal White Paper for the World Bank
World Bank Blog, March 16, 2017, "The potential gain from regional electricity trade in South Asia." Retrieved at
    https://blogs.worldbank.org/developmenttalk/potential-gain-regional-electricity-trade-south-asia.

Conference Session Extracts

From a conversation with participants considering the paper with the author

Speaker 3: Was there a team? Was it you, or was a group of you?

Speaker 2: Me and one other, maybe two. That's it. It was a very small team. That's another big misnomer. You don't need armies. We need a few. The World Bank people were holding the container, and they were also helping deliver. They were helping figure out how delivery would happen.

Speaker 4: And you had trained them? At the World Bank?

Speaker 2: All the directors in the World Bank had all gone through our leadership program. The vice president had gone through it. All of them, four years prior.

Speaker 5: About the architecture. If we start delivering a structure and process to an inquiry, then we have to sell it in a way that we don't know, because it's an acknowledgement of their complexity. And I really don't know.

Speaker 2: Well, it's a paradox, right? I never once said "nothing will come of it." I just said, "I don't know exactly what will come of it." Well it was a little more than that. I said, "What will come of it is an understanding of why the problem looks the way it does," and not some other way. And that would give us access to change. But until we get to that . . .

There's an internal development component, which I'm calling now the vertical component, coming into people's experience. Without that the external pattern doesn't work. Then there's an external architecture to figure out, how the context works, to read it, and to put the right people together in the right ways, to set the right containers. But then what happens in those settings is a function of the qualitative nature of the exchange. And that has to be cultivated.

Speaker 6: Why do you call it a vertical dimension?

Speaker 2: One reason is, I think of perspective as height. Which is another way of talking about a different understanding of identity. Most human beings already identify with subsets of who they are, not who they really are. They identify with reactive patterns that are basically sub-personalities that they think are them. "I feel like this." "I'm like that." No you're not. That's the part of you that feels that way. Now that's a big conversation. What I just said in that one little sentence. And to the extent that people are involved in those sub-personalities, their sub-personality tries to fix other people's personality, and off we go! It's a mess. Well it's true, right?

Speaker 6: That's why the fixes don't stick?

Speaker 2: Well they don't stick because someone will generate another problem out of it.

Speaker 4: So the vertical is "big S" self, the yoga self?

Speaker 2: I call it who they really are. Use whatever word you want. The very notion that there is such a thing present in people is generally missed. People can go through therapy for years and years and understand all their bits, and never change. Why? Because they haven't actually shifted. One part is talking to another part, so you have this museum of parts and you understand what they all are, but none of it changes. You can only transform it from a place of not being identified with it.

Speaker 4: It's the spiritual dimension that you getting at?

Speaker 2: I'm calling it the vertical dimension.

Speaker 3: As a consultant, what strategic or tactical moves do you rehearse in your mind to say, "This fellow is talking from a partial identity that he's in touch with at the moment, but it's not his true self." How do I get him to recognize that his true self is other? You don't say, "You asshole. Why did you step out of yourself and get bit?"

Speaker 2: That wouldn't be very compassionate, would it?

Speaker 7: What's going on there in that space? You can begin with vision, then there's a space where there's discovery, and then a diagnostic. Then, it can lead to a need for a crystallized vision?

Speaker 2: They were diagnosing but it was . . . they were really very personal about it.

Speaker 8: You have to go in, and you have to generative to diagnose those situations. And then to respond, or to react. You may have gone into the situation with a plan, but that's not the plan that played out, because you had to shift and change.

Speaker 1: The plan we had was, if we don't get the real conversation happening among the most senior people at the highest levels, the actual real conversation, this region has no hope of changing. No chance.

Speaker 8: The most important thing, and where most of the time is spent, is creating the container, creating the architecture. We may be fooled into thinking it is about facilitating the dialogue.

Speaker 2: The facilitator. Yeah. That's the least of it.

Speaker 8: The dialogue is relevant, but most of all it's the container, and then the sustainability of the structure. The dialogue is important, it's critical, but it's the least of it.

Speaker 9: When I think back when, when you refer to it as architecture, there's a certain mindset around that and I think we're talking about completely special architecture that avoids . . . I think that as things get going, there's a natural human tendency to try and formalize it. In this case that's going to kill it. It's how to maintain a generative architecture.

Speaker 2: So what's the generative architecture? That's a really good question. I used the phrase *formalized in formality*. To try and give people a language. We're going to be deliberately informal. Every time we interact, all the time. We're going to go out to dinner together. We're going to hang out. They would sing, and they would do stuff. After hours. Actually hanging out together. People would bring their wives. All kinds of stuff. There were three basic components: create the container, create the setting, create the seed in which a new possibility could be seen. That does involve getting people to talk together who wouldn't otherwise, mapping, articulating stuff that's somewhat hidden. There's a bunch of to do.

Postscript
The author's reflections, written some months after the conference

In the months since last year's conference, as I have reflected on my work in South Asia, a number of thoughts have emerged about how such endeavors unfold. What is most striking about the Champions process is its generative and organic nature. Each step built on the last, and each expanded its reach and the depth of understanding of participants, leading now to a global effort on climate change. In retrospect the process looks as if it was carefully planned, when in fact we had little idea of each next step until we were nearly upon it. And yet looking back, a remarkable series of significant strategic investments did get made, and a fundamentally new level of engagement across the region formed that continues to this day.

Several technical insights also emerged. First was the essential nature of the architecture of containers—a wide, holistic design process that creates the space, or "holding environment" for the organic unfolding. Second, the need to shift "accepted boundaries" among all participants, to expand their frames at all levels about what is possible. Third, the necessity that the champions own the process as something *they* are doing. Finally, for organizations sponsoring these efforts, the need to be less insistent on announcing and taking credit for developments under way, and to be sensitive to the right timing to make these efforts more visible. Premature institutional insistence on visibility and credit only hinders innovation and the generative nature the process.

Facilitating this process required that I develop a deep appreciation of and respect for the nuances of context—the historic context within each country, and the personal contexts each Champion brought to the table. This does not mean learning the details of their history; it means listening for the music behind the words, the unconscious factors seeking to emerge. I also have come to see that generalized approaches to dialogue, or didactic efforts to "teach" dialogue, would have instantly failed. People learned by seeing dialogue in action.

What emerged most prominently for me is the need to deepen my model of teaching how to facilitate dialogue. The most important skills and tactics are subtle ones that are difficult to convey, leading to a wide gap between people's intellectual ideas about dialogue and their ability to evoke the experience of it. This is the learning edge I am focused on now.

The Netherlands in Dialogue: A Structural Approach to Dialogue Across Society

Olga Plokhooij

I consider dialogue to be the method of the future. It is a method that connects, and of which listening to the other is perhaps the most essential element. Dialogue can be used much more than discussion and debate, in which one's own interests are often paramount, to develop shared views and support for the major societal changes that are currently under discussion.
— Herman Wijffels, former Executive Director of the World Bank, quoted as ambassador of *The Netherlands in Dialogue* (2009)

It is the ninth of September, 2009: coordinators, trainers and dialogue facilitators from 36 cities are gathered at the Okura Hotel in Amsterdam for the national meeting of *The Netherlands in Dialogue* (NID). National ambassadors and partner organizations are present, and they express their wish to strengthen social cohesion in the Netherlands by organizing dialogue gatherings across all segments of society.

I feel butterflies in my stomach as I wander across the room. It is a festive gathering; we celebrate the fact that, since its inception in 2005, we have grown into a national dialogue network with 56 local Days of Dialogue across the country. On this day we will explore the future of *NID* by hosting 25 dialogue round tables with some 200 stakeholders. Nearly all committed colleagues with whom we have worked on both a national and local scale are present. Copies of the book we created about the first years of *The Netherlands in Dialogue* are displayed.

We have also invited people from other dialogue movements in the Netherlands. We see this meeting as both an impetus to increase the number of Days of Dialogue and for more exchange between the various schools of thought shaping dialogue across the country. It is a collaboration that is obvious, but it is one that has not yet been established. My butterflies flutter restlessly.

Fast-forward to September 2019: ten years have passed since that memorable meeting at the Okura Hotel. I'm surrounded by boxes of archive material: 15 years of correspondence, photos, flyers and reflections pass through my hands. I reflect on how this national social movement, *The Netherlands in Dialogue*, came into being. I'm looking back on what we've accomplished, what dilemmas we've faced. I'm writing down my personal story to express my appreciation and recognition to all concerned, and to show what we're proud of. I want to share lessons and dilemmas so that they can be used by people who work with dialogue in society and also by other social entrepreneurs who will most probably recognize our journey in their own work.

The recent decision to terminate *The Netherlands in Dialogue* in its old form is another incentive to write this article, as well as an invitation I received from the Academy of Professional Dialogue to write a paper for their conference in October.

Story of Our Evolution

The first Day of Dialogue was organized in Rotterdam in 2002, initiated by the municipality of Rotterdam and a large number of social organizations. The urban debates in Rotterdam, among other places, following the attacks in New York on 11 September 2001, did not appear to contribute to the cohesion of the city. The group of active Rotterdammers foresaw that *dialogue* would be more suitable to building understanding and connection than *debate*, so they initiated the facilitation of dialogue round tables during what they called a Day of Dialogue. The Brahma Kumaris spiritual movement proposed *Appreciative Inquiry*, first developed by David Cooperrider, as a form of dialogue. Appreciative Inquiry focuses on determining what is already going well and what we dream of for the future. All participants' experiences contributed to the joint research for this first Day of Dialogue. The event in Rotterdam turned out to be very successful.

Roos Nabben, co-initiator of the Day of Dialogue in Rotterdam and active partner in *NID* said of this event:

> *[The] Day of Dialogue offers people safety to experiment with accepting others. People take a few hours to really talk to each other, to listen to someone with whom they wouldn't easily come into contact in their daily lives. By doing so, you will overcome your prejudices and practice unbiased listening . . . Everybody is part of me. The dialogue makes me realize that.*

Personal Commitment

In 2002 I was working as a board advisor on Diversity Policy at the Municipality of Amsterdam when a colleague from Rotterdam called to tell me about the success of their dialogue initiative. I was about to leave for Guatemala at that moment, where I was working on a political agenda for the Mayan people with former Guatemalan congresswoman Manuela Alvarado. The way she applied dialogue fascinated me. Throughout the country we organized gatherings at which Manuela hosted conversations in circles varying from 10 to 150 people. She made sure that everyone always spoke in an atmosphere of respect and equality. Because of the 36 years of civil war that the country had known, the experiences that were shared had an emotional charge. I was intrigued by the depth of the conversation that came from letting each other talk without interruption, knowing that everyone would have their say, and by the way she held the space for the conversation. I spent the last leg of my trip in Ojai, California, studying the dialogues between Krishnamurti and David Bohm about consciousness. I returned to the Netherlands full of inspiration and the calling to contribute to dialogue in society. I chose the Day of Dialogue as the vehicle to do so.

An Action Plan for Amsterdam

Upon my return in 2004 I started working at Nieuwe Maan [New Moon], a partnership of independent entrepreneurs who formed coalitions around social themes through cooperation between the government, business community, social organizations and others. My colleague Danielle Driessen and I decided to organize the Day of Dialogue in Amsterdam. We visited the organizers in Rotterdam and participated in their dialogue training for facilitators. Based on this, we developed an action plan for Amsterdam that would include, among other things, greater involvement of the business community.

What appeals to me about the concept of the Day of Dialogue is that it makes dialogue accessible. By taking it out of an intellectual sphere and placing it in society, we found that it was attractive to a wide audience. The dialogue approach is simple, and the threshold for participation is low. Although dialogue can be conducted in more sophisticated ways, the simplicity makes the approach well suited to a social initiative aimed at strengthening social cohesion. I look at this approach as a form of Spanish tapas. You taste a little bite, which hopefully makes you long for more.

The tragic murder of cinematographer Theo van Gogh on 2 November 2004 in Amsterdam increased the urgency for people to talk to each other about the ways different population groups relate to each other. It reinforced the commitment of the municipality, and it ensured significant participation of civil society and religious organizations, schools, the police and the business community. On this first Amsterdam Day of Dialogue in December 2004, a hundred dialogues took place. Afterwards the mayor called for a year-round dialogue. In 2005 we organized the second and third Days of Dialogue in cooperation with a growing number of organizations and participants.

National Roll-Out of the Day of Dialogue

After a visit to the Knowledge Centre for Large Cities Policy in 2005, I found myself at the train station in The Hague with my colleague Danielle Driessen and Marcel Kreuger of the LBR [Landelijk Bureau Racismebestrijding, or National Bureau Against Racism, now Art.1].

For some time before this auspicious meeting we had been investing in building a coalition of national partners who would jointly spread the Day of Dialogue throughout the Netherlands. It turns out it was not an easy assignment we had given ourselves. We got a lot of sympathy but no active participation or financial contribution. I felt many of my colleagues had second thoughts about our mission. Now, standing at the train platform as if struck by lightning, I experienced clarity and an ardent drive to spread the dialogue on a large scale. It was vocational call that I would later recognize in a number of my other dialogue colleagues. It gave me the energy to draw from in good times and bad. This moment at the station is still very much in my mind.

A breakthrough followed in December 2005, when then-Princess (now Queen) Máxima was present at the third Day of Dialogue in Amsterdam. Shortly after her visit, the royal Orange Fund, which supports projects that build social cohesion and participation, announced that it would invest in the roll-out of the Netherlands Day of Dialogue for the next three years. Over the previous months we had gathered a number of people from government, business, science and civil society organizations and asked them to commit to our initiative. We now asked them to join us and provide support through their network by a financial contribution and by organizing dialogue round tables. For them, the added value lay not only in the social objective, but also in cross-sectoral collaboration.

In addition to the Orange Fund, the University of Amsterdam, the Knowledge Centre for Large Cities, Rabobank and, later, the Albert Heijn supermarket chain, social housing provider Ymere, the LGBTI support network COC, the Red Cross Netherlands and coworking and meeting space network Seats2meet participated. The strength of this national coalition proved to be enormous. The partners organized their own dialogue round table and invited their customers and employees to join in. Because of the variety of national partners, local initiators of a Day of Dialogue could involve the local branches of these national partners. An important condition for the success of the event was the diversity of those involved. Through contact with the national coalition, the local organizing working groups and at the dialogue round table themselves, target groups that would not normally meet with each other found themselves in conversation, greatly enriching the sense of diversity.

What Does a Day of Dialogue Look Like?

The idea behind the Day of Dialogue is simple and effective. The core of the time consists of one or more dialogue circles of six to eight people gathering and exchanging experiences around a central theme. The conversation follows a predefined process and is hosted by a trained facilitator. On the Day of Dialogue, these conversations take place in all kinds of different places in a city, village or district. There are dialogue round tables at the town hall, in the mosque/church/synagogue/temple, at police stations, schools, banks, supermarkets, the market, the library, the COC centre, welfare organizations and in people's homes. A local coordinator ensures that the backgrounds of the participants at a dialogue round table are diverse. The mix of people in a dialogue increases the probability that new connections are made between those who would otherwise not easily have met.

Dialogue Facilitator
A facilitator guides the dialogue, which lasts at least two hours. He or she will be trained for this a few weeks in advance. In this training we practice the basic principles of dialogue facilitation and the questions that have been developed for the specific theme that is of relevance to the local community.

Dialogue Approach
As mentioned, the dialogue approach of *NID* is based on the Appreciative Inquiry method. AI is the art and skill of asking questions about the desired future. The assumption is that by visualizing the ideal situation we create our own reality, and one held in common. The components of AI were translated into four steps in the dialogue and complemented with moments of silence and introspection.

> **Four Steps in the Dialogue**
> 1. **Getting to know** each other and the subject of the dialogue
> 2. **Sharing experiences** about the subject
> 3. **Dreaming** about the ideal situation
> 4. **Doing it!** Sharing the first step are you going to take to make your dream come true

These four steps, framed as four questions to guide the conversation (outlined in the 'Questions for the Four Steps' box below), have proven to be effective. They offer participants the opportunity to share personal experiences and listen to others while setting aside judgement. Also, by describing the ideal situation in the form of a dream (Step 3 in the box below), a positive, forward-looking energy is created. It is not uncommon for participants' dreams to touch or overlap. The connection that is experienced in sharing dreams creates fertile ground to name your first step after the dialogue.

Facilitator Training
The training we offer to large groups of dialogue facilitators in preparation for the Day of Dialogue offers a basic introduction to Appreciative Inquiry. It mainly focuses on engaging in dialogue, practicing as a facilitator and getting feedback. The organizers prepare the guiding questions in advance and provide a compass for the dialogue.

Theme

The theme for a local Day of Dialogue is determined by the local organizing parties who know what is happening in their community. Over the years, themes such as *Belonging*, *Me and The Other*, *Freedom*, *Living and Working Together* and *Peaceful Together* have been chosen. Here are four questions used to guide a session of the theme of Belonging:

Questions for the Four Steps: Belonging
Step 1: Introduce yourself briefly. What does belonging mean to you?   **Step 2:** When did you feel completely at home? Where was that? How did that happen?   **Step 3:** What does the city look like when everyone is part of it?   **Step 4:** Which step will you take tomorrow to contribute to this?

Conversation Rules

In the dialogue we use conversation rules that help bring the participants into the right state of mind and encourage joint responsibility. The facilitator outlines these at the start:

- Let the other person tell his or her story
- Don't interrupt
- Don't immediately respond with your own story
- Treat each other with respect and kindness
- Speak from personal experience ("I find" instead of "they say")
- Ask for an explanation if there are any generalities on the table
- Postpone judgements and examine them
- Allow silences

Foundation for the Day of Dialogue

As a foundation for the day, we create six pillars that emphasize our working values:

Six Pillars
1. It is a social initiative for the city of citizens and organizations. It is not the property of one person or organization.   2. Dialogues take place in varied groups of six to eight people at round tables throughout the city/population.   3. The dialogues focus on one central theme and follow a fixed approach with four steps.   4. The dialogues are led by facilitators who have followed a preparatory dialogue training.   5. The personal responsibility of the participants is central to the conversation.   6. A central organizer coordinates and takes care of communication and publicity.

Nationwide Offer

Based on the experiences in Rotterdam and Amsterdam, in 2006 we drew up a handbook for organizers, containing the six pillars of the Day of Dialogue and an outline of the dialogue approach. People who wanted to start a Day of Dialogue in their town or village could attend the national training courses free of charge. What we asked in return was commitment to the six pillars, the dialogue approach and membership in the national network of coordinators. Together we would learn from the local successes and dilemmas.

The Impact of Dialogue

Jos Kessels, philosopher and author on the topic of Socratic conversation, has been involved from the beginning of the Day of Dialogue in Amsterdam. For a number of years, he kept track of the development of our dialogue training courses. When we asked him about the power of dialogue, Kessels emphasized that it gives people the feeling of belonging, which is an existential desire. As he said,

> *When the traditional ways of belonging disappear and our permanent identities become more fluid, temporary communities take on a more important role. After all, identity is no longer a fixed, lifelong fact, but the sum of those to whom you want to belong at some point. Cohesion is temporary involvement. On a Day of Dialogue, the dialogue is used as a form of conversation that creates space to jointly give meaning to the experiences of participants. By investigating an issue on the basis of their own experiences, participants get to know each other's vision, points of view and backgrounds. The vulnerable setup is disarming.*

When I was interviewed by the local broadcaster as to why I found the dialogue so valuable, my answer was that it is a form of conversation that can help to turn *fear into curiosity* through clear principles – curiosity about what is going on in yourself and in the relationship with others. You don't have to defend yourself. There is time, you can listen, you can ask questions. This way you can quietly investigate your own ideas and the way others think and feel. You can consider any new perspectives that open up and decide whether you want to adjust your ideas and actions. You don't *have* to change the way you think; you decide for yourself. It's enriching, whatever the outcome. In addition to a personal, inspirational experience, the dialogue often leads to new initiatives that strengthen mutual ties.

The exact magic of dialogue is not easy to explain in words. It has to do with the very personal character of the conversation. By asking participants about their experiences and not about their views or opinions, everyone is asked to show something of themselves. If one of the participants takes up this invitation and shares their personal story, it is almost a given that the other participants will do the same. Stories will emerge about situations that have touched or inspired people. Participants are often touched or even confused by the fact that their experiences are so similar, while still perceiving each other as being so different.

Loes de Jong, a philosopher who was involved in the Day of Dialogue for many years, put it this way:

I have been working with all kinds of dialogue for years, and I still do not understand exactly how the magic of dialogue arises. The strength lies in a listening attitude, not judging what you hear instantly, but asking questions. Put aside the easy "yes but . . .". Then you start to see what moves others and ask yourself what your own motives and beliefs are – and whether they are correct.

The transcending of one's own experience or vision, precisely because it is articulated, can lead to a common experience of flow where words seem to form themselves in space, apart from the individuals and the group. They come from another place, another consciousness.

Research into the Impact of the Day of Dialogue

In 2006, we decided to have the Day of Dialogue in Amsterdam studied for effectiveness by Evelien Tonkens, Professor of Active Citizenship of the University of Amsterdam. At this point we were regularly asked about the results of a dialogue and the Day of Dialogue. Sceptics wondered if it really is more than a nice conversation with a cup of tea with like-minded people, and they assumed it wouldn't have an impact on the social climate in the city. Participants, on the other hand, were invariably surprised by the impact that a 2.5-hour conversation with strangers had on their ideas, and the sense of connection with others. The results of the study, which included attendance at dialogue round tables, in-depth interviews with participants, round table organizers and dialogue facilitators, were promising. The study's findings were presented in a report entitled 'Talking Helps'*. The report concluded that 'incidental, structured group dialogues between citizens from different backgrounds can also make a meaningful contribution to greater mutual understanding and connection'.

Some results of the study:

- 65% of the respondents met people they wouldn't otherwise get in touch with so easily.
- 80% learned a lot from the conversation.
- 41% changed their minds about the subject under enquiry. More than half of them felt more connected to other Amsterdammers.

---

* Tonkens, Evelien (2006). *Talking helps! Evaluation of the effects of the Amsterdam Day of Dialogue by Evelien Tonkens, Professor of Active Citizenship.* UvA, Amsterdam.

After another four months, all respondents were approached to see to what extent the effects had lasted. The 64 surveys and 17 in-depth interviews showed that:

- 81% were stimulated to think by the conversation.
- 64% gained new insights.
- 50% were interested in a return day.

National Evaluation
In 2009, seven years after the first Day of Dialogue, we decided to carry out a large-scale evaluation. This time we researched the national network. The evaluation focused on the experiences of the participants during the dialogue. Among other things, the study examined the motivation and goal of participation, the satisfaction of the participants and the possible consequences of the Day of Dialogue.

Among the 12,000 people who entered into dialogue during the National Dialogue Week of 2009, 6,950 forms were distributed by participating local coordinators. Of these, 2,414 were returned, a surprisingly high response rate of almost 35 percent. The national evaluation, based on the surveys and individual interviews, showed that participants experienced the dialogue positively in ways that paralleled the initial study of the Day of Dialogue in Amsterdam.

The evaluation results also showed that, while people with a variety of different personal characteristics (e.g., gender, age, ethnicity, sexual orientation, education) participated in the Day of Dialogue, diversity deserves more attention in the future. The distribution in terms of age, gender, education and ethnic origin was disproportionate; that is, more women than men took part in the survey, the majority were of Dutch descent and almost half of all respondents were highly educated. The dialogue round tables tend to become more homogeneous the longer the Day of Dialogue is established in a community. The need to focus on diversity in the organization and the network every year remains strong. If the organization of the Day of Dialogue consolidates into a small group of people or even one organization, the diversity decreases.

Activities Over the Years

National Program and Handbook
In addition to a handbook we produced in 2006 about the organization of a Day of Dialogue, we designed and later promoted the training for organizers of a Day of Dialogue at a wide range of national and local events. We offered experiences with a dialogue as part of the promotion. We developed workshops, a dialogue facilitator training and, over two years' time, refined our offer. By the end of 2007 we had a solid national program that included training new local dialogue coordinators and meetings with existing coordinators, a train-the-trainer program for dialogue facilitators and a completed national evaluation with all stakeholders.

Butterfly Power, Butterfly Simplicity

In 2008, we decided to produce a book on our experiences in order to increase national awareness and increase the number of dialogue sites. The book was titled *Butterfly Power, Butterfly Simplicity,* referring to the impact that the apparently small movement of a butterfly wing can have. In the book, prominent figures and participants spoke about the value of engaging in a dialogue. We also explored what *dialogue* actually means. The frequent use of the word does not always do justice to the specific conversation type. In the Netherlands, *dialogue* is widely used in political contexts. There it seems interchangeable with *discussion*, *debate* and *negotiation*. In the book we draw attention to the value of dialogue by explaining how essential attentive listening, equality and enquiry rather than persuasion are in this type of conversation.

Ahmed Aboutaleb, former Dutch State Secretary and now mayor of Rotterdam, writes in the foreword of the book:

> *Ideally, people should give their housekeys to their neighbours. Trust is the basis of a stable community. But at the moment, mistrust is the most important thing in society and that worries me. If we're afraid of each other, everything stops . . . We have to build bridges to get together and take away distrust. I regard Amsterdam and Rotterdam as social laboratories. The Day of Dialogue is a great initiative that originated from the Rotterdam society. Day of Dialogue should therefore be nominated for the Peace Prize.*

National Dialogue Week

2008 was also the start of the National Dialogue Week, taking place the first week of November. By working together and organizing all local Days of Dialogues in one week, the movement became more visible. We filled the week with national events and asked ambassadors to speak out about the social value of dialogue. An example of this is the quote of Wijffels at the beginning of the article. As coordinators, we provided national press releases that could also be used locally to get attention through the newspaper, radio and TV, and we were regularly successful.

European Year of Intercultural Dialogue

The movement continued to gain momentum. As part of the European Year of Intercultural Dialogue, we organized a European Conference on the Day of Dialogue in 2008, with the participation of representatives from 16 countries.

Network of Local Coordinators

In addition to the national program, which included the offer to train new local coordinators, we deepened and sharpened our offerings, including in-depth dialogue training. The national network meetings, where local coordinators and trainers were asked to share their successes and dilemmas, grew rapidly. The meetings gave rise to more and more substantive exchanges and an annual selection of a national theme for the Dialogue Week. Also, we began to see more diversity in how the different local coordinators shaped their Day of Dialogue. Some organized the event deliberately without the need for payment, while others focused on specific target groups such as young people or migrants.

The National Organization

Looking back, the dialogue movement went through a number of stages of development.
From an inspired intention in 2005 and learning while doing, we grew into a movement with:

- 100 local dialogue coordinators for a Day of Dialogue
- 40 trained trainers
- About 3,000 trained dialogue facilitators
- 10 national and hundreds of local partner organizations
- Well-known ambassadors
- A foundation with a board

Between 2006 and 2011 we provided national coordination with a budget between 35,000 and 125,000 euros per year, with a peak in 2012 of 300,000 euros because of income from a new partnership. From 2013 onwards, the funds decreased, and it became more difficult to find a budget for the national activities. In 2012 and 2013, we explored the possibility of becoming a social enterprise, maximizing the good we could do while providing income for stakeholders.

Bruce Tuckman's team-phase model provided a framework for categorizing our stages of development:

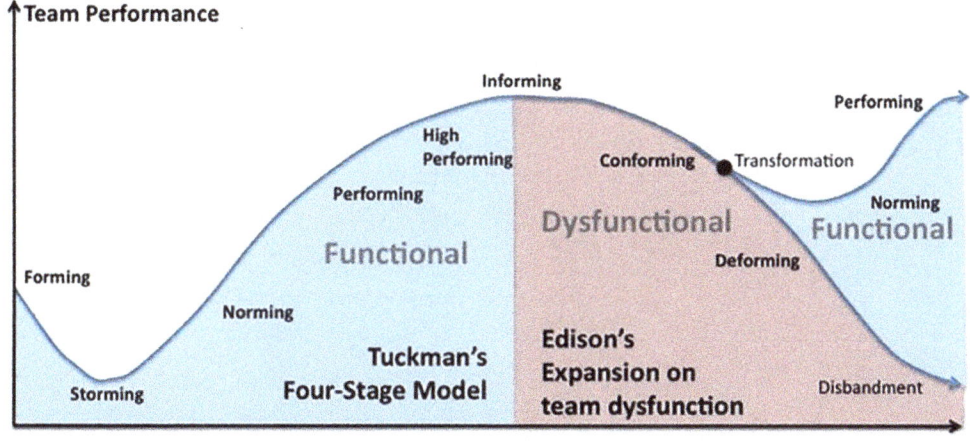

Figure 1 – this illustration shows the full-cycle of a team's development, from its initial formation to its potential decline unless there is a transformation initiated (adapted from Edison [6])

Forming Phase

As outlined, in the early years of 2005 to 2007 we worked part-time with three professionals from Nieuwe Maan and Art.1 to build up the initiative. Thanks to the financing of the Orange Fund and the fact that the professionals weren't dependent on *The Netherlands in Dialogue* for their funding, an idealistic motive prevailed over a commercial one. This allowed progress also to be made in less successful stages of the initiative. From 2006 we were able to financially cover a number of the professionals' hours. Other partners also contributed financially and offered manpower and training locations. We developed materials such as the organizers' handbook and we offered presentations and experiences of dialogue throughout the country. This national aspect of the initiative is still called 'The Day of Dialogue Everywhere in the Netherlands'.

We offered our training courses and materials free of charge for the local coordinators, who were responsible for setting up and funding their own local Day of Dialogue. In exchange for this, they became participants in the national network of coordinators; we asked them to use the house style of the Day of Dialogue so that their events were recognizable as part of the country's overall program. From 2005 to 2013 the number of villages or cities with a Day of Dialogue grew from three to 100.

Storming Phase

To our joy, the Orange Fund honoured our request for two years of additional funding in 2009 and 2010. Because of this we were able to continue to build on the growth of the national network of local coordinators. However, this growth brought new challenges. Coordinators were now faced with such issues as cooperation with their municipality, applications for subsidies, working with unpaid volunteers and creating communications plans. At the same time, the demand for facilitator trainings and trainer prep continued to grow, which led to more investment in trainings and marketing, including a website and a digital meeting place.

The increasingly active national partner organizations such as Albert Heijn and Rabobank organized dialogue round tables at their offices across the country. The telephone at the national coordination was ringing off the hook and we were flooded by a daily stream of emails. We worked from a mix of proactive vision creation and reactive answering of questions coming to us from the network. In other words, we were *learning by doing*.

It was an energetic, successful, informal period that we enjoyed with many people. It was also a period that helped build a more well-oiled national organization, where quicker answers could be given to questions asked by both local coordinators and national partners.

Norming Phase

In 2010 the national coordinators started to collaborate with students of the Breda University of Applied Sciences who were taking part in ImaginHeroes, a program for social entrepreneurship. Together we created a good back office. The students took care of meeting planning, trainings for local coordinators and the National Dialogue Week. We now called this part of the activities the Foundational Program. The students developed new concepts for marketing and communication and improved the organizational model. The national coordination was complemented by a National Advisory Committee with ambassadors and an Advisory Board. In 2011 we reflected as a total network – national and local – on a sharpened vision and mission for *The Netherlands in Dialogue*.

Until the end of 2011, the *NID* movement had no legal structure. However, due to the increasing number of activities, the development of a much larger budget and more brand awareness, a growing number of partners wanted to create a legal framework for our movement. We undertook a comprehensive review of legal requirements.

Establishing a Foundation – and a Pioneer's Heart

After extensive consultation and deliberations, we set up *The Netherlands in Dialogue* Foundation at the end of 2011. Although this would help keep the work transparent, some had doubts as to whether the network, which had hitherto been organized on an equal footing, would benefit from a more hierarchical form with a director and a supervisory board. The ownership of the initiative would no longer rest with the initiators and implementers, but formally with the board in which financing partners take part.

From the very beginning of the foundation, I experienced tension around the role of managing director. I discovered that I am more of a pioneer than a manager. More and more time was needed to write annual plans and reports. Meetings became more formal and the board now had the final say. My ambivalent attitude to take on the role of managing director and preference to remain a member of the network retrospectively impacted both the network and my enthusiasm. We were 'suddenly' an organization with a planning cycle and a program. My pioneer's heart hurt a bit.

Performing Phase

As a foundation we strove for a wider spread of our dialogue approach than just during the Day of Dialogue. The dialogue could be added to existing national initiatives such as the Peace Week, the Week of Respect and the National Integration Dinners. In this heyday of 'performance', our three main activities were all beginning to face their own challenges:

I. Foundational Program for Organizing the Day of Dialogue
The national offer for coordinators was called the foundational program. It consisted of the

training courses for new coordinators described above. In addition, there were three meetings a year where coordinators met to exchange experiences, share ambitions and deepen their knowledge on issues that arise in connection with questions about infrastructure and development. Together we organized the National Dialogue Week for the first week of November. The network was becoming more tightly knit.

II. Methodology Group

We next noticed that some local trainers had started to experiment with variations on our form of dialogue. The positive side of this was that the dialogue offer was being broadened, but it made it difficult to guarantee the quality of the dialogue on a national level. Dialogue facilitation trainings have a major influence on the quality of the dialogue facilitators, and thus have a direct influence on the quality of the dialogue experienced by the participants.

Tension arose here and there around the agreements with local coordinators to base their dialogues on Appreciative Inquiry on the Day of Dialogue. We communicated this approach on the national website and in press releases, which created expectations among participants and organizations.

The first real challenge in terms of network growth was beginning to emerge. The network had become so large, diverse and independent that some network members began to express their own preferences. As national coordination body we were celebrating this development but, at the same time, we were concerned about the quality of dialogue guidance. We did not have the people or resources to provide thorough monitoring. We decided to set up a training and methodology working group to examine, in consultation with the network, the concerns and opportunities about quality. This working group consisted of trainers with whom we had worked from the very beginning, supplemented by people who brought experience from different dialogue approaches.

Together with Danielle Dietz from Imaginheroes we worked out the foundation for professionalizing the training courses and monitoring quality.

In 2012 we organized an informal national gathering about the methodology, with stakeholders who also have experience with other forms of dialogue. The gathering was chaotic, with personal pleas for the right form of dialogue and the associated methodology. Some people were of the opinion that dialogue could not be conducted without a talking stick, while others stood behind a Socratic, Bohmian or Appreciative Inquiry approach. I was overwhelmed by the dogmatism; together with my colleagues, we took a good look in the mirror. Was this an effect of our own clear preference for a single dialogue approach? And did we, by choosing the name *The Netherlands in Dialogue*, perhaps made too great a claim on dialogue for the country? It was valuable that the undercurrent came up and that we were talking.

III. Innovation

With decreasing financial contributions from the business community or funding subsidies, we began researching other ways to generate revenue. I personally put a lot of time and effort in this. Significantly, we developed a partnership with Rabobank and the World Wildlife Fund under the name World=U. Our goal was to bring young people together in dialogue on the themes of world citizenship, food and climate. *The Netherlands in Dialogue* contributed dialogue as a form of conversation, and we provided professionals who could guide groups of young people and facilitate dialogue. The partnership around World=U was a great success, with 35 dialogue groups totalling more than 200 young people who initiated local programs. Could *this* be a way to independently gain income?

Despite the success, selecting the guiding professionals was a source of tension within the network of *The Netherlands in Dialogue*. On what criteria was the selection of these professionals based? Whose decision was it to choose who could be professionally hired? Who was going to earn money within the network?

Consolidation and Contraction

The year 2013 was the beginning of a particularly challenging time. The means for organizing national events was drying up. The economic recession was causing the Corporate Social Responsibility budgets of companies to decline. We also had to deal with the 'not invented here' syndrome when we try to involve new partner organizations, underlining the common preference for innovation over supporting established initiatives. We explored a number of ideas for creating alternative income, including setting up a national facilitator database, offering paid dialogue trainings and creating new partnerships and pilot programs. However, the ideas generally did not come to fruition, partly because they caused tensions between the national organization and the local network of coordinators. At several regional meetings it became clear that some local coordinators were afraid that inequality would creep into the network if we started earning money. Who would then decide which trainers, dialogue facilitators and advisors would be eligible for professional deployment? How would this relate to the people who organized the local Days of Dialogue on a voluntary basis?

After several regional meetings we came to the conclusion that we would not transform into a social enterprise with its own revenue model. The majority of the network was not in favour of that path. As national coordination, we decided not to force the choice.

Decision-Making and Dialogue

Personally, I experienced this as a difficult juncture as I strongly believed in the possibilities, and professionally I foresaw the difficult times into which we were entering as a foundation. We received several rejections of financial applications from new and existing partners. In retrospect I think the national coordination and the network of local coordinators had different priorities, and we had no clear decision-making process. When we consulted with our coordinators and partners, for example, most of the underlying questions that arose seemed to be about the decision-making jurisdiction of the managing director and foundation board: who decides the future of a network that you have built up with some 100 local coordinators? Is 'centralized power' at odds with what we stand for in dialogue? Does the voice of everyone involved count equally?

Personal Transition

Because I had committed to making the transition to a social enterprise based on the positive experience with World=U, I decided to resign my position as managing director.

In 2013 Karin Oppelland succeeded me. She had been involved in the Day of Dialogue Rotterdam for many years and had collaborated intensively with me in *The Netherlands in Dialogue* for the past year. Karin chose to continue her work with *The Netherlands in Dialogue* on a voluntary basis, with the focus on the Day of Dialogue and Week. Her motto was, 'Together we are *The Netherlands in Dialogue*'. Due to a shrinking budget, national activities were decreasing. As time passed, the national partners withdrew. The network of active dialogue coordinators became smaller but tighter.

And these years of consolidation and contraction were marked by good highs. A number of national partnerships on themes such as happiness, peace and freedom were created in cooperation with civil society organizations such as Pax Christi, the National Happiness Route and the National Committee on 4 and 5 May. The National Dialogue Week continued, with more and more dialogue locally throughout the year. The focus turned to local and regional dialogue. In 2017, people celebrated 10 years of the National Dialogue Week with a dialogue festival in Venray.

The total activity in the network decreased further in 2016 to 2018. There were no more national partners or resources. Dialogue training courses that offered more depth in the choices of theme, consideration of the moderator's position, and different levels of listening were discussed, and the courses were still offered nationwide. However, the attendance at national gatherings was decreasing and some training sessions were cancelled because of last-minute cancellations by participants.

Transformation

In 2017 Karin invited six thinking partners, including me, to explore with her the future of *The Netherlands in Dialogue*. Without resources or partners, and low attendance at national meetings, the question arose as to whether and how the initiative could be transformed or reinvented to meet the needs of our time.

In a few intensive sessions we considered the origins of the Day of Dialogue, the methodology, the emergence of *The Netherlands in Dialogue* and the course of the movement. During the process Karin decided to resign her position. As her partners, we took on the role of interim board to make her departure possible.

After a few sessions as interim board with the still-active network, we decided that it was time to dissolve the foundation. It no longer had any function as a legal entity and it stood in the way of real transformation because of its hierarchical structure. By abandoning the form, the network of local coordinators could jointly address the question of *whether* and *how* they wanted to build up dialogue in society – perhaps under the same name, maybe in a whole new capacity.

We communicated the decision to the network on 19 June 2019. The foundation will be dissolved in October 2019. We decided to put all the developed materials on the website under a Creative Commons license. This way, the lovingly created material would be donated to the world and can move outward. The active members of the network have already met a number of times. Until they come to a conclusion about the future of the network, we have reserved the name of *The Netherlands in Dialogue* in order to be able to transfer it if necessary.

Social Context

The spirit of the age has an important influence on the origin and course of its initiatives. Around the time of 2006, more and more social pioneers in the Netherlands were embracing social themes that they did not see the government or any welfare organizations take up. Similarly, many factors influenced the later transitions of the dialogue movement in the Netherlands: the economic recession, a growing appreciation of entrepreneurship, a retreating government, the emergence of networks of freelancers who work together on social themes.

The rise of social media such as Facebook and Twitter and information technology created different kinds of opportunities. It is now possible, for example, to involve large groups of people in activities in a short period of time and in new ways.

Because we live in an era of change or, as Herman Verhagen and Jan Rotmans put it, even in a change of era, there were not many successful social enterprises with a focus on welfare when we started. Femke Zwaal (my colleague from Nieuwe Maan) and I therefore had decided to contribute to joint learning by setting up a growth program for social enterprises with the Orange Fund and the McKinsey and Company consulting firm in 2010. At the moment we look back on ten years of social entrepreneurship in the Netherlands with an eye to where the chances are of next achieving sustainable social enterprises in the welfare sector.

The Dilemmas and Questions over the Years

Over the years, we have achieved great successes with *The Netherlands in Dialogue*, as evidenced by the Active Citizenship Award we won in 2011 and the recognition we received for both World=U and *The Netherlands in Dialogue* from Liesbeth Spies, Minister of the Interior, at the Power in the Netherlands meeting in 2012. Yet we have learned at least as much from the dilemmas we have encountered and the questions with which we've wrestled – most of which are mentioned in this article. I'll briefly summarize these dilemmas, with some questions that accompany them:

Learning-Opportunity Dilemmas and Questions

Dialogue Approach
Our dialogue approach is easily transferable and introduces many people to the value of dialogue for the first time. However, there are also restrictions. Dialogue requires a specific attitude and awareness that cannot be captured in a structure. Due to the size of the network and its success it became more difficult to keep addressing both the strength *and* limitations of the approach. *How do you allow and propagate other forms of dialogue without creating confusion in our own network and constituencies?*

The Name of The Netherlands in Dialogue
The name *The Netherlands in Dialogue* expresses a clear, national mission and has contributed to its success. Specifically, we propagate the use of Appreciative Inquiry, so the name is associated with only this approach for dialogue. The name has therefore evoked resistance and a sense of competition in various long-standing schools of thought about dialogue. *How do you maintain a clear, national mission and explore the 'right' way of conducting dialogue with differing perspectives?*

Decision-Making
By becoming a foundation our network was formalized. However, the distance between the national partners, the national coordination and the local coordinators grew despite the gatherings and exchanges of thoughts. As national coordination, we ended up in a split. *How do you make decisions in an organically grown dialogue network – democratically or by partners in the board?*

Growth and Quality
Due to strong growth, at one point we worked with dozens of local trainers who transferred a form of dialogue to local dialogue facilitators. We trained about 3,000 people over the years. Because of the number of dialogue facilitators and trainers, and a poor administration in the first years of the movement, we lost sight of who had been trained and whether someone might be suitable as a dialogue facilitator. *How do you maintain quality across a rapidly growing network with limited resources?*

Organizational Form
The shift from a network of intrinsically motivated people to a more professional body organized as a foundation was impactful. The formal structure brought clarity and financial transparency, but also structures that were less inspiring and more formal. *How do you reconcile the benefits of an organic and personally motivated network against the clarity and transparency brought by a more formally structured entity such as a foundation?*

Voluntary Work
Locally, The Day of Dialogue often was organized by volunteers who worked without pay. Sometimes this was a conscious choice and sometimes it was for lack of resources. This high level of voluntary labour did not always make cooperation with national partner organizations easy. The national partners expected to be able to reach organizers all year round, but many local dialogue networks were only accessible around Dialogue Week or sometimes on one fixed day a week. *How do you balance the personal needs of unpaid volunteers with the more structured needs of partner organizations?*

World=U
The successful youth dialogue World=U, which we set up in partnership with local branches of Rabobank, meant that we needed about 10 dialogue professionals who were not only able to properly guide the dialogue in the manner of *NID* but also able to act as consultants. *On what criteria do you select these consultants? Whose decision is it to choose who could be professionally hired?*

Social Enterprise
Dependence on subsidies and donations makes us vulnerable. *How do you design a revenue model that delivers sufficient returns and from which everyone benefits sufficiently?*

Interest of the Government
In 2009 an advisor to the Prime Minister expressed his interest in The Netherlands in Dialogue. In exchange for funding, he wanted us to establish a national dialogue on sustainability. However, we would have had to impose the theme of sustainability top-down on all local Day of Dialogues. The national coordination chose not to do so. The reason was a matter of principle, as we were a bottom-up initiative, so time and energy was invested at the local level in the selection of a suitable theme that would attract people from all segments of society. How do you combine these fruitful opportunities with the principles of your organisation?

A Promising Time for Dialogue

Parallel to the developments within *The Netherlands in Dialogue*, beautiful encounters between people from different dialogue movements were taking place. The initial ambition for cooperation in 2009 is now shared by many dialogue enthusiasts in and outside the country. Slowly but surely, the field is ready for more mutual cooperation.

The establishment and first conference of the international Academy of Professional Dialogue, set up by Peter Garrett and Jane Ball among others in 2018, has given a current impulse to the national exchange between dialogue movements. As Dutch participants in the conference, we exchange experiences beyond feelings of competition, and we explore opportunities to connect with each other as dialogue professionals from different approaches. Together we bring decades of experience in the application and training of dialogue in social and organizational contexts.

Personal Reflection

Back in my office among the boxes of materials from *The Netherlands in Dialogue*, I realize that these experiences were the beginning of my working with dialogue and applying it professionally. I have developed a dialogical attitude and have increased my awareness by feeling and thinking constructively with others.

The fervent realization that I had at the train station in 2005, knowing that I would contribute to the spread of dialogue in society, feels in hindsight like a vocation. It gave me the opportunity to stand up for what I believe in. It gave me courage, guts and patience. It challenged me to take leadership without stepping out of the dialogue. It taught me to work with others and also to experience limits to growth. I made me aware of the high demands I place on quality and integrity. It brought with it the path of Socratic dialogue, Native-American Talking Circles, Kgotla, Deep Democracy, Bohmian dialogue and the work of William Isaacs, Joseph Jaworski, Peter Senge and Margaret Wheatley.

It was a deep experience with social entrepreneurship, and I was allowed to pass on many lessons to others. I got to know my limits by crossing them. This work has taught me when to let go of playing my role. It taught me that you can come back when your contribution is wanted again. It made me experience what transformation really means. But most of all, I learned so much from all those moments when I myself was in dialogue with others. I listened as a participant, allowed myself to be surprised, made myself vulnerable and asked for help when things became difficult.

My focus has been on personal and leadership development for a number of years now. Dialogue plays an important role when it comes to joint research into experiences and wisdom. At Leerweg Dialoog [Learning Dialogue] I give trainings with Renate van der Veen about what we believe are basic principles of dialogue, and we let people get acquainted with different approaches to dialogue. From Spirit of the Age, Femke Zwaal, Renate and I, together with a large network of partners, investigate the spirit of the age and the co-operation society demands of us around social issues.

Over the past five years, together with Rabobank, we have built up a professional and structured form of dialogue within their organization and with stakeholders. This collaboration has resulted in a dialogue centre of expertise within Rabobank. This centre is staffed by four professionals who provide internal advice on dialogue and shape regional dialogue processes. We were delighted to support Rabobank in learning to value, structure and implement dialogue. We trained more than a hundred dialogue facilitators within their organization. At the beginning of 2019, we concluded the partnership and Rabobank continued to develop its own training courses and now professionally organizes internal and external dialogue. We have completed a similar process with the Social and Economic Council, the National Employee Insurance Agency and the Royal Auris Group. Internationally, we promote the dialogue within the Council of Europe's network for Intercultural Cities.

From a relentless passion for dialogue, I continue to contribute to the national and international development of dialogue initiatives. And I look forward to working with other professionals.

References

Cooperrider, D. & Whitney, D. (2001). A Positive Revolution in Change: Appreciative Inquiry. Available at http://www.tapin.in/Documents/2/Appreciative%20Inquiry%20%20Positive%20Revolution%20in%20Change.pdf

Masselink, R., van den Nieuwenhof, R., Joep de Jong, et al. (2008). Waarderend organiseren – Appreciative Inquiry: Co-creatie van duurzame verandering.

Nederland in Dialoog (2008). *Vlinderlijke kracht, vlinderlijke eenvoud. Over de beweging Nederland in Dialoog*. Amsterdam. http://nederlandindialoog.nl/mediatheek/2

Nederland in Dialoog (2006). Handbook for organizing a Day of Dialogue. http://nederlandindialoog.nl/mediatheek/2

Tonkens, E. (2006). *Talking helps! Evaluation of the Effects of the Amsterdam Day of Dialogue*. Amsterdam: UvA.

van der Veen, R. and Plokhooij, O. (2018). Basisprincipes Dialoog. http://leerwegdialoog.nl/wp-content/uploads/2018/05/1801-Basisprincipes-Dialoog-Renate-van-der-Veen-Olga-Plokhooij.pdf

Useful Websites

www.nederlandindialoog.nl
www.leerwegdialoog.nl
www.spiritoftheage.nl

Conference Session Extracts

From a conversation with participants considering the paper with the author

Speaker 1: I was fascinated to read about the charity that you set up, and your experience of that. It's very relevant to me because of where the Academy's going with setting up charities in different countries. I was intrigued by your question, and it's mine as well: What is the magic that happens in dialogue? What brings that about so spontaneously?

Speaker 2: When I read the paper, I liked very much that you also reflected at the end with your own questions concerning the process. You're questioning what you have been doing. I think this kind of reflective approach helps us to really learn from what we're doing, and what we achieve or don't achieve. I've heard that many people are interested in what made it die. I'm more interested in what could it make *rise*. What are the conditions and what do we need to do, and what can we learn from your experience in order not to let something like that die in the future? To consider that collectively about different cultural backgrounds, because I think there could be differences. In South Africa maybe there are other needs than in Finland or Holland, or wherever. I'm interested in going into all your questions. I don't remember them in detail, but I think they're a good guideline for our conversation.

Speaker 3: Accountability. Yes, that's the word I wanted, thank you. That's my lack of English . . . Yeah. I'm not sure that a structure, or a hierarchy, or writing reports is the way to organize accountability. It is one way, but you take a high risk as well because you end up thinking – that if you do it, if you write reports, and make new plans, and get the money, and it's all organized properly – you might start to believe that the structure is what makes it work.

Speaker 4: I'm just thinking in my head like, Why do we establish an organization? Is it that we think about dialogue as being so fundamental and new that we don't trust that there is dialogue in other people in their workplaces? There is a little bit of dialogue, everywhere!

Speaker 5: But that's the systemic challenge isn't it? How did you get dialogue into the system? That's the systemic change. Because I was thinking something like, "Who cares about the organization? What matters is what's needed". I'm asking: Did *The Netherlands In Dialogue* achieve what it was trying to achieve? And if it did, then it could [close], and anything could happen next. Whether it's a one-off event or an organization that lasted 10 years or 100 years – in order to do what? And if you have achieved what it was trying to achieve, then you are probably done. Whereas in contrast, in systemic work it is getting it embedded so that it's continuous in the organizations that we have. These are two slightly different things, I think.

Speaker 6: Take the great European experiment. It was begun in the face of fascism, with the intention to remain vigilant about fascism, which seems to me is critically important. Fascism appears and reappears, and we need organizations to resist fascism. You can't just make speeches about it on platforms and then disappear, because those fascist guys are working hard. They are well-known names, and we accept them as politicians, when actually they have no interest in the politic, the body politic. And then when I think of what the present government has done to education, distributing responsibility to let every local school decide for itself, let every local health unit decide for itself. Why? We don't want to take responsibility for the whole.

I think it's important that in the discussion about going beyond organizations, we don't dismiss the value of organization. We don't have to do it all locally. We need the authority of government. Greta Thunberg, the 16-year-old Swedish girl, knows that she needs governments to act – forcibly and powerfully.

Speaker 7: How would we ideally organize a large-scale dialogue initiative in society? Can we dream about that? What would be the ingredients? What would that look like? Who would like to start sharing his or her dream?

Speaker 8: We're doing an experiment with 25 people just to see what the interest is. We wanted some climate activists and some climate experts involved, so we put the invitation out and 25 people signed up in three days. And now what we plan in 2020 is to have a series of seven big-venue meetings. And this all emerged in the conversation the five of us were having. We're going to bring in experts, activists, scientists and so on to present a big piece up front. We'll give them 45 minutes and then open the dialogue. I don't know where it's going to go but that's what has emerged.

We want to bring together politicians, who have such a hard time, and scientists, on the issue of climate change and in such a way that it becomes televised. We want their dialogue to become available on the television networks so that the dialogue is visible. That is the critical thing for us. That it's not just a cosy discussion, and that's the aspiration. And I could imagine some little collaboration with you. And so what gets televised is bigger than this small country.

Speaker 9: I am very interested. We work in Austria and we train practitioners, but my great worry with that is that the training institute is so disconnected from society. The point where I am is that I have no idea how, but I would like to find a way to see how we can be in dialogue. How can we get dialogue from this more elite training place into society? And I just carry this dream, but I feel like when you do a training institute, you can just make a plan and do it. There are some people who want to do it too. But something like this, where do you start? And what I do now is that I'm just talking to people and finding the people out there who are already [taking action]. Somehow we are engaged in initiatives or in the same spirit to bring dialogue into community, to bring it throughout.

Speaker 10: It seems to me, looking at all the people here, that the people who have experienced dialogue in some situation or another, are sort of inherently drawn towards it again. What I'd like to have in Finland would be the possibility in people's minds that dialogue is something you can actually learn. We have this mystifying language of personal chemistry and charisma, and what else? Atmosphere. Things that people say when they experience dialogue: "Oh, it was such a nice atmosphere, and we've got such a good personal chemistry despite our differences". It is a skill, it's an art, and it can be learned, but it's something that people think is sort of somewhere beyond learning. I would like to bring it into focus on the learning as an art, a skill.

Postscript
The author's reflections, written some months after the conference

The request by the Academy to write an article about our 15-year process with *The Netherlands in Dialogue* (NID), coincided with the moment we decided to terminate the foundation in its present form. The NID network was in need of transformation. The mission to build locally rooted dialogue networks was more than successful. The national foundation no longer added any concrete value. In fact, the impasse in which the national foundation had found itself seemed to inhibit the start of a new phase. The writing of the paper became a precious process. For weeks I searched through the archives. It helped to reflect, learn lessons and created a sense of pride in what we had achieved.

Renate van der Veen, my business partner at Leerweg Dialoog and I, facilitated the workshop at the conference. The central question was: "What is your dream for dialogue in society?" A conversation unfolded around questions such as why we ended a successful initiative, what had gone wrong and whether we would choose a specific method again. It was an inspiring conversation because we saw the completion of the foundation as a logical phase in a country where dialogue is growing. It marked the end of an era – an era of 15 years in which many dialogue professionals were dedicated to spreading the dialogical conversation. It was an era in which dialogue 'currents' such as Socratic conversation, Bohmian dialogue, Talking Circles and Appreciative Inquiry were separated into different foundations and companies. This suited the *zeitgeist* of emancipation.

The exchange in the conference workshop helped to articulate all this more clearly: what it means; what we learned; what the spirit of the times is; what this requires in terms of grasping momentum; and letting go and moving on. As many experiences from other countries were shared, we were overwhelmed by the energy in the room!

Meanwhile, in the Netherlands, we have been steadily building a network consisting of various dialogue currents for almost two years now. It is a network in which abrasive views are just as much a part of the collaboration as the richness of the overlap we experience in vision and practice. The Academy dialogue conferences have stimulated this.

In addition to these developments, Renate and I continue our thriving business in professionally facilitating and training dialogical conversations in organizations. We are thankful for the inspiration that came from both the writing of the article and the exchange in the workshop in October 2019!

Dialogue for Social Change: A Practical Case Study

Ove D Jakobsen and Vivi ML Storsletten

In Western societies, where the mechanical world view has dominated since the 18th century, we tend to evaluate developments through measurable indicators such as economic and technological growth. One of the most important features of this kind of thinking is that technical solutions are to be universally applied regardless of the cultural or natural context. The market economy, based on competition between autonomous actors, is an illustrative example of a mechanical system that is supposed to stimulate growth and increase welfare wherever it is implemented and practiced. The idea is that the business model is all-seeing; therefore, technology becomes the most important tool for social change. Today's global economy is a network of financial flows that are mechanically constructed without a culturally conditioned ethical framework. The result is that social inequality is "widening the gap between the rich and the poor and increasing world poverty" (Capra and Jakobsen 2017, p. 842). In a mechanical world view, models for development are unfailingly transportable and can be applied anywhere in the world.

Today, social development is dominated by market economics. Because competitive market economics is abstracted from both nature and society, it leads to a whole lot of unintended negative consequences that are difficult, if not impossible, to cure within the system. A major consequence, or perhaps even the aim, is that opportunities are reduced to bringing about genuine solidarity between people and care for nature. Worldwide, these problems are being confronted through the UN's definition of the 17 Sustainability Goals. Within the system, money and power are used to reduce the negative symptoms. These approaches are insufficient, so we are compelled to reflect far more deeply on the ontological prerequisites for today's economic and political systems.

Solidarity requires dialogue processes aimed at increasing and deepening our insights into social, political, cultural and economic realities. Solidarity rooted in dialogic practice goes deeper than other approaches, and 'bottom-up' developments initiate solidarity and help everyone to be committed to mutual aid principles (Kropotkin 1909). Such developments question the assumptions and reasons behind the problems. A consumer society rooted in growth, competition, smartness, new public management and efficiency, is now ready and ripe for a deep thorough and critical review.

In this paper we explore the degree to which dialogue is suitable for the development of societies based on quality, development, cooperation, wisdom, freedom and meaning. These thoughts are not new and have been advocated by many pioneering philosophers and social scientists throughout history. What *is* new is that these ideas are back, and a growing proportion of the population is expressing them all over again. The feeling is growing that if we are to create viable societies characterized by a high quality of life in harmony with culture and nature, then we need deep and real changes at many levels.

Dialogue between people – and between man and nature – is central to dynamic social development. A dialogue-based community is rooted in processes that give people influence over themselves and the society in which they live. We believe such an approach is more constructive and effective than warnings based on dramatic descriptions of upcoming crises and breakdowns. As we will see below, a dialogue-based community involves, engages, and inspires people to contribute to creative processes where individual and collective potential are clarified and realized. Dialogue, then, is not primarily a means of finding solutions but rather is the very energy of social development. The goal is to develop communities and regions in which it is attractive to live. Facilitating individual participation and involvement is an important driving force in all change processes. Dialogue is thus more than a way of finding good solutions to specific challenges; dialogic relationships represent an integral part of vibrant societies. Through dialogic interaction people are interconnected with each other, with culture and with nature. Dialogue plays a key role in the development of living communities characterized by a high quality of life for people within the framework of sustainable ecosystems. The reason is that dialogue contributes to establishing and developing dynamic ethical frameworks which are necessary conditions for co-responsible decisions and action. The starting point is to accept that life is all about relationships and that all forms of life are interdependent. Humans are physically connected to ecosystems through air, water and soil. As social beings, people are connected through various forms of communication. Dialogues thus become an important prerequisite for cultural development. In order to develop a common understanding of norms and values that are both ethical and political, dialogic interaction is central.

In addition to active reflection on one's own thoughts, a constructive dialogue requires reciprocity and trust between the participants in the exchange of thoughts, ideas and opinions. Through the development of judgement and dialogue, participants become more conscious of their own values and attitudes. By introducing one's own and others' values and assumptions, dialogic processes lead to the development of a common context for interpreting the challenges society faces. In order to arrive at the meaning behind what is being said, or the thoughts behind the words, it is every bit as important to listen to the views of others as it is to express oneself. As an example, we can mention that dialogue helps to increase the ability to reach common understanding through philosophizing in a qualified way. Dialogues also improve the skills to express one's own thoughts and ideas in a clear way so that others understand what is being said.

Instead of highlighting environmental, social and economic crises, which threaten from all directions, we can inspire participants in dialogues to provide examples of how they can contribute to constructive social development. We can focus on activities we can do more of and put less emphasis on eliciting detailed, alarming images. Inspired by Georgescu-Roegen (1975), we do not ask how the future *will* be, as if the great machine takes all the decisions, but rather we can ask how we *want* the future to be. The core value is 'freedom in solidarity' (Bjørneboe 1972), which contributes to creating commitment, action and co-responsibility.

The Gildeskål Dialogues

Gildeskål is a coastal municipality in Nordland county municipality with approximately 2000 inhabitants, consisting of both a mainland and a number of islands. The largest islands are Sandhornøya, South Arnøy, North Arnøy, Fugløya, Fleina and Femris as well as the archipelago Fleinvær. The mainland consists of a beach plain that extends to mountainous areas east of the municipality. Gildeskål is an agricultural and fishing municipality. Today tourism, as well as private and public service facilities, are important arenas for employment.

Gildeskål's vision is captured in the phrase 'Oh I know about a country'. It is drawn from the beloved song 'Childhood memory from Nordland', written by the theologian, linguist, politician and psalmist Elias Blix, who grew up here. Firstly, the vision tells of a place with a long and proud past, which traces all the way back to the Iron Age, including Vikings, hunting, the production of clipfish [dried and salted cod, an unusually exciting church history, and Gildeskål as the seat for county officials and county governors for the whole of Nordland. Secondly, the vision of the perpetual present reflects and is preserved by the magnificent spread of nature that characterizes Gildeskål so beautifully. No matter where you are in the municipality, you are at the intersection of high mountains and deep fjords. Beaches, valleys, caves, steep slopes, green valleys and fertile land, and hundreds of islands and islets make up this beautiful setting. Thirdly, if the lines to the future lie in vision, there are endless new possibilities here. This vision describes the Gildeskål people's great love for this area and an indomitable belief in a good future for old and young.

We held four dialogues in Gildeskål as part of a project we called 'Site development'. At it, the political administration of the municipality, in collaboration with the population of the city – as well as local, regional, national and international actors in the public and private sector – carried out a number of sub-projects to develop ideas, proposals and frameworks aimed at sustainably developing the local society in a way that is anchored in quality of life. The project focuses on housing, business, and destination development. It explores ways to involve, engage, and inspire the municipality's employees, inhabitants, culture and businesses to actively participate in creative processes to actualize the municipality's potential. These sub-projects are goals in themselves because they contribute to creating activity and involvement in the municipality and are a tool for defining problems and working out solutions to various challenges. Through the four dialogue workshops that took place in different local centres spread over Gildeskål (a café in Inndyr, a school in Nygårdssjøen, a restaurant at Arnøy Brygge and in the local community hall in Våg), the purpose was to engage and inspire the participants to be active in creating a community with a high quality of life. Two of the dialogues took place in October 2018 and the other two in March and April of 2019. An average of about 50 people from each of the locations where the dialogues took place met for the three-hour workshops.

Dialogue is an integral part of vibrant societies; e.g., it is a crucial element of active local democracy. Dialogue connects people with each other, with culture and with nature. Dialogue engages the public, and it is a method for coming up with ideas, proposals and frameworks for development that provide good solutions to specific challenges. In the dialogue meetings in Gildeskål we asked the question, What is a viable municipality in which you really want to live? The question relates to the overall purpose of the Gildeskål project. The project description emphasized the importance of actively involving the population in the process of determining what development they want and are willing to implement through active participation. The question about what development the citizens themselves want is paramount: it mobilizes engagement and action to a far greater extent than an approach in which the challenge is merely to find out which development is likely from statistics and forecasts, and then adapting that to the expected development.

Social development as a concept understood as a bottom-up process has its roots in history. In this paper we firstly will shed light on and discuss different perspectives on dialogue. Secondly, we look at different approaches to development and societal change based on the tension between ideology and utopia, as discussed by Mannheim (1936), Ricoeur (1986) and Levitas (2013). Their argument is that all societies, like individuals, have potential for development. Thirdly, we describe and reflect on the results from the Gildeskål case. Our challenge was to facilitate creative processes that actualize potential; in other words, helping to realize the dynamic utopias. Finally, we share some reflections on how dialogue can initiate the deep changes that are needed to bring about a sustainable society based on high quality of life for humans and whole ecosystems.

We consider communicative processes as inherent ingredients of 'living societies'. This contrasts with the instrumental value of dialogue in, for example, the 'smart city' concept where dialogue is a top-down initiated method for finding technological solutions. Our goal was to facilitate and inspire processes that create dynamic relationships. By these means we wanted to develop a dialogue-based society where economy balances human needs with nature's 'sink and source capacity', or the effect of habitat quality on population growth or decline. To make this goal as clear as possible, we refer to the United Nations 17 Sustainable Development Goals (SDGs) and the objectives expressed in the Earth Charter. Both statements make it clear that the principles of sustainability, justice and peace are interconnected. All living systems interact cognitively with their surroundings in ways that are determined by their own internal structure. In a societal perspective, "these cognitive interactions (involve) include consciousness and culture, and in particular a sense of ethics" (Capra and Jakobsen 2017, p. 842). In the dialogue meetings the idea was to connect directly to the participants' own experiences. The participants were encouraged to explore issues of fundamental importance based on their own experiences. Instead of pointing to experts and theory, they were encouraged to move between their own experiences and abstract reflection.

Perspectives on Dialogue

Dialogue primarily consists of a conversation between two or more people. Dialogue is thus different from monologue in that it stimulates active relationships between people. Dialogue is an ongoing exchange of views that aims to create understanding and to equalize contradictions. Dialogue can also be a communication process that highlights collective thinking and learning. The goal of dialogic communication is to develop common understanding, not to convince, control, manipulate, persuade or influence. Dialogue can thus be described as a stream of statements that provide the basis for creative development processes that help to form a holistic picture of reality. Dialogue helps to strengthen mutual understanding and improve the quality of human relationships.

Practicing dialogue is important for creating energy and direction in social development. Dialogical processes open to the unknown, expand rather than constrain, include rather than split and lay the foundation for synergies. The prerequisite for dialogic communication is that the participants are open and willing to listen actively to often-conflicting perspectives in order to arrive at a common understanding that transcends the individual's insight. Dialogue is thus a necessary prerequisite for creating dynamic processes where everyone becomes co-creative and co-responsible.

Dialogue is a conversation where the goal is to understand other people. A good dialogue requires the ability and willingness to listen on several levels, and to be open to surprises and change. Dialogue is also characterized by reciprocity and respect for each other's differences. Dialogue is often described as an alternative to debate, discussion and negotiation. While participants in a dialogue try to understand the other, participants in a debate are more concerned with winning over the opposing party by using hard-hitting arguments and by putting issues at the forefront. In a debate, it is assumed that participants disagree about what is true or what is right. The various parties try to influence each other in the direction of their own perceptions through linguistic arguments. In a debate, it is more important to conquer the opponent than it is to find a common solution. A discussion is characterized by demands for objectivity and relevance, but a dialogue opens up personal expressions and personal narratives where emotions are included as natural parts. Unlike discussion, where issues are atomized in smaller parts, dialogue seeks out holistic solutions. Through dialogue, hidden knowledge comes to the surface and it becomes possible to develop a common cultural foundation for understanding and solving specific challenges. All that is said has roots in experience, knowledge, understanding, beliefs, opinions. By shifting the focus from conflict and competition to collaboration, partnership and inclusion, dialogue contributes to strengthening cohesion and thus the commitment and drive of society. Everyone becomes a winner in a dialogue because everyone develops increased insight and understanding.

In negotiations, various instruments are used to reach agreement on practical solutions to defined questions or problems. In dialogues, the challenge is to elucidate a common theme to gain better insight or understanding. Dialogue as narrative is often associated with Plato's anecdotes about Socrates provoking dialogues with people in Athens. Plato distinguished between persuading and convincing. He accuses the rhetoricians of persuading the audience into specific conclusions by manipulating their beliefs and opinions. Anyone who attempts to persuade is not interested in changing his own mind. Conviction occurs in an I-you relationship through critical reflection and logical argumentation where the goal is to arrive at a common understanding of a case. Persuasion refers to a one-way communication in which participants are reduced to objects. Conviction occurs through a dialogue where all participants are subjects. In recent times, dialogue has been a central theme in several directions in philosophy, pedagogy, psychology and sociology. The importance of dialogue has also become a central theme within economics and business administration.

The prerequisite for creating good dialogues is that participants accept that nobody knows everything and that everyone has something to contribute. According to Holbæk-Hanssen, we can give up the dream of the individual's total overview and control, as "only the interaction between people with different experiences can provide the necessary complementary understanding" (Holbæk-Hanssen 1984, p. 61). It is therefore important that the speaker expresses everything clearly and the listener hears and interprets what is being said. In a dialogue, it is also important to allow room for reflection, that is to think about what is being said and how we perceive what is being said. There are three forms of listening:

- Listening to another person;
- Listening to your own interpretation of what is being said; and
- Listening to the common understanding that develops through the dialogue process.

In such a process, the thoughts behind the words are central and it is always important to ask if anyone can help shed light on the matter at hand.

Plato maintained that the purpose of dialogue is to clarify what is unclear and to find out what is right and wrong in ethics, economics and politics. He therefore valued "the experience of being corrected or becoming convinced by others more than the experience of convincing them to adopt his views" (Westoby and Dowling 2013, p. 116). Reflecting on experiences makes sense in a critical dialogue process. By practicing reflexive thinking, we become aware, individually and collectively, of the complexities that characterize human societies. How we understand the world we live in has a direct impact on our actions. Every society has a distinctive worldview that regulates social and political processes that contribute to influencing "people in certain ways of ethical being, thinking and behaving that are consistent with such a view" (Westoby and Dowling 2013, p. 117).

Results from the Gildeskål Dialogues

The dialogue workshops were characterized by great attendance, positivity and optimism. The people of Gildeskål expressed a high degree of pride in the municipality and they believed there is great potential for development. The goal was to describe some principles for the development of a vibrant local democracy, where the inhabitants of the municipality are drawn into processes to find the solutions that are best for the local community.

In the dialogues, several basic values were exemplified in many interesting ways. In all four dialogues, cooperation and good relations between the inhabitants were highlighted as values that should be nourished and enhanced. Interaction with nature, as self-esteem and resource, was prioritized at all dialogue meetings. Security and peace were also highlighted as important positive features of Gildeskål. Many also pointed out that the municipality gives room for freedom in relation to both people and nature. Finally, it is important to note that many people felt that the cultural roots of the municipality must be part of the development of the future Gildeskål society.

To be more concrete, the findings from the dialogues could be categorized in three different classes: nature, culture and economy. Each add important ingredients in the future quality of life in Gildeskål:

Nature	**Culture**	**Economy**
Varied nature, mountains and fjords	Good neighbourhood, relationships	Economy and jobs
Nature's dignity	Safety	Short distance between production and consumption
	Cultural understanding and historical roots	Infrastructure
	Pride over the countryside	Production in accordance with principles in nature
	Freedom, independence	
	Sound cohesion	
	Possibilities, venues	
	Collaboration	

As can be seen from the overview, it is clear that the results all agree that the good life in the municipality is linked to a good social environment, where individual freedom combined with good cohesion is the most important factor for well-being. The results also emphasize nature as an important contribution to the good life – not primarily as an economic resource but as an intrinsic value. Economics is mentioned as an important prerequisite for viable development, but as the results from the dialogues demonstrate, a sustainable economy must be rooted in vibrant nature and local culture.

The results are consistent with positive psychology (Seligman 2002), which claims that good life in good society can be divided into three levels:

- A comfortable life – satisfying basic needs;
- A good life – the opportunity to make the most of their potential;
- A meaningful life – helping to realize values beyond oneself

An important element in making Gildeskål a municipality in which people want to live will be to stimulate development and interest among all levels of the community. An important contribution to the creation of such an atmosphere is the establishment of meeting places where the citizens can participate in decision-making for the municipality. Active participation helps to bring about co-responsibility.

The Participants' Evaluation of the Dialogues

We prepared a questionnaire to provide empirical evidence of how meaningful and useful the participants found the dialogue workshops in light of the overall goal of the Gildeskål project. The questions referred to some of the criteria for using dialogue as a method for social improvement. We need insight into, and understanding of, our own and others' perspectives, and to see the connection between our own understanding and group understanding. We also included questions related to the willingness to help decode the consensus into practical action. We asked about gender and age to examine if, in terms of our project, there are differences between women and men and between the young and the elderly.

To analyse the results, we used two simple statistical methods: frequency analysis and factor analysis. The first indicates how the answers are distributed (as a percentage) while the second tells how the answers to the different questions are related. Factor analysis is used to detect any correlation between a number of observed variables using a smaller number of factors. The purpose of a factor analysis is to find out if there are groups in the population that have common traits suitable to distinguish them from groups with other common traits.

The questionnaire contained the following questions; the answer options are divided into a seven-point Likert scale, from 'a small degree' to 'a large extent':

1. I have become more aware of the challenges Gildeskål faces
2. I have acquired a clearer picture of the future society of Gildeskål
3. I agree that Gildeskål has a great potential for development
4. The results we achieved through the Socratic dialogue are in line with my wishes for the future of Gildeskål
5. I believe it is possible to realize the results we came up with through Socratic dialogue
6. It is likely that I will make an active contribution to achieving the goals

Respondents were also asked about their gender, age, occupation and interests.

Frequency Analysis

Respondents returned 89 forms with answers to all the questions, a response rate of approximately 60%. Of those who submitted the completed form, 41 were women and 48 men. The age distribution was three persons under 20, 14 persons between 21 and 40, 42 persons between 41 and 67, and 30 persons over 68. The age distribution was almost equal between women and men.

Figure 1. Frequency gender

Gender / Age	<20	21 - 40	41 - 67	>67
Women	3 7%	18.4%	47.4%	26.3%
Men	0%	14.3%	46.9%	33.8%

Figure 2. Frequency on all questions

Question \ Answer	1-2-3 Negative	4 Neutral	5-6-7 Positive
1	13.6%	19.3%	67.1%
2	12.3%	11.2%	76.5%
3	1.1%	2.2%	96.7%
4	2.2%	10.1%	87.7%
5	2.2%	13.5%	84.3%
6	5.7%	12.5%	81.8%

As the table indicates, a large majority say that they had become more aware of the challenges Gildeskål faces (question one) through participation in the Socratic dialogue. That is, the dialogue contributed to raising awareness of common challenges. A small group (13.6%)

answered the question negatively. The number of positive answers is even higher (76.4%) on question two, asking the participants if they have developed a clearer picture of the future society of Gildeskål through participation in the dialogue. That is, the dialogue has helped to make the potential for development more manifest through participation in the dialogue workshop. A small minority (12.3%) answered this question negatively. Question three, asking whether the group's perception of potential for development corresponds to the individual's experience, was answered unequivocally positively (96.6%). Almost none responded to the three lowest levels (1.1%). The distribution of answers on question four (87.7%) confirms that the results of the dialogue largely correspond to the wishes of the individual. A great majority (84.2%) on question five believe that it is possible to implement the proposed changes in practice. Most of the participants (81.8%) also responded on question six that they will help to achieve the goals.

Figure 3. Frequency Women and Men

Question \ Answer	1-2-3 Negative	4 Neutral	5-6-7 Positive
1	5.2% - 20.9%	18.4% - 20.8%	76.4% - 58.3%
2	5.3% - 18.3%	5.3% - 16.3%	89.4% - 65.4%
3	2.0% - 2.0%	2.6% - 2.0%	97.4% - 96.0%
4	0% - 4.1%	7.9% - 12.2%	92.1% - 83.7%
5	2.6% - 2.0%	7.9% - 18.4%	89.5% - 79.6%
6	5.3% - 4.2%	15.8% - 10.4%	78.9% - 85.4%

When we look at differences between women and men, there are tendencies for women to respond more positively to most questions. The differences are greatest for questions one, two, four and five, where women were more positive. Both groups scored highest on the question about Gildeskål's potential for development. Men responded markedly more negatively to questions one and two than women. This can either mean that they have a clear picture of the situation already, and a clear idea of the future. It may also mean that the dialogue was not as rewarding for men as for women. However, the differences are too small to have practical relevance. The only question in which men are more positive than women is in their willingness to contribute actively in practical action to create the future society in Gildeskål.

From the empirical material we draw the conclusion that a great majority of those who participated in the dialogues benefited greatly from taking part in the dialogical process. In addition, they generally agreed that there is a potential for development in the municipality and they are willing to contribute actively in the work to achieve the goals.

Figure 4. Frequency positively (5-6-7) by age

Question \ Answer	> 20	21-40	41-67	>67
1	100%	64.3%	61.9%	67%
2	100%	50%	73.9%	90%
3	100%	100%	100%	90%
4	100%	85.8%	88.1%	86.6%
5	100%	85.7%	88.1%	76.6%
6	100%	92.9%	88.0%	65.4%

The answer to question one, "I have become more aware of what challenges Gildeskål is facing", is evenly distributed across all age groups. On question two, "I have a clearer picture of the future Gildeskål", there is a marked rising trend with higher ages, from 50% in the group 21 to 40 years to 90% for those over 67. All age groups agree with question three that "Gildeskål has a great potential for development". There is also a great deal of agreement on question four that "The results we have achieved through the Socratic dialogue are in line with my wishes for the future Gildeskål". The same goes for question five, "I think it is possible to realize the results we came up with through the Socratic dialogue". There is a marked decreasing tendency to respond positively to question six, "It is likely that I will contribute actively to achieving the goals": 92.9% for the age group between 21-40 years, and 65.4% for the age group over 67 years.

The results indicate two interesting findings; firstly, that there is a significant positive attitude to developing the potential that everyone believes is present in Gildeskål. It is also interesting that the younger participants, to a large degree, are keen to contribute to realizing the potential. Secondly, the results show that dialogue helps to create a common understanding of what the challenges consist of and about the values that should be used in shaping the Gildeskål community of the future. In other words, dialogue inspires not only change in concrete knowledge but also, and maybe more importantly, a change in the interpretative context. This is an absolute prerequisite for deep societal change.

Factor Analysis

Through the factor analysis it is possible to find out if there are any groups in the population that have common traits different from other groups in the same population. The results of the factor analysis indicate that two different groups stand out. The first group, with the highest scores on variables three, five and six, we have named 'Active optimists'. The second group, which scores highest on variables one, two and four, we have called 'Passive realists'.

The Active optimists believe that Gildeskål has a great potential for development and they believe it is possible to realize the potential; also, they will actively contribute to achieving the goals.

Group 1: Active optimists
Q. 3: 0,700   I agree that Gildeskål has a great potential for development
Q. 5: 0,749   I think it is possible to realize the results we came up with
Q. 6: 0.838   I want to make an active contribution to achieving the goals

Group 2: Passive Realists
The Passive realists have become aware of the challenges Gildeskål faces, they have a clearer picture of the future society and they agree with the results that emerged in the Socratic dialogue. In other words, they see the challenges and the possibilities but do not think it is possible to reach the goals. They do, however, express a willingness to participate in active action to actualize the goals.

Q. 1: 0,850   I have become more aware of the challenges Gildeskål faces
Q. 2: 0,884   I have acquired a clearer picture of the Gildeskål of the future
Q. 4: 0,463   The results we came up with in the Socratic dialogue agree with my wishes for the future Gildeskål

Political Implications

An important purpose of the Gildeskål project was to get input relevant to the municipal administration and the politicians on how to develop the community into something which would "appear as an attractive municipality to live in and be characterized by good and adapted high-quality services to the population". We interpret this expression to mean that the municipality must not only *appear* attractive, it must *be* attractive. In order to become attractive, a number of key factors are synthesized: "Create well-established and robust urban areas with adapted living and business areas, as well as good services and social meeting places. Facilitating the participation and involvement of inhabitants is an important driving force in the development of the community".

The purpose of the dialogue meetings was to facilitate participation and engagement. Next we will take a closer look at how the participants in the dialogue meetings believed the basic values of an attractive Gildeskål could be put into practice. In the review, we distinguish between economy, nature and culture, although the different areas often intersect. This interconnectedness is interesting and suggests that the relations between the various agencies in the municipality is a topic of great importance that administrations and politicians must deal with.

Economy

Safe jobs that are rooted in diverse decentralized networks of smaller firms and a place to live are the foundation of an attractive municipality. Local production and processing of food from agriculture and fishing is important. In order to stimulate the establishment and development of small- and medium-sized firms, the establishment of a sharing economy is fundamental; that is, farmers and fishermen should have the opportunity to borrow instead of buying their own very expensive machinery. In order to develop sustainable societies it is necessary to develop an infrastructure that facilitates creativity and innovation. Through the dialogue meetings it became clear that Gildeskål has a culture based on individual freedom rooted in community responsibility and solidarity. 'Freedom in solidarity' can be developed to become the main integrating value in an attractive and viable municipality.

In order to stimulate the development of interesting workplaces it is important that the municipality facilitates and practices open dialogue with the population where the business community is developed through collaborative networks. Instead of perceiving the neighbouring company as a competitor, there is great potential in developing an integrated and sustainable business sector characterized by synergy. In order to stimulate the development of integrated solutions, both businesses and the local population should make use of the services provided nearby. In this way, the local trade and service offerings are stimulated.

Open channels for dialogue between the population and the municipal administration increase the possibility of interaction. In order to stimulate new start-ups and financing of development, it is also important that the municipality offers assistance in writing applications and filling out forms. The goal is to open up creativity in a long-term perspective.

Culture

In all the different dialogue workshops participants agreed that further development of social activities must be facilitated, including physical spaces for different activities. We also saw that it is important that the municipality be better connected. Specifically, this means facilitating joint activities that will connect the inhabitants of the municipality more closely. Joint events help create common meeting places for all the inhabitants of Gildeskål. In this regard, we discovered that the municipality should facilitate better public transport. It is also important to facilitate good contacts with the neighbouring regions, the whole country and the rest of the world. Likewise, it is important to facilitate good public transport solutions to the nearest city. Meeting places for multicultural interaction are also central to the attractive Gildeskål of the future.

To create a viable municipality, we must bring the local culture to life through yearbooks, and the yearbooks should be actively used in the schools. It is a shared responsibility to communicate local history and culture. Local business should also be invited to contribute to teaching at schools. The older part of the population should be invited to contribute storytelling about the development of the municipality from a historical perspective. The story can also be dramatized through performances in which locals are active, both as writers and actors. The cultural heritage can be internalised by looking at people who have stood for important values. The renewal of the culture can take place through meeting places for cross-cultural activities.

The dialogues also made clear that an attractive municipality provides a well-developed kindergarten, school and health services, home nursing and elderly care. The schools must contribute to psychosocial security for all, including a school day without bullying – safe schools for everyone, with good communication and the ability to get back and forth safely between school and home.

In order to stimulate participation and engagement, it is necessary to facilitate the development of attractive meeting places for associations and interest groups of various kinds that can help to link communities together. The participants in the dialogues agreed that great emphasis was being placed on creating good relationships, affiliation, sharing, new forms of good neighbourliness. The activities should have local roots and be future-oriented. Such an approach includes activities where generations meet. In other words, the municipality must contribute to a good flow of information between politicians, the administration and the population. The dialogue must be two-way; dialogue arenas must include both bottom-up and top-down initiatives.

Nature

On the one hand, the population wants to preserve nature; on the other hand it wants to use nature. The coastal culture in Norway has a tradition of sustainably using the sea and the cultural landscape. The population wants more active participation in processes that lead to sustainable management of cultural landscapes, animal husbandry, grazing and vegetation, including the sea.

Final Remarks

Through the dialogue workshops in Gildeskål, it was clear that the inhabitants of the municipality appreciate the local culture. It meets their needs on several levels, and they want to participate in development that facilitates the fulfilment of basic needs such as good living conditions, access to healthy food and other necessities. In other words, they want to facilitate a quality-of-life society. Through the development of a diverse business and cultural life that gives the individual the opportunity to actualize their potential, the foundation is laid for a good life in a good society. In addition, it is important that meeting places are established for cooperation and interaction within both business and cultural life. Through practicing dialogic processes, people are inspired to contribute to realizing values beyond themselves, thus creating a meaningful life.

In order to stimulate a balanced development where economics, nature and culture are perceived in context, it is important that no sector becomes dominant. The dialogue meetings show that the population perceives 'a sustainable nature' as a necessary condition for an attractive Gildeskål. That is, nature's intrinsic value must be safeguarded if a conflict arises with the instrumental view of the economy. The dialogues show that the population will participate in the processes that determine this balance. In an attractive Gildeskål, a viable local-based economy is central. Through the development of dialogue-based collaborative networks, the population wants to contribute to the development of a viable business based on diversity. The dialogue workshops also indicate that the participants want to help develop a flourishing cultural life based on great variety.

Through the establishment of meeting places for cultural activity, the municipality can stimulate the population to become active members of social development, which in turn leads to increased co-responsibility. Such a development is realistic if the 'optimistic people of action' are given good conditions to participate and contribute in interaction with the municipality's administration and politicians. It is therefore important that the municipality makes sure that creative individuals and groups have access to resources that enable them to actualize the potential that exists. The survey showed that the inhabitants of Gildeskål have a positive outlook on the future. The dialogue also showed that this positive attitude is largely linked to their own ideas and creative suggestions. It is therefore important that the municipality does not fall into the trap of having the administration and politicians taking the initiative from the active optimists, but instead gives them the opportunity to explore the possibilities. Everything is ready for the dialogue-based Gildeskål model to turn out as a well-functioning methodology for site development.

History offers many examples of societies that are very different from ours, so it is not only possible but also likely that the society of the future will be very different from today's modern societies.

References

Jens Bjørneboe, J. (1972). *Politi og anarki*. Oslo: Pax.

Capra, F. & Jakobsen, O. (2017). "A conceptual framework for ecological economics based on systemic principles of life." *International Journal of Social Economics,* 44(6), 831–844.

Georgescu-Roegen, N. (1975). "Energy and economic myths." *Southern Economic Journal,* 41(3), 347–381.

Holbæk-Hanssen L. (1984). *Et samfunn for menneskelig utvikling*. Oslo: Tano-Aschehoug.

Kropotkin, P. (1909). *Mutual Aid: A Factor in Evolution*. New York: Doubleday.

Levitas, R. (2013). *Utopia as Method: The Imaginary Reconstruction of Society*. Basingstoke, UK: Palgrave Macmillan.

Mannheim, K. (1936). *Ideology and Utopia*. New York: Harvest Books.

Ricoeur, P. (1986). *Lectures on Ideology and Utopia*. New York: Colombia University Press.

Seligmann, M. (2002). *Authentic Happiness: Using the New Positive Psychology to Realize Your Potential for Lasting Fulfillment*. New York: Free Press

Westoby, P. & Dowling, G. (2013). *Theory and Practice of Dialogical Community Development – International Perspectives*. Abingdon, UK: Routledge.

Conference Session Extracts

From a conversation with participants considering the paper with the author

Speaker 1: It's interesting what you did. In the paper I think you referred to it as Socratic dialogue, but actually you've got your own particular method, which is very effective, but it doesn't come out so much in the paper itself. First there is what I call *convening*, how you get the right people in the room. You began with the logic of utopian thinking, and the work is actually dependent on that logic. Without introducing that in your invitation, you couldn't get to where you want to go. The next bit is showing pictures and images that activate feeling, which related in different ways from the thinking logic. With the feeling you can get into the narrative stories. Everybody has personal experience to tell.

From there, I think you have a reflective description of the good life – things we already know about what the good life is – what it's like to live well and be happy and so on. We can forget because we're so busy dealing with life. Then you hear 15 stories, involving real participation, because there's no right or wrong, and people's titles and labels fall away to experience. You select just one, that surprised me, but with that one, you go deeper into it to find the characteristics. Without the characteristics you can't go to change.

And from there, then you apply the characteristics to all the other stories which pulls people back in, and everybody is deeply proud to find their characteristics confirmed, and they can add more. But again you pull them down to just four. Lastly you ask how can people contribute? I kind of know what I want, but I understand the characteristics of it, and I can actually do something about it, which then comes down to action. There is a flow there, and a method that is interesting, effective and quite replicable by other people. It probably doesn't have a name, but you could call it the ... I don't know ... the Jacobsen-Storsletten Dialogue Pattern, or something like that.

Speaker 2: Thank you! Can we include that in the paper? One difference between ecological economics and neoclassical economics is that we have a different paradigm. There are few things that connect people talking about the ecological economics and the first thing is that we learn from nature, and what we learn from nature is that everything is integrated. There are circular connections between everything, and there is no waste in nature. In human society there is waste everywhere, so something is wrong. We have not connected, and we are not a circular economy.

The other thing we find in nature is that Darwin was wrong when he said that "everything is in competition with the others". Instead of being atomistic, the economic view that man is an autonomous actor, we see that everything is connected. There are some other principles too, and you will come up with economic practice that is very different in different places — just as the ecosystems are different in northern part of Norway and in South Africa and in India and in the US in California. It's very different ecosystems but they are the same principles. There are some principles that are common, such as cooperation and networks.

Speaker 3: When you were speaking, [the not-for-profit organisation] *Imagine Chicago* came up for me — do you know it? Between 1993 and 2003, *Imagine Chicago* did visioning work on a massive scale — 10,000 people were involved through schools, faith groups, voluntary professions, the statutory networks, professional networks. They managed to create a structure whereby the one vision, the one story connects with 10,000 others. It was massively resourced. They've done it all over the world now, so if you are interested in how to upscale these things, *Imagine Chicago* is a fantastic model.

Speaker 4: I was thinking about how good and bad experiences both affect ideas about the good life.

Speaker 5: About experiencing the worst or the best . . . We had one refugee in the first dialogue meeting who, when expressing what she experienced as the best thing there, then also said something about the worst thing that she had experienced. Whilst others were talking about the weather, and things like that, her story was about how "I love being here. There's no war here! It's peace and quiet and I feel safe."

Speaker 3: I think you've raised a really important point there about the need to deal with the past, to banish the past, before you can envision the future. I think there are a lot of dangers in storytelling about the past. You can trap people in powerless victim positions. You can sometimes re-traumatise people — you can isolate them. I think it's really important, if you're going to go down that road, to actually work with those stories, and not just accept them. For instance, there's a lot of really interesting work in Northern Ireland on this. If someone tells you a story of really bad things happening, even in those bad situations there are moments of human kindness or compassion or whatever. The question may be: "What enabled you to survive that? How did you come through this?" You can begin to reframe the story of disaster as a story of change or a story of hope. And that's quite a skilled process I have to say.

Speaker 6: We used the circles to heal that, to see each other in a different way and to show emotions. It was indeed the challenge to contain that. And after that, then they could see how much they had in common, and how many dreams they shared. It was very small scale in the neighbourhood. And then we started to say: "How can we? . . . How do we? . . . What does a happy neighbourhood look like?" If we can get rid of this, and feel that, and we all actually want the same things . . . and then we could move on.

Speaker 9: If we are going to emulate nature, we have to accept diversity. But it's not only collaboration in nature. We have all these wonderful metaphors, but we also have to accept competition. We are competing because it's part of human nature. And you can go to animals you will see pecking orders. Go to a chicken farm and see what happens there. The lowest, those at the bottom, they have no feathers.

Speaker 2: Yes, but I think the main thing here is that the from the mental level the source of life is interconnectedness. Without interconnectedness everything is dead. In a future economy you will have competition between different producers of pizza, for example. There's no problem. But the fundamental idea behind economics should be cooperation.

Postscript
The authors' reflections, written some months after the conference

Participating in the Academy of Professional Dialogue conferences over the past two years has inspired us to develop our own research-based practice. We focus on dialogue-based methods to develop organisations and local societies. The idea is that if the participants in organisations and the inhabitants in local societies are involved in the process of creating the future, they will behave more responsibly.

Our paper represents a report of the first steps in developing what we today call Utopian Workshops. A Utopian Workshop is a combination of different methods anchored in the dialogue philosophy and philosophy of science reflections. In agreement with Karl Popper, we distinguish between the context of discovery and the context of justification.

We start with a modified version of Socratic dialogue, where the participants are free to tell their own experienced-based story in a non-restrictive context of discovery – they are free to refer to all kinds of experience. In the next stage the main ideas are concretized in an improvised version of Open Space dialogue. In the third and final stage the projects are critically evaluated in a plenary session.

Many interesting and relevant questions from participants at last year's conference dialogues inspired us to develop our approach further. Several helpful questions were raised: How do you get the right people in the room? How should we introduce utopian thinking in the invitation to the workshops? Another comment pointed out the dangers connected to storytelling about the past. The argument was, "You can trap people in powerless victim positions" and "You can sometimes re-traumatise people – you can isolate people". These are serious arguments that we must find good answers to. The dilemma is, should we work with those stories and not just accept them? Another thought-provoking comment was connected to our positive image of humankind: "We have all these wonderful metaphors of synergy in nature's ecosystems, but we also have to accept competition". We noted an interesting comment concerning the need for a physical room for dialogue in every street in every town.

We hope to develop our cooperation with the Academy of Professional Dialogue in the years to come in preparation for the Bodø European Capital of Culture in 2024 (https://bodo.kommune.no/les/ECC/ – The AofPD is mentioned on page 21.) What the EU panel said about the bid-book from Bodø is promising: "The intention is to bring to the urban vision development of the 'smart city' approach a social (as opposed to the mere technological) dimension, based on dialogue within society and between society and nature. In the panel's view, this is forward-looking and a strong element of the bid".

The World Needs Dialogue!
2019 Conference Participants

Lars-Åke Almqvist
Sweden

Jane Ball
UK

Whitney Barton
UK

Mechtild Beucke-Galm
Germany

Chro Borhan
Norway

Joop Boukes
Netherlands

Rebecca Cannara
USA

Harold Clarke
USA

Vicky Coates
South Africa

Eelco de Geus
Austria

Nancy Dixon
USA

Jonathan Drury
UK

Linda Ellinor
USA

Jackie Elliott
UK

Lena Eriksson
Sweden

212 | Participants

Bobby Frazier
UK

Jenny Garrett
UK

Peter Garrett
UK

Mirja Hämäläinen
Finland

Geir Harald Hagberg
Norway

Ewa Östlund Henschen
Sweden

Peter Hill
Canada

Gerd Holmboe-Ottesen
Norway

Bernhard Holtrop
Netherlands

Sam House
USA

William Isaacs
USA

Ove Jakobsen
Norway

Simon Keyes
UK

Thomas Klug
Germany

Harriet Krantz
Sweden

Sabine Kresa
Austria

Katharina Lobeck
Germany

Marie-Ève Marchand
Canada

Steve Marshall
UK

Timo Nevalainen
Finland

Participants

Siv Nystedt-Claesson
Sweden

Tom O'Connor
USA

Hugh Pidgeon
UK

Olga Plokhooij
Netherlands

Liv Ronglan
Norway

Robert Sarly
USA

Mark Seneschall
UK

Peter Sorum
Norway

Vivi Storsletten
Norway

Nima Taylor
South Africa

Kati Tikkamäkï
Finland

Renate van der Veen
Netherlands

www.ingramcontent.com/pod-product-compliance
Lightning Source LLC
Chambersburg PA
CBHW042358280426
43661CB00096B/1154